#1 *NEW YORK TIMES* BESTSELLING AUTHOR
MIKE EVANS

SEE YOU
iN NEW YORK

"We will raise the flag of Allah
over the White House" —ISIS

TIMEWORTHY
·BOOKS·

P.O. BOX 30000, PHOENIX, AZ 85046

*This book is dedicated in memory
of those cherished men, women and children
who perished on September 11, 2001
in the attacks on the World Trade Center,
the Pentagon, and on United Airlines flight 93.*

PREFACE 7

PART ONE: THIS PRESENT STRUGGLE

1 / *The West Meets ISIL* 27

2 / *Can We Win?* 39

3 / *A Prophetic Storm Gathers* 51

4 / *Recalibrating America's Moral Compass* 75

5 / *Only Moral Clarity Will Bring True Peace* 89

6 / *Filling the Void* 99

7 / *The Centers of Gravity* 113

8 / *The Real Battle Begins* 125

9 / *Iran Rises* 135

10 / *The World War against Terrorism* 149

11 / *Iran's Burgeoning Nuclear Ambitions* 159

PART TWO: A BATTLE OF TWO BOOKS

12 / *Fumbling Our Ally, Iran* 173

13 / *The Rise of Islamofascism* 187

14 / *Jimmy Carter's Liberal Legacy* 199

15 / *The Nuclear Bomb of Islam* 217

16 / *The Rise of the Mahdi* 229

17 / *How Possible Is a Terrorist Nuclear Attack?* 241

18 / *The Battle for the Soul of America* 253

19 / *The Broad Reach of Islamofascism* 269

20 / *Rapture: The Return of the Messiah* 287

APPENDIX A: 297
    Excerpts from an Interview with
    Benjamin Netanyahu

APPENDIX B: 307
    Excerpts from an Interview with
    Retired IDF General Moshe Ya'alon

APPENDIX C: 323
    A 21-Day Study of Iran (Persia), Iraq (Babylon),
    and Israel in Biblical Prophecy

ENDNOTES 325

PREFACE

IN PARIS, FRANCE, 2015 burst on the scene, not with fireworks, but with gunfire and jihad. Shortly after the French magazine, *Charlie Hebdo*, tweeted its latest satirical offering its offices were stormed by three gunmen who opened fire inside the building. The January 8, 2015 attack left twelve journalists dead and at least eleven injured—four critically. Among them were Editor, Stephane Charbonnier, Jean Cabut, Georges Wolinski, Bernard Verlhac, and Bernard Maris.[1] Also killed were two policemen, one identified as a 42-year old Muslim man, Ahmed Merabet. A policewoman was murdered the following day in a separate, but allied, terrorist attack on the streets of Paris.

Police identified two persons of interest, brothers Cherif (32) and Said Kouachi (34), both believed to have trained with al Qaeda in Yemen. A third suspect, Hamyd Mouradan (18), surrendered to police in Charleville-Mézières, a town close to the border between France and Belgium. After two days, the suspects were tracked to an industrial complex outside Paris where both were shot. Many who reported on the incident referred to the men as "martyrs" when, in reality, they were nothing more than murderers.

A cohort of the Kouschi brothers, Amedy Coulibaly, and his accomplice, a 26-year old female, Hayat Boumeddiene, stormed a kosher grocery on the eastern edge of Paris and took a number of hostages. The pair threatened to execute their captives if the police rushed the building where the Kouschis were entrenched. Boumeddiene and Coulibaly were suspected of having killed the policewoman the day before. Coulibaly and several hostages were killed during the attempted rescue; Boumeddiene escaped capture during the melee at the grocery, and reportedly left France for Syria.

A tweet released by the magazine shortly before the assault contained a drawing of ISIL leader, Abu al-Baghdadi speaking into a microphone, saying, "Greetings from al-Baghdadi as well . . . and especially health."

The attack was the second directed at the magazine. In 2011, the weekly's offices were targeted with firebombs for printing an offering it called its "Sharia" edition with a depiction of Muhammad on its cover.

As the three gunmen escaped, one was captured on a video feed from a nearby building as he shouted in fluent French, "We killed *Charlie Hebdo*. We avenged the prophet!"[2] On another video, one of the men, clad in black from head to toe, was heard to shout, "Allahu akbar!" Its translation from Arabic to English is, "Allah is the greatest."[3] It is not the first time God has been lauded amidst a brutal attack, and it won't be the last as fanatical Islamic terrorists become more brazen. In 2009, Army Major Nidal Hasan stationed at Fort Hood, Texas, uttered that cry as he calmly murdered 13 people and injured more than thirty. Such a heinous attack should not come as any surprise. In 1999, years before the 9/11 attack I released a book, *The Jerusalem Scroll*, which included an attack on the Twin Towers in New York City. I was ridiculed by many for daring to even think in fictional terms of an attack on the continental United States.

This offering was followed by my 2007 bestseller, *The Final Move Beyond Iraq: The Final Solution While the World Sleeps,* in which I wrote that the results of the Iraq war would be the formation of an Islamic army that would wreak havoc in the region and spread its poisonous tentacles even wider. The result was an all-out attack by the Liberal Left on the premise of the book during network television debates and interviews.

As France reeled under the assault and its gendarmes tracked down the perpetrators of this heartless and brutal attack, other countries have responded by tightening security. France's President Francois Holland called the assault an "act of exceptional barbarism" while President Obama "strongly condemned" the attack on *Charlie Hebdo.* Other freedom-loving nations and organizations quickly followed suit.

As a journalist and writer, I was appalled by the news of the assault. Freedom of speech is one of the guarantees of the United States Constitution and is treasured within the borders of those countries who value that liberty. Such independence is not welcomed among radical Islamists the likes of which carried out the attack on the French weekly. It was not the first such assault against the magazine which had been the target of firebombs by radical Muslims in November 2011.[4] France is the record-holder—according to Europol—among European countries for the highest number of arrests of religiously-motivated terrorists scheming to launch strikes within its boundaries.

Following the disaster in Paris, Andrew Parker, Director General of Britain's MI5, warned of possible plots to wreak massive destruction on the West. Parker was quoted as saying that al

Qaeda operatives in Syria were prepared to "cause large-scale loss of life, often by attacking transport systems or iconic targets" in the West.[5] This warning came despite the death of Osama bin Laden in 2011 after which the terror threat from al Qaeda seemed to abate.

The speech delivered by Parker had been planned before the Paris terrorist attack. According to Parker, approximately 600 British jihadists had made their way to Syria hoping to join ISIL in its jihad against the West. Parker also decried the blatant use of social media networks to recruit terrorists and plot against Britain and her allies in the West. He added:

> We face a very serious level of threat that is complex to combat and unlikely to abate significantly for some time . . . . My sharpest concern as Director General of MI5 is the growing gap between the increasingly challenging threat and the decreasing availability of capabilities to address it.[6]

Calling upon the giant technology companies to bolster security services and allow those agencies intent on tracking and stopping terror attacks better gateways to gain information, Parker warned:

> The dark places from where those who wish us harm can plot and plan are increasing . . . . We need to be able to access communications and obtain relevant data on those people when we have good reason.[7]

It has become obvious that the United States of America and her European allies need to have the same resolve in dismantling the worldwide radical Islamist terrorist network as it did when fighting the Axis powers during World War II. The threat is as great in the twenty-first century as was that of Hitler's Nazi regime in the twentieth century. During the Iraq War, too few Americans seemed to realize that the "insurgents" being fought by the US in the streets of Iraq were not simply disgruntled Iraqis caught in a cycle of incomprehensible ethnic intolerance, but rather it was a terror-network that would be unleashed in its full ferocity once the last US vehicle departed Iraq's borders. The vipers that had been multiplying underground have been freed now to surface and spread their venom unfettered in the form of ISIL and restructured *al Qaeda* to become an even more radically militant form of Islam.

What many fail to realize is that the West is fighting the newest world power, based not on an ideology such as Communism or Nazism, but on an over-zealous, distorted form of Islam whose constituents are willing to both kill and die in the hope of spreading it worldwide. The goal is to chase democracy and freedom from the Middle East, then from the world at large. This newly-formed "Islamic State" and its fanatical members have the mentality of suicide bombers willing to blow themselves up in order to achieve its purpose.

In July 2014 an al Qaeda splinter group seized some of Iraq's largest cities and marched toward Baghdad with thousands of well-armed *jihadists*. Their ultimate goal was and is the creation of an Islamic State. The group is sometimes called the Islamic State of Iraq and Syria (ISIS); but their all-inclusive name is ISIL— the Islamic State of the Levant (a large area in the Middle East bordered by the Mediterranean, the Arabian Desert, and Upper Mesopotamia)—meaning the terrorist group initially has designs on the entire region.

Recent news disclosed in *The Fiscal Times* by journalist Riyadh

Mohammed indicates that the ISIL strategy has taken a predictable course: infiltration of rebel groups located along the border between Syria and the Israeli-occupied Golan Heights. Such a move would open the door to ISIL members of Ansar Bait al-Maqdis in Egypt and other ISIL cells in the south of Syria that have seemed to overshadow US-supported groups in the region. Three additional jihadist groups joined forces with ISIL in late December 2014: The Yarmouk Martyrs Brigade and two much smaller factions.

Professor Geoffrey Levin, an alumnus with New York University, weighed the implications:

> If Israel was attacked by ISIS, America would expect a proportionate response by Israel, which is militarily capable of defending itself. America would counsel against sustained Israeli involvement because it could threaten the tacit alliance between America, Iran, Turkey, and several Arab states against ISIS.[8]

Israel responded by increasing security measures in the Golan Heights in the event ISIL leaders adopt tactics from Saddam Hussein's "book of war strategies." During the height of the 1991 Gulf War, the late dictator ordered SCUD missiles lobbed into Israel, hoping to entice Israeli retaliation. That plan failed. ISIL's desperate attempts to draw the Jewish State into its web of war has, at this writing, taken the same path as that of Saddam.

Israel has maintained a vigilant outlook in order to intercept weapons transfers from radical Islamic countries such as Iran before they could fall into the hands of ISIL fighters.

This news of increased ISIL activity near Israel's borders makes the speech delivered by Israeli Prime Minister Benjamin Netanyahu on September 29, 2014, of paramount importance. He stood before the United Nations General Assembly and issued a grave warning to those assembled:

> But our hopes and the world's hope for peace are in danger. Because everywhere we look, militant Islam is on the march. It's not militants. It's not Islam. It's militant Islam.
>
> Typically, its first victims are other Muslims, but it spares no one. Christians, Jews, Yazidis, Kurds—no creed, no faith, no ethnic group is beyond its sights. And it's rapidly spreading in every part of the world. . . . For the militant Islamists, "All politics is global." Because their ultimate goal is to dominate the world.
>
> Now, that threat might seem exaggerated to some, since it starts out small, like a cancer that attacks a particular part of the body. But left unchecked, the cancer grows, metastasizing over wider and wider areas. To protect the peace and security of the world, we must remove this cancer before it's too late. . . .
>
> ISIS and Hamas are branches of the same poisonous tree. ISIS and Hamas share a fanatical creed, which they both seek to impose well beyond the territory under their control.
>
> Listen to ISIS's self-declared caliph, Abu Bakr al-Baghdadi. This is what he said two months ago:

> A day will soon come when the Muslim will walk everywhere as a master ... The Muslims will cause the world to hear and understand the meaning of terrorism ... and destroy the idol of democracy.

Now listen to Khaled Meshaal, the leader of Hamas. He proclaims a similar vision of the future:

> We say this to the West ... By Allah you will be defeated. Tomorrow our nation will sit on the throne of the world.

As Hamas's charter makes clear, its immediate goal is to destroy Israel. But Hamas has a broader objective. They also want a caliphate. Hamas shares the global ambitions of its fellow militant Islamists.

That's why its supporters wildly cheered in the streets of Gaza as thousands of Americans were murdered on 9/11. And that's why its leaders condemned the United States for killing Osama Bin Laden, whom they praised as a holy warrior. So when it comes to their ultimate goals, Hamas is ISIS and ISIS is Hamas.

And what they share in common, all militant Islamists share in common:

✧ Boko Haram in Nigeria;

✧ Ash-Shabab in Somalia;

✧ Hezbollah in Lebanon;

✧ An-Nusrah in Syria;

✧ The Mahdi Army in Iraq;

✧ And the al Qaeda branches in Yemen, Libya, the Philippines, India, and elsewhere.

They operate in different lands, they target different victims and they even kill each other in their quest for supremacy. But they all share a fanatic ideology.

They all seek to create ever-expanding enclaves of militant Islam where there is no freedom and no tolerance—where women are treated as chattel [slaves], Christians are decimated, and minorities are subjugated, sometimes given the stark choice: convert or die.

For them, anyone can be an infidel, including fellow Muslims. . . .

So don't be fooled by Iran's manipulative charm offensive. It's designed for one purpose and for one purpose only: to lift the sanctions and remove the obstacles to Iran's path to the bomb. The Islamic Republic is now trying to bamboozle its way to an agreement that will remove the sanctions it still faces and leave it with a capacity of thousands of refugees—of centrifuges, rather—to enrich uranium. This would effectively cement Iran's place as a threshold military nuclear power. And in the future, at the time of its choosing, Iran, the world's most dangerous regime, in the world's most dangerous region, would obtain the world's most dangerous weapons. Allowing that to happen would pose the gravest threat to us all. It is one thing to confront militant Islamists on pick-up trucks armed with Kalashnikov rifles; it's another thing to confront militant Islamists armed with weapons of mass destruction . . . .

Militant Islam's ambition to dominate the world seems mad. But so too did the global ambitions of another fanatic ideology that swept to power eight decades ago. The Nazis believed in a master race. The militant Islamists believe in a master faith.

They just disagree about who among them will be the master . . . of the master faith. That's what they truly disagree about. Therefore, the question before us is whether militant Islam will have the power to realize its unbridled ambitions.

There is one place where that could soon happen: The Islamic State of Iran. For 35 years, Iran has relentlessly pursued the global mission which was set forth by its founding ruler, Ayatollah Khomeini, in these words: We will export our revolution to the entire world.

Until the cry "There is no God but Allah" will echo throughout the world over . . . And ever since, the regime's brutal enforcers, Iran's Revolutionary Guards, have done exactly that.

Listen to its current commander, General Muhammad Ali Ja'afari. And he clearly stated this goal. He said: Our Imam did not limit the Islamic

Revolution to this country . . . Our duty is to prepare the way for an Islamic world government . . .

Iran's President Rouhani stood here last week, and shed crocodile tears over what he called "the globalization of terrorism."

Maybe he should spare us those phony tears and have a word instead with the commanders of Iran's Revolutionary Guards. He could ask them to call off Iran's global terror campaign, which has included attacks in two dozen countries on five continents since 2011 alone.

To say that Iran doesn't practice terrorism is like saying Derek Jeter never played shortstop for the New York Yankees.

This bemoaning of the Iranian president of the spread of terrorism has got to be one of history's greatest displays of doubletalk.

Now, some still argue that Iran's global terror campaign, its subversion of countries throughout the Middle East and well beyond the Middle East, some argue that this is the work of the extremists. They say things are changing. They point to last year's elections in Iran. They claim that Iran's smooth talking President and Foreign Minister, they've changed not only the tone of Iran's foreign policy but also its substance. They believe Rouhani and Zarif genuinely want to reconcile with the West, that they've abandoned the global mission of the Islamic Revolution. Really?...

Imagine how much more dangerous the Islamic

State, ISIS, would be if it possessed chemical weapons. Now imagine how much more dangerous the Islamic State of Iran would be if it possessed nuclear weapons . . . .

Would you let ISIS enrich uranium?

Would you let ISIS build a heavy water reactor? Would you let ISIS develop intercontinental ballistic missiles?

Of course you wouldn't. Then you mustn't let the Islamic State of Iran do those things either. Because here's what will happen:

Once Iran produces atomic bombs, all the charm and all the smiles will suddenly disappear. They'll just vanish. It's then that the ayatollahs will show their true face and unleash their aggressive fanaticism on the entire world. There is only one responsible course of action to address this threat:

Iran's nuclear military capabilities must be fully dismantled.

Make no mistake—ISIS must be defeated. But to defeat ISIS and leave Iran as a threshold nuclear power is to win the battle and lose the war.

To defeat ISIS and leave Iran as a threshold nuclear power is to win the battle and lose the war. . . .

Israel is fighting a fanaticism today that your countries may be forced to fight tomorrow.

For 50 days this past summer, Hamas fired

thousands of rockets at Israel, many of them supplied by Iran.

I want you to think about what your countries would do if thousands of rockets were fired at your cities. Imagine millions of your citizens having seconds at most to scramble to bomb shelters, day after day.

You wouldn't let terrorists fire rockets at your cities with impunity. Nor would you let terrorists dig dozens of terror tunnels under your borders to infiltrate your towns in order to murder and kidnap your citizens.

Israel justly defended itself against both rocket attacks and terror tunnels.

Yet Israel also faced another challenge. We faced a propaganda war.

Because, in an attempt to win the world's sympathy, Hamas cynically used Palestinian civilians as human shields.

It used schools, not just schools—UN schools, private homes, mosques, even hospitals to store and fire rockets at Israel.

As Israel surgically struck at the rocket launchers and at the tunnels, Palestinian civilians were tragically but unintentionally killed. There are heartrending images that resulted, and these fueled libelous charges that Israel was deliberately targeting civilians. We were not. We deeply regret every single civilian casualty. And the truth is this:

Israel was doing everything to minimize
Palestinian civilian casualties. Hamas was
doing everything to maximize Israeli civilian
casualties and Palestinian civilian casualties.

Israel dropped flyers, made phone calls, sent
text messages, broadcast warnings in Arabic on
Palestinian television, always to enable Palestinian
civilians to evacuate targeted areas.

No other country and no other army in history
have gone to greater lengths to avoid casualties
among the civilian population of their enemies.

This concern for Palestinian life was all the more
remarkable, given that Israeli civilians were being
bombarded by rockets day after day, night after night.

As their families were being rocketed by Hamas,
Israel's citizen army—the brave soldiers of the IDF,
our young boys and girls—they upheld the highest
moral values of any army in the world.

Israel's soldiers deserve not condemnation,
but admiration. Admiration from decent people
everywhere.

Now here's what Hamas did:

Hamas embedded its missile batteries in
residential areas and told Palestinians to
ignore Israel's warnings to leave.

And just in case people didn't get the message,
they executed Palestinian civilians in Gaza who
dared to protest.

No less reprehensible, Hamas deliberately placed its rockets where Palestinian children live and play. . . . As Israeli children huddled in bomb shelters and Israel's Iron Dome missile defense system knocked Hamas rockets out of the sky, the profound moral difference between Israel and Hamas couldn't have been clearer:

> Israel was using its missiles to protect its children.
>
> Hamas was using its children to protect its missiles. . . .

Despite the enormous challenges facing Israel, I believe we have an historic opportunity.

After decades of seeing Israel as their enemy, leading states in the Arab world increasingly recognize that together we and they face many of the same dangers: principally this means a nuclear-armed Iran and militant Islamist movements gaining ground in the Sunni world.

Our challenge is to transform these common interests to create a productive partnership. One that would build a more secure, peaceful and prosperous Middle East.

Together we can strengthen regional security. We can advance projects in water, agriculture, in transportation, in health, in energy, in so many fields. . . .

Just look around you.

The Middle East is in chaos. States are disintegrating. Militant Islamists are filling the void.

Israel cannot have territories from which it withdraws taken over by Islamic militants yet again, as happened in Gaza and Lebanon. That would place the likes of ISIS within mortar range—a few miles—of 80% of our population.

Think about that. The distance between the 1967 lines and the suburbs of Tel Aviv is like the distance between the UN building here and Times Square.

Israel's a tiny country.

That's why in any peace agreement, which will obviously necessitate a territorial compromise, I will always insist that Israel be able to defend itself by itself against any threat.

Yet despite all that has happened, some still don't take Israel's security concerns seriously.

But I do, and I always will.

Because, as Prime Minister of Israel, I am entrusted with the awesome responsibility of ensuring the future of the Jewish people and the future of the Jewish state.

And no matter what pressure is brought to bear, I will never waver in fulfilling that responsibility. . . .

Isaiah, our great prophet of peace, taught us nearly 3,000 years ago in Jerusalem to speak truth to power.

For the sake of Zion, I will not be silent. For the sake of Jerusalem, I will not be still. Until her justice shines bright,

And her salvation glows like a flaming torch. . . . Let's light a torch of truth and justice to safeguard our common future.[9]

What Mr. Netanyahu did not divulge was where the materials for the tunnels originated. In August 2014, it was revealed by Dennis Ross, senior Mideast policy adviser to Secretary of State Hillary Clinton (2009–2011) that it was his responsibility to pressure the Israelis to loosen the reins on the military blockade against Gaza. Ross admitted:

> I argued with Israeli leaders and security officials, telling them they needed to allow more construction materials, including cement, into Gaza so that housing, schools and basic infrastructure could be built. They countered that Hamas would misuse it, and they were right.[10]

According to the *Wall Street Journal*:

> The sophisticated underground passageways were reinforced with concrete, and phone and electrical wires ran the length of the structures. The Israeli military said it found rocket-propelled grenades, mortars, AK-47 assault rifles and motorcycles in the tunnels, and that Hamas invested between $1 million and $10 million for the construction of each underground passageway.... The average tunnel required 350 truckloads of construction supplies—enough to build 86 homes, seven mosques, six schools or 19 medical clinics, the Israeli military says. It estimates Hamas spent $90 million on building the 32 tunnels that were uncovered, so their destruction has dealt a major setback to the Islamist group.[11]

As Mr. Netanyahu reminded the world, an unrestrained Islamic revolution is spreading from Iran through Iraq, Syria, Lebanon, the Palestinian territory, and threatens the border with Turkey, all while the world sleeps. The goal is to take over the Middle East and then the entire world. Many of us don't understand the true nature of what it will take to defeat this global web of terror. At the time, we didn't seem to understand that Iraq was not a war in itself, but only one of the first battles in the overall war on terrorism. Too many didn't recognize that the next World War had already started and we were right in the middle of it.

In *See You in New York*, we will take a walk back through history to look at the beginning of today's spike in terrorist activities—where and how it began, and what that portends for the world today.

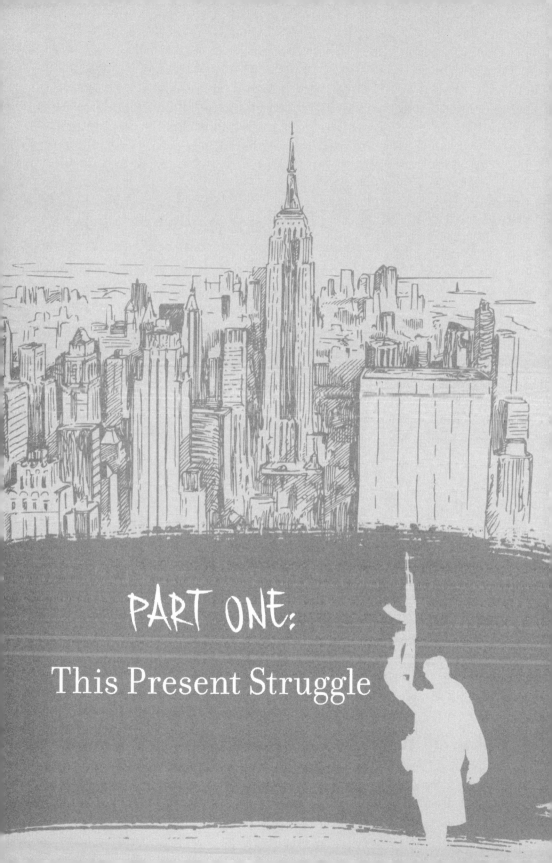

PART ONE:

This Present Struggle

CHAPTER ONE

The West Meets ISIL

I say to America the Islamic Caliphate has been established and we will not stop. Don't be cowards and attack us with drones. Instead send your soldiers, the ones we humiliated in Iraq. We will humiliate them everywhere, God willing, and we will raise the flag of Allah [over] the White House.

ABU MOSA, ISIS SPOKESMAN[12]

TODAY, THE UNITED STATES of America needs to have the same resolve in dismantling the terrorists' worldwide network that we did in fighting the Axis powers during World War II. The threat is as great as was that of Hitler's Nazi regime. Too few Americans seemed to realize at the time that the "insurgents" the US was fighting in the streets of Iraq were not simply disgruntled Iraqis caught in a cycle of incomprehensible ethnic intolerance, but the fighting was against a terror network that would be unleashed in its full ferocity once the last US vehicle departed Iraq's border. The vipers that had been multiplying underground were then free to surface and spread their venom unfettered in the form of ISIL and its radically militant form of Islam.

Joining ISIL and al-Nusra, another terrorist group, is Khorasan, an offshoot of al Qaeda. It, too, has also been targeted by US and ally-led bombings in Syria. Khorasan is led by thirty-three-year-old Muhsin al-Fadhli. The US State Department refers to al-Fadhli as a "senior facilitator and financier" for Khorasan. A news report stated:

> In 2012, the State Department was offering up to $7 million for information about [al-Fadhli's] whereabouts. Born in Kuwait, he has operated in Chechnya, fighting Russian soldiers, according to the United Nations, and has been wanted in connection to al Qaeda attacks in Saudi Arabia.
>
> In a conference call with reporters after the air strikes, several senior administration officials . . . said that Khorasan had established a safe haven within the chaos of Syria to plot attacks against the United States and other Western nations. One official reported that this planning was "nearing the execution phase." A senior administration official also said that Khorasan . . . was recruiting Westerners fighting in Syria for "external operations," and that Khorasan plotting had prompted the United States to beef up aviation security measures a few months ago. One administration official noted that President Obama had been contemplating strikes against Khorasan for months "separate and apart from the growing threat from ISIL."[13]

A CBS *60 Minutes* segment featuring FBI Director James Comey relayed further information about Khorasan:

"Khorasan was working and may still be working on an effort to attack the United States or our allies, and looking to do it very, very soon," he said . . .

"I can't sit here and tell you whether their plan is tomorrow or three weeks or three months from now," he said.

"Given our visibility, we know they're serious people, bent on destruction. And so we have to act as if it's coming tomorrow."

He said that terrorist networks in Syria are a product of "the metastasis of al Qaeda" with the two major groups, al-Nusra and the Islamic State in Iraq and Syria (ISIS).

"They are both vicious, sort of the inheritors of a lot of the mantle of al Qaeda and present different threats in a lot of ways," Comey said.

He described the al-Nusra group as experienced bomb makers, killers, and planners seeking international targets.

"These are people who have thought about bringing terrorism on a global scale," he said.

"ISIL is as sophisticated, maybe more than any of the others in its media presence and its recruiting and training efforts online," he said, using another acronym for ISIS.[14]

These are not the only two groups targeting the West, but are currently the most dangerous. When ISIL leader Abu Bakr al-Baghdadi was released from Camp Bucca, an Iraqi detention center, he said to his American captors that he would see them in New

York. He seems intent on rallying every jihadist globally in order to achieve that goal. In 2014, al-Baghdadi clearly defined the aim of his Islamic State:

> The Muslims today have a loud, thundering statement, and possess heavy boots. They have a statement that will cause the world to hear and understand the meaning of terrorism, and boots that will trample the idol of nationalism, destroy the idol of democracy and uncover its deviant nature.[15]

In a 9/11 anniversary speech, President George W. Bush predicted the peril of an early withdrawal from Iraq: "Whatever mistakes have been made in Iraq, the worst mistake would be to think that if we pulled out, the terrorists would leave us alone." His warning clearly proved to be prophetic with the rise of ISIL.

We fail to realize that we are fighting the newest world power based not on an ideology such as Communism or Nazism, but on an overzealous, distorted form of Islam whose constituents are willing to both kill and die in the hope of spreading it worldwide. Their goal is to chase democracy and freedom from the Middle East, then from the world at large. This newly formed "Islamic State" and its fanatical members have the mentality of suicide bombers willing to blow themselves up in the hope of wiping Judaism and Christianity off the map. Sadly, its targets are not just Christians and Jews but even other Muslims who refuse to embrace the extremist mentality flaunted by ISIL.

As President Obama's hastily put-together coalition battles ISIL with air strikes and arms support for troops in Iraq, it may be that the al-Baghdadi organization will falter and fall by the wayside. But one thing has become abundantly clear:

Jihadists worldwide have rushed to the aid of a group whose sole aim is to form a global Muslim caliphate. As my good friend and former Mossad head, Isser Harel, said to me, "You kill a fly and you celebrate. We live with flies daily. One dies and 100 flies come to the funeral." A report of al-Baghdadi's having been wounded or killed by a coalition air strike is a case in point. The void left by his absence—whether temporary or permanent—will be rapidly filled by numerous volunteers. While ISIL may fade into the background or even coalesce into something else, the desire of its members will remain the same: world domination.

And one can but wonder how long it would be before Iran embraces ISIL members and takes that poisonous snake to its bosom. Will its displaced denizens be allowed access to its nuclear enrichment program? What horrors would an ISIL like mentality with nuclear capabilities unleash on an unsuspecting world?

Iran's leadership is maniacally set on obtaining nuclear weapons and advancing their missile technology so that it has the power to destroy Israel and cripple the United States and Europe. Just as Ayatollah Ruhollah Khomeini joined with and then ruthlessly turned on his allies in the Islamic Revolution in the 1980s, transforming Iran into his own kingdom on earth, so Iran now may be willing to cut any deal to get what it wants. Iran's leaders hope to keep the international community at bay long enough to develop their own small nuclear arsenal—and once that is done, all previous bets will be off. Wiping Israel "off the map" is seen as the first step toward a world without Zionism and the United States.

To avoid such a scenario, we need to take a look back at the plan Mr. Netanyahu offered in his 2013 UN General Assembly speech. The prime minister laid out restraints that it would be wise to follow, a guideline that has been largely ignored by the West:

1. Totally halt uranium enrichment in Iran;

2. Confiscate Iran's already enriched uranium;

3. Disassemble plants at both the Qom and Natanz nuclear facilities;

4. Halt the production of plutonium;

5. Keep all sanctions in place until Iran has complied.

The key to victory against ISIL and its terrorist offshoots will take a concerted effort by the West, joined by its Muslim allies who are in equal danger. The world stands at a critical crossroads, but unfortunately it does so wearing politically correct blinders. Because of this, we mistakenly see our friends—namely Israel—as the root of the problem; and our enemies—Islamists set to destabilize the democracies and moderate governments of the Middle East—as misunderstood militants fighting for religious and political freedom. If we don't correct our view, we may soon abandon our friends to appease these "militants," only to find a nuclear knife in our back as the reward.

If we don't find a way to turn the right corner against radical, fanatical Islam, the road ahead may never again be as clear or as safe as it is now.

Why We Fight

As a nation, we have been blinded by liberal rhetoric to the purpose of the war against terror. It is time we set our blinders aside and acknowledge the truth.

We have only to look as far back as the presidency of Jimmy Carter to find where Pandora's box was opened, and the Islamic

Revolution was unleashed. In an 800-word diatribe against Israel co-written by former president of Ireland Mary Robinson, the two opined regarding the recent Gaza/Israel conflict:

> There is no humane or legal justification for the way the Israeli Defense Forces are conducting this war. Israeli bombs, missiles, and artillery have pulverized large parts of Gaza, including thousands of homes, schools, and hospitals.[16]

Of course, the former president has shown his disdain for Israel in countless ways and in a myriad of diatribes against the Jewish state. Carter has met several times with Hamas leader Khaled Meshaal in Damascus in an ongoing attempt to push Israel toward a one-sided peace agreement—in favor of Hamas. His personal relationship with Meshaal rivals that of Carter's long-time liaisons with the late Yasser Arafat.

Journalist Dwight L. Schwab, Jr. penned an article entitled "Jimmy Carter doesn't know when to shut up." In it he wrote:

> There is little doubt Carter is no fan of Israel. Carter has never met a terrorist leader he didn't have good relations with, including the late Yassir Arafat. In retrospect, he also criticized former President Clinton for offering a two-state solution to the Palestinians and Ehud Barak in 2000–2001. The same Jimmy Carter who thinks the terrorist group Hamas is a legitimate political party. Yet, out of nowhere, Carter now condemns President Obama

for being too soft on ISIS. Not only that, he condemns Obama for employing drone strikes against terrorists in general . . . .

Carter supports the terrorists who attack Israel, but ISIS apparently is "different." Why? The flow of money to Hamas and other organizations Carter favors will be cut off by the influence of ISIS, that's why.[17]

Carter's same ideology was alive and well during the time of the shah of Iran, and leaves no question in my mind that it was responsible for the destabilization of Iran, a pro-Israel and pro-Western ally. Khomeini could never have succeeded with the birthing of the Islamic Revolution without the assistance and support of President Jimmy Carter. Khomeini's Islamic Revolution, in turn, generated the onslaught of terrorism by which the entire world has been gripped and victimized.

On the occasion of his recent ninetieth birthday, Mr. Carter has again pushed the limits of rhetoric by declaring that he could have defeated Ronald Reagan in the 1980 presidential election by bombing Iran. Said the former president, "I could've been reelected if I'd taken military action against Iran, shown that I was strong and resolute and, um, manly and so forth." He added, "I could have wiped Iran off the map with the weapons that we had, but in the process a lot of innocent people would have been killed, probably including the hostages and so I stood up against all that."

Perhaps few remember that it was 4:31 a.m. on the morning of the Reagan inauguration that Carter wire-transferred $7.9 billion dollars through a series of banks including the Federal Reserve to the Bank of England. The funds to buy the hostages back were from money that had been controlled by the shah of Iran. At the same time, the president signed the Algerian Accord, committing the United States to respect Iran's territorial integrity and not to attack. That little stroke of the pen still haunts and fetters the US in the Persian Gulf region.

Mr. Carter's most recent comments regarding his role in Iran might well have been challenged by the late French President Valery Giscard d'Estaing, leader of France during the time of America's first crisis with Iran. In my interview with him several years ago, I was told that in 1979 he met with Carter in Guadalupe for a summit, as did Helmut Schmidt of Germany and James Callahan of Great Britain and that Carter informed this group of men that the US was going to support Khomeini instead of the shah of Iran. In essence, Mr. d'Estaing said he realized the US was trading its strongest pro-Western Persian Gulf ally in favor of a terrorist Muslim cleric. "I was horrified," said d'Estaing. "The only way I can describe Jimmy Carter is that he was a 'bastard of conscience.'"

Mr. Carter seems to have conveniently forgotten that he listened to the advice of those who had an agenda regarding the shah and turned a blind eye while the ruler and his family were summarily expelled from Iran. It paved the way for Khomeini and his terrorist element to seize control of the country. Today, the world continues to pay the price for President Carter's actions.

Asadollah Alam, appointed prime minister by the shah in July 1962, was Pahlavi's personal confidant. Alam, in his autobiography, wrote of Pahlavi's concerns over the election of Carter. The shah had asked: "Who knows what sort of calamity he [Carter] may unleash on the world?"[18] Today, we do know, as radical Islam seeks to create a global caliphate that would institute a "bow or die" philosophy.

The US went to Iraq and Afghanistan initially to take the fight to the terrorists. Every terrorist organization in the world is now in the Middle East in some form, and the West and its allies are struggling to hold them at bay. The chaos that has gripped Iraq, Syria, Kurdistan, and threatens to spill over into Turkey, Jordan, and Israel is a palpable sign of ISIL's primitive caliphate and the very difficult war that is being fought. Even with US air strikes ordered by President Obama in September 2014, the battle is far from over, and we must hold to our resolve to see it through to victory.

Could it be that the administration of President Barack Obama has simply taken up where Mr. Carter's presidency ended—with an agenda to discredit Israel and elevate terrorists in the Middle East to sainthood status? Based on past experience with the United States, Iran and other terrorist nations can look at the US under the current leadership of yet another Liberal Left president and ask, "Crime pays; what will be our reward this time?"

Success is dependent on tenacity—especially against the likes of ISIL and its heinous assault on humanity. One example is that of Australian terrorist Khaled Sharrouf, whose Twitter account was suspended after posting a shocking photo of his seven-year-old son holding aloft a severed head in the city of Raqqa, Syria. The caption beneath the photo read, "That's my boy." This is but one illustration of the viciousness and barbarism inflicted by ISIL militants on those who fail to kowtow to their demands.

Another instance was the threat issued to an entire village in Iraq: Become Muslims or we will kill you all. ISIL radicals have already enforced a primitive Islamic caliphate on a portion of that country. The remainder of Iraq as well as Syria, Lebanon, Turkey, and Cypress are in their crosshairs. Their tactics are brutal and the corpses left in the wake are reminiscent of the killing fields in Cambodia.

When ISIL troops encircled the walled town of Kosha, inhabited by members of the Yazidi sect with ancient Zoroastrian ties, the ultimatum was delivered to the town mayor who, in turn, made the demands known to the villagers. The village official said money was offered to ISIL, but was refused. It seems only blood and mayhem, death and destruction, will satisfy the fanatics.

One Iraqi government leader reported that some 500 men, women, and children had been slaughtered by the extremists, some buried alive, with more than 300 women reportedly captured and taken away as slaves. That again proves that these bloodthirsty terrorists will stop at nothing in order to achieve their goal of total domination—one region at a time.

CHAPTER TWO

Can We Win?

*Half-hearted or tentative efforts, or airstrikes alone, can
backfire on us and actually strengthen our foes' credibility . . . .
We may not wish to reassure our enemies in advance that
they will not see American boots on the ground.*

GEN. JAMES MATTIS, USMC (RETIRED)

MILITARILY, THE UNITED STATES appears to have lost
ground since the 2008 presidential election of Barack Obama. At
least 197 military officers have been given their walking papers by
the chief executive, some with good reason, others dismissed under
a dubious list of infractions. Added to that list are nine generals
with varying degrees of seniority, giving way to speculation that the
Obama administration is determined to purge the US military of its
seasoned veterans. Army Major General Paul Vallely (US, retired), a
vocal opponent of the president's handling of military affairs has said:

> Obama will not purge a civilian or political
> appointee because they have bought into Obama's

ideology. The White House protects their own. That's why they stalled on the investigation into Fast and Furious, Benghazi and ObamaCare. He's intentionally weakening and gutting our military, Pentagon and reducing us as a superpower, and anyone in the ranks who disagrees or speaks out is being purged.[20]

What could be the purpose of such house cleaning in a once-globally feared army? Could it be a move to emasculate and render impotent the American military whose might has been a stimulus for peace worldwide? Conversely, it has been a deterrent for the enemy—terrorists all—whose purpose is fundamentally evil. Without a strong military, the US will be drawn into one global disaster after another until our troops are decimated and the country is left at the mercy of the wolves circling outside the door.

Sadly, too many of the Liberal Left genres fail to recognize the deliberate and debilitating disassembly of our first line of defense. Major General Patrick Brady wrote:

> I believe that Obama has no knowledge of or interest in military matters. Nor does he have the capacity to deal with crisis—the reason for a military—and he knows it. A feeble military would give him cover. A lack of resources is the perfect excuse for doing nothing, an Obama hallmark. And there are no votes in military spending—this man lives for votes. In a world aflame with uncertainty and violence, watch the president's campaign media. You will never hear a word about increasing or preserving our military

strength, only that the troops are coming home. Ignorance of military matters is one thing and can be overcome, but ignorance of the importance of military might in promoting peace worldwide and protecting America is deadly.[21]

Unfortunately, there are those who believe that the US military is an outdated indication of a country whose uniqueness and global leadership necessitate frequent justification. As penance, the United States, or so it seems in Mr. Obama's world, must be altered to fit his mold of lackeys bearing overcoats and umbrellas in preparation for a coming cold front. It will do little to thwart a nuclear winter should ISIL or any of the other fanatical threats facing the world decide to overrun a country with atomic weapons capabilities.

While the US armed forces defeated Hitler's Nazi machine in World War II, and President Ronald Reagan challenged Mikhail Gorbachev with, "Mr. Gorbachev, tear down this wall," which ended the Cold War, there seems to be little backbone in Washington these days when it comes to facing down evil. Appeasement has become the weapon of choice; weakness is preferable to power.

By a refusal to take a stand against Bashar al-Assad in Syria, Vladimir Putin in Russia, and ISIL in its early stages, terrorism and its adherents are now running amok. Who can forget the open-mic aside that occurred between then Russian president Dmitry Medvedev on the eve of the 2012 election? According to a Reuter's news story in the Huffington Post:

> President Barack Obama was caught on camera on
> Monday assuring outgoing Russian President Dmitry

Medvedev he will have "more flexibility" to deal with contentious issues like missile defense after the US presidential election.

Obama, during talks in Seoul, urged Moscow to give him "space" until after the November ballot, and Medvedev said he would relay the message to incoming Russian president Vladimir Putin.[22]

One can but question what other promises were made to the thugocracies, or family-owned corporations in the Middle East, the card-carrying, mafia-like cartels that control much of the world's oil. The way terror organizations are kept from turning on them is by paying baksheesh (bribes) and by funding and fueling their causes. It is a "don't ask, don't tell" policy. In that light, Saudi Arabia continued to fund terrorist-Sunni rebels in Iraq hoping to keep democracy as far from its borders as it could, even though the same tactic didn't work for them with al Qaeda—and is unlikely to work with ISIL.

Islamic State leaders have been vocal in their criticism of the House of Saud and its hold over Saudi Arabia. There is a wide rift between what ISIL sees as the modernists in that country and its own members.

What exactly does the Islamic State plan for the cradle of Wahhabism in the Middle East? The purpose is to cause a total disintegration of the Kingdom of Saudi Arabia. The plan is to return the region to the teachings of al-Wahhab and legislate that Wahhabism, an Islamic "reform movement" to restore "pure monotheistic worship,"[23] becomes the sole foundation for Islamic beliefs. What would that entail? Every Muslim would be forced to accept Wahhabism or be slaughtered. All property would revert to ISIL as spoils of war—including that of any family members. Any hesitation or reservation would result in execution.

If the Kingdom of Saudi Arabia were to be overcome by ISIL zeal, the region would be forever changed—for the worse. The Middle East would become grotesque and distorted in ways we cannot even conceive. The Islamic State is a time bomb waiting to explode with a hatred for all the trappings of wealth—without which the organization would perish due to lack of funding.

While an enemy is needed in order to have an army, today's Liberal Left leaders seemingly have determined that "We have met the enemy, and he is us."[24] The Liberal media has little regard for the truth that the Islamic world doesn't want the Palestinian crisis resolved. The thugocracies and Islamofascists do everything in their power to keep that from happening. If the Palestinian crisis were resolved, there would be no enemy, and they need Israel to be the "Little Satan" of the Middle East in order to have some entity to blame for their problems. With the advent of the Islamic State, the microscope has been moved from the Palestinian issue to open assault against other Muslims, Christians, and Jews. This allows Mahmoud Abbas to fly under the radar and focus on making an end run around Israel to achieve the goal of dividing Jerusalem and establishing a Palestinian state recognized by the UN.

Abbas was aided in his plot to circumvent peace talks with Israel in October 2014 when the British Parliament voted to acknowledge Palestinian statehood. Even though the vote was non-binding because less than half the members of Parliament were in the House of Commons, it is seen as a wave of the future. Paul Hirschson, spokesperson at Israel's Ministry of Foreign Affairs said the move sends the message that the Palestinians "could get what they want without making compromises."[25]

The question begs asking: Will the United States follow suit and engage in Israel-bashing, as have some European countries?

While many Muslims are not opposed to democracy, as noted by statistics that the majority of Muslims are not Islamofascists, they simply want to live freely by the dictates of their own consciences just as the rest of the world does. Islamofascists do not, and will do anything to keep Islam under radical control and moving toward a caliphate and Sharia Law.

But the question remains: "Is America strong enough?" I am concerned that it is not. The US certainly has the technology, but does it have the will to stay the course until victory is realized? Can the American people overcome the seeming lack of will to win, the self-loathing, and the unconcern that seems to surround the War on Terror?

The Liberal Left has convinced many Americans that the War on Terror cannot be won through military action and has shattered our will to win. The liberals point to the US pullout in Lebanon, in Korea, and in Vietnam, or to the Soviet Union's withdrawal from Afghanistan to support their pronouncements. What these pundits do not seem to understand is that it was political pressure exerted on a military force that precipitated each decision to leave the field of combat—the Viet Cong, the North Koreans, Hezbollah, and the Afghan fighters. The results were military victories for each of those groups and a loss of respect for US armed forces.

Appeasement is the offshoot of self-loathing; we hate war. General William Tecumseh Sherman said, "War is hell." Rather than believe those who wage war against us are evil, we mistakenly begin to see ourselves as evil for retaliating, or even worse, preemptively striking to prevent a sure danger to regional or world security. Self-loathing replaces righteous indignation—and begets appeasement. The desire to negotiate no matter the cost gives rise to those in the West who become unwitting cohorts to the jihadists. These individuals rationalize the presence of evil and attacks by terrorists based on their perception of our own past sins.

The result is unconcern, complacency, or lack of motivation—the disorder has many names. Whatever the label, it results in simply not taking the threat of terror attacks seriously. The first World Trade Center attack in 1993 should have been a wake-up call; however, few realized the import of that momentous explosion: It was a precursor to 9/11.

If we refuse to act now—before terrorists have further access to nuclear weapons—for what will the 9/11 attacks be a precursor?

There is only one way to win in this clash of civilizations. Winston Churchill understood this when he spoke these unforgettable words before Parliament on June 4, 1940, following the dark days of defeat at Dunkirk in which 338,000 Allied troops had to be evacuated to English shores:

> Even though large tracts of Europe and many old and famous States have fallen or may fall into the grip of the Gestapo and all the odious apparatus of Nazi rule, we shall not flag or fail. We shall go on to the end, we shall fight in France, we shall fight on the seas and oceans, we shall fight with growing confidence and growing strength in the air, we shall defend our Island, whatever the cost may be, we shall fight on the beaches, we shall fight on the landing grounds, we shall fight in the fields and in the streets, we shall fight in the hills; we shall never surrender.

It was Winston Churchill who said that the world lacked the "democratic courage, intellectual honesty, and willingness to act" to stopping Hitler's war machine in 1938. If they had, 61 million people would not have died in concentration camps and on the battlefields during World War II.

The terror of 9/11 should have gotten our collective attention; but our attention span seems to be measured in nanoseconds rather than the years it will take to win this struggle. We tend to ridicule the ragtag armies of many of the world's superpower pretenders—Iran being a case in point. We refuse to admit that the US, like Israel, could suddenly become a repository for suicide-belted jihadists intent on our destruction. We dismiss as a mere nuisance the threats made by the likes of Iran's former leader President Mahmoud Ahmadinejad. After all, what weapons can the fanatical practitioners of Islam really have at their disposal?

✧ Weapons of mass destruction, or the ability to obtain them;

✧ Rabid religious fanaticism;

✧ Funds flowing into their coffers from oil-rich Middle Eastern countries such as Saudi Arabia and Iran, among others;

✧ Broad appeal—from beggars in the streets to university professors in the halls of academia; from Riyadh to Boston; from Tehran to Toronto;

- ✧ Immigration and infiltration—legal immigrants to largely non-Muslim countries such as the United States, Great Britain, France, Germany, Canada, and Spain are well versed in using the legal and political systems in those countries to further their agenda of ultimate domination;

- ✧ Sheer numbers—if the radical element of Islam measures only ten percent of Muslims as a whole, the number is still a staggering 125 million plus. That is a sizeable army of radicals with only one ultimate aim: kill infidels wherever they may be found.

Will the lack of resolve, the self-loathing, and the absence of motivation cause the US to end the war on terror? Will the West fall victim to disastrous losses of human life and goods? How long will it take to recognize the truth that no one, I repeat, no one—no American, Britain, Frenchman, German, Spaniard, not even a Muslim—is safe from the assault of the radical Islamists' hatred? And the most pressing question of all: Can the civilized world survive the onslaught of such fanaticism? What will it take to jar the West from its comfortable complacency? I pray it is not another devastating attack or series of attacks on US soil.

The Road Ahead

Now, with the appearance of ISIL and the resurgence of al Qaeda in the form of Khorasan, it is imperative the Liberal Left realize that the war was not only justified but is also part of a much larger picture. Whatever form it takes, we will pay much more dearly down the road if we fail to find a strategy for victory over this latest rise of fanatical Islamism and its adherents.

When the US pulled out of Iraq it simply meant the coming of another, bloodier fight down the road. Had we stopped Hezbollah in Lebanon in the 1980s, winning this war might have been much simpler—or might never have had to be fought.

In the coming months, the United States must find a path to victory over ISIL, Khorasan, Hamas, Hezbollah, and other terrorist organizations worldwide—not the path of appeasement and premature withdrawal—but a clear track of moral clarity. If we let the terrorists off now, it will simply mean more devastating attacks in the future.

In the following pages we will explore why we are where we are today in the Middle East, the reasons for pushing forward with the fortitude and courage necessary to win the war on terrorism, and what the best road ahead will be. It is time for our nation to come together.

In the midst of the American Civil War on April 30, 1863, Abraham Lincoln called the nation to prayer based upon 2 Chronicles 7:14:

> If my people, who are called by my name, will humble themselves and pray and seek my face and turn from their wicked ways, then I will hear from heaven, and I will forgive their sin and will heal their land.

Lincoln's proclamation read:

We have been the recipients of the choicest bounties of Heaven. We have been preserved, these many years, in peace and prosperity. We have grown in numbers, wealth and power, as no other nation has ever grown. But we have forgotten God. We have forgotten the gracious hand which preserved us in peace, and multiplied and enriched and strengthened us; and we have vainly imagined, in the deceitfulness of our hearts, that all these blessings were produced by some superior wisdom and virtue of our own. Intoxicated with unbroken success, we have become too self-sufficient to feel the necessity of redeeming and preserving grace, too proud to pray to God that made us! It behooves us then, to humble ourselves before the offended Power, to confess our national sins, and to pray for clemency and forgiveness.

President Ronald Regan once told me after I spoke briefly at the end of an event he hosted that the greatest political body in America is not the Republican Party, but the Church. With a smile, he also said, "I am not as worried about the left wing or the right wing—I want God to heal the bird." He was sworn in twice; both times his hand rested on 2 Chronicles 7:14. During his first Inauguration, the hostages were being released in Iran. During his second term, Communism fell

I believe this is a battle between two books, two kingdoms, and two spirits; and that the key to victory lies more in the hands of the Church crying out to God than in the hands of politicians in Washington, D.C.

God does answer prayer—indeed, America needs to become a purpose-driven nation once again.

We have had a rude awakening; now we need a great awakening.

CHAPTER THREE

A Prophetic Storm Gathers

*And then that day when we attack Israel, even the trees and
the stones will have mouths. They will cry out. They will say,
"There is a Jew hiding behind me. Come, oh Muslim. Come, oh
slave of Allah. Come and kill him 'till not one male Jew is left."*

WALID SHOEBAT, FORMER TERRORIST[26]

*"Tell us, when will these things happen? And what will be the
sign that they are all about to be fulfilled?" Jesus said to them:
"Watch out that no one deceives you. . . . When you hear of wars
and rumors of wars, do not be alarmed. Such things must happen,
but the end is still to come. Nation will rise against nation, and
kingdom against kingdom. There will be earthquakes in various
places, and famines. These are the beginning of birth pains . . .
"Brother will betray brother to death. . . . All men will hate you
because of me, but he who stands firm to the end will be saved."*

MARK 13:4–5, 7 8, 12, 13

THE VAST MAJORITY of students of prophecy have always
believed that the end of the age would begin with a worldwide battle
between the descendants of the two sons of Abraham: Isaac, the Jew,
and Ishmael, the Arab. Such a battle would center on the Middle

East—mainly Israel—and increase like a pandemic until it engulfs the entire globe. This battle grows ever closer.

The apostle John received the vision from God on the Isle of Patmos in AD 95 that became the book of Revelation. In that vision, John saw four riders on horseback galloping across the earth, bringing deceit, death, destruction, and devastation. Those four riders are commonly known as the Four Horsemen of the Apocalypse. If you listen closely, you can almost hear the hoofbeats of those four horses across all the news channels and throughout the pages of today's newspapers and magazines.

The Revelation of John begins with the unveiling of a scroll written on both sides and sealed with seven seals. Seals, in that day, were impressions made with wax, clay, or some other soft material that assured unauthorized persons had not accessed the contents. The seals must be broken, one by one, to divulge the contents of what is inside. As John broke each seal, another portion of God's revelation about the final days of the earth was disclosed, each time divulging a worse horror than the previous one.

Let us briefly look in Revelation 6 at the impact that the breaking of the seal indicative of the four horsemen will have on the earth. In verses 1 and 2, we are introduced to the rider of the white horse. It is believed that this rider is equipped with a bow but no projectiles and represents the coming Antichrist. Pastor and author Dr. David Jeremiah refers to him as "the most despicable man who will ever walk the earth."[27] He will not have to earn his crown through war, but will be acclaimed the conquering hero because of his promises of peace and safety. (See 1 Thessalonians 5:3.) The rider will craft a peace treaty with Israel, only to break the accord after three and a half years and ensnare a totally gullible world population. (See Daniel 8:25.)

The red horse of Revelation 6:4 depicts carnage—death and destruction from wars that will erupt following the introduction of the Antichrist.

The rider of the third, black horse in Revelation 6:5–6 will introduce worldwide famine. A denarius during the time of John the Revelator symbolized a day's wages. The vision signified that a person would work all day for barely enough to feed oneself. Food prices would rise to approximately ten times the norm. It is reminiscent of the terrible famine in 2 Kings 6:25–29:

> There was a great famine in the city; the siege lasted so long that a donkey's head sold for eighty shekels of silver, and a quarter of a cab of seed pods for five shekels. As the king of Israel was passing by on the wall, a woman cried to him, "Help me, my lord the king!" The king replied, "If the LORD does not help you, where can I get help for you? From the threshing floor? From the winepress?" Then he asked her, "What's the matter?" She answered, "This woman said to me, 'Give up your son so we may eat him today, and tomorrow we'll eat my son.' So we cooked my son and ate him. The next day I said to her, 'Give up your son so we may eat him,' but she had hidden him."

Such horrors await an earth gripped by famine, and the climactic result of the rise of the Antichrist, ensuing wars, and famine, will be the fourth, pale horse, which represents death. (See Revelation 6:7–8.) Matthew 24:21 tells us, "For then there will be great distress, unequaled from the beginning of the world until now—and never to be equaled again." Even more distressing is that the arrival of the four horsemen is only the onset of sorrows as God's judgment begins to fall upon the earth.

Daniel, the prophet who lived in ancient Babylon (modern-day Iraq), wrote this of the mystery of the end times in the twelfth chapter of Daniel. It begins:

> At that time Michael, the great prince who protects your people, will arise. There will be a time of distress such as has not happened from the beginning of nations until then. But at that time your people—everyone whose name is found written in the book—will be delivered. Multitudes who sleep in the dust of the earth will awake: some to everlasting life, others to shame and everlasting contempt. Those who are wise will shine like the brightness of the heavens, and those who lead many to righteousness, like the stars forever and ever. But you, Daniel, close up and seal the words of the scroll until the time of the end. Many will go here and there to increase knowledge . . . I heard, but I did not understand. So I asked, "My lord, what will the outcome of all this be?" He replied, "Go your way, Daniel, because the words are closed up and sealed until the time of the end. Many will be purified, made spotless and refined, but the wicked will continue to be wicked. None of the wicked will understand, but those who are wise will understand" (Daniel 12:1–4, 8–10).

On the Mount of Olives, Jesus' disciples asked Him, "What

will be the sign of your coming, and of the end of the age?" [Jesus answered] "You will hear of wars and rumors of wars, but see to it that you are not alarmed. Such things must happen, but the end is still to come. Nation will rise against nation, and kingdom against kingdom. . . . If those days had not been cut short, no one would survive" (Matthew 24:3, 6–7, 22).

As I write this, Israel is overshadowed by a threatening apocalypse from the terrorists that surround her—the very land God promised to Abraham and His descendants in the book of Genesis. Understanding the biblical backgrounds and cultures of the Middle East and its nations and peoples can be very enlightening for the student of prophecy.

From the Cradle of Civilization

The kingdoms of Persia and Babylon inhabited the region that played host to the world's earliest civilizations. They are thought by most archaeological scholars to contain the site named in the Old Testament book of Genesis as the Garden of Eden. Ur of the Chaldees, the home of Abraham, was also a part of the region that was once Babylonia—later controlled by the Persians.

At its zenith, the Persian Empire encompassed the landmass from India to Greece, from the Caspian Sea to the Red Sea, and included the Arabian Sea. Its modern-day equivalent would be the countries of Pakistan, a portion of India, Afghanistan, Iran, Iraq, Syria, Turkey, Jordan, Israel, and Egypt—all combined into one vast empire.

For three millennia, Iran has maintained its existence as an autonomous territory, changing its name from Persia in 1935. Unlike its neighbors, Iran is not Arab—it is Persian, or more correctly

Indo-European. While the Iranians write in a script nearly identical to Arabic, the official language of the nation is not Arabic, but Farsi. Unlike its neighbors, Iran's history is not rooted in Islam, but rather in a time when kings were like gods and massive structures were erected in their honor. Even today, Iran celebrates *No Ruz* (new day or New Year). This is not a tradition of Islam, but rather of the days before Islam conquered Persia.

Cyrus the Great, the first Achaemenid Emperor—and incidentally, the first king to add "Great" to his title—established the Persian Empire by uniting the Medes and the Persians, two of the earliest tribes in Iran. He ruled the extensive empire from 550–529 BC, when he was succeeded by his unstable son, Cambyses II.

Within four years of his ascension to the throne, Cyrus subjugated Croesus, the king of Lydia (of "rich as Croesus" fame), and controlled the Aegean coast of Asia Minor, Armenia, and the Greek colonies along the Levant. Looking eastward, Cyrus seized Parthia, Chorasmis, and Bactria.

Cyrus ruled over one of the largest empires in early recorded history. Though he conquered people after people, he was known for his unparalleled forbearance and charitable posture toward those whom he subjugated.

In 539 BC, Babylon fell before the advance of Cyrus's army. He was greeted by roars of welcome from the Jews who had been carried captive to Babylon. Following his conquest of that great city, Cyrus permitted some 40,000 Jews to return to their homeland in Canaan. With such an unprecedented move, Cyrus displayed great deference toward the religious tenets and social mores of other peoples.

Let me stop here a moment and point out that under the leadership of Cyrus, the Persians exhibited great compassion in allowing the Jews taken captive by Nebuchadnezzar to return to Judah, and to Jerusalem. What prompted the conqueror to allow the conquered to make their way home? None other than Jehovah God! God can move the heart of a king just as surely as He can move the heart of a pauper. As Proverbs 21:1 says:

> The king's heart is in the hand of the LORD; he directs it like a watercourse wherever he pleases.
>
> Cyrus was lauded as "upright, a great leader of men, generous and benevolent. The Hellenes, whom he conquered, regarded him as 'Law-giver' and the Jews declared him to be 'the anointed (sic) of the Lord.'"[28]

In biblical history, Cyrus is first mentioned in 2 Chronicles 36:22–23, and again in Ezra 1:1–3. Both passages record that God "moved the heart of Cyrus king of Persia" in order to fulfill "the word of the LORD spoken by Jeremiah":

> In the first year of Cyrus king of Persia, in order to fulfill the word of the LORD spoken by Jeremiah, the LORD moved the heart of Cyrus king of Persia to make a proclamation throughout his realm and to put it in writing:
>
> > This is what Cyrus king of Persia says: "The LORD, the God of heaven, has given me all the kingdoms of the earth and he has appointed me to build a temple for him at Jerusalem in Judah. Anyone of his people among you—may his God be with him, and let him go up to

Jerusalem in Judah and build the temple of
the LORD, the God of Israel, the God who is in
Jerusalem" (Ezra 1:1–3).

When King Nebuchadnezzar of Babylon captured Jerusalem
in 604 BC, every precious vessel was looted from the Temple and
carried away to Babylonia. When nations were conquered by the
Babylonians, the idols worshipped by that people were placed in
a position of subservience to Marduk, the idol worshipped by the
Babylonians. The Israelites were an exception. They did not worship graven images; therefore the vessels taken from Solomon's
Temple were likely placed in close proximity to, but not in subservience to, Marduk.

Daily food offerings were presented to the idol, and the food,
blessed by being in the presence of their god, was then presented
to the king. It was on such an occasion that Belshazzar, in a fit of
drunken frenzy, demanded that the vessels from Solomon's Temple
be brought to the banquet hall.

Daniel 5:3–4 gives us this picture:

> So they brought in the gold goblets that had been
> taken from the temple of God in Jerusalem, and the
> king and his nobles, his wives and his concubines
> drank from them. As they drank the wine, they
> praised the gods of gold and silver, of bronze, iron,
> wood, and stone.

The holy God of heaven was not amused by Belshazzar's antics.
The banquet hall was silenced, and the king became a quivering

mass as the fingers of a man's hand appeared and wrote a divine message on the wall:

This is the inscription that was written:
MENE, MENE, TEKEL, PARSIN

Here is what these words mean:

Mene: God has numbered the days of your
reign and brought it to an end.
Tekel: You have been weighed on the
scales and found wanting.
Peres: Your kingdom is divided and given to the
Medes and Persians (Daniel 5:25–28).

Belshazzar didn't have long to wait for God to fulfill this indictment against him:

That very night Belshazzar, king of the
Babylonians, was slain, and Darius the Mede
took over the kingdom (Daniel 5:30–31).

Darius was later conquered by Cyrus the Great.

It may surprise you to know that God doesn't predict the future; He creates it. God foretells events to His prophets, who in turn prophesy to the people those things that God has revealed. God disclosed His future plans to the prophets of old—Isaiah, Jeremiah, Daniel, Ezekiel, and others. Then in His perfect timing, He caused the prophesied events to become reality. He used ancient kings and kingdoms to chastise and direct His errant children, the nation of

Israel, and He used those same kings and kingdoms to return them to their rightful place.

As ruler of Persia, Cyrus was heir to all the vessels looted by the Babylonians from Solomon's Temple in Jerusalem. Unlike other conquerors, Cyrus did something that was completely uncommon. Seventy years after they were taken captive by Nebuchadnezzar, Cyrus allowed the Jewish people to return home to Israel. (This is what Daniel had prayed for in Daniel 9:17–19.) Not only were they allowed to return, Cyrus provided everything they needed to rebuild the Temple and the walls of the city. With their return to Jerusalem, he relinquished into their care the items that were taken from the Temple.

Cyrus was unique, not only because he allowed the Jews to return to Israel but also because his birth and his name were foretold by the prophet Isaiah almost 150 years before he was born. God also revealed Cyrus's mission to the prophet. Isaiah recorded that Cyrus would accomplish specific tasks under God's direction during his life-time. King Cyrus was destined to carry out God's plan as it related to His chosen people. It was through Cyrus that the Babylonian Empire and seventy years of Jewish captivity came to an end.

Isaiah 44:28:

> Who says of Cyrus, "He is my shepherd and
> will accomplish all that I please;
> he will say of Jerusalem, 'Let it be rebuilt,' and
> of the temple, 'Let its foundations be laid.'"

Although Cyrus was a practicing pagan, a worshipper of the idol Marduk, he would achieve noble feats as an instrument in the hands of Jehovah God. He would contribute, albeit indirectly, to the coming of the Messiah, God's anointed One:

> Moreover, King Cyrus brought out the articles belonging to the temple of the LORD, which Nebuchadnezzar had carried away from Jerusalem and had placed in the temple of his god. Cyrus king of Persia had them brought by Mithredath the treasurer, who counted them out to Sheshbazzar the prince of Judah (Ezra 1:7–8).
>
> However, in the first year of Cyrus king of Babylon, King Cyrus issued a decree to rebuild this house of God. He even removed from the temple of Babylon the gold and silver articles of the house of God, which Nebuchadnezzar had taken from the temple in Jerusalem and brought to the temple in Babylon.
>
> Then King Cyrus gave them to a man named Sheshbazzar, whom he had appointed governor, and he told him, "Take these articles and go and deposit them in the temple in Jerusalem. And rebuild the house of God on its site." So this Sheshbazzar came and laid the foundations of the house of God in Jerusalem. From that day to the present it has been under construction but is not yet finished.
>
> Now if it pleases the king, let a search be made in the royal archives of Babylon to see if King Cyrus did in fact issue a decree to rebuild this house of God in Jerusalem. Then let the king send us his decision in this matter (Ezra 5:13–17).

In the first year of King Cyrus, the king issued a decree concerning the temple of God in Jerusalem:

> Let the temple be rebuilt as a place to present sacrifices, and let its foundations be laid. It is to be ninety feet high and ninety feet wide, with three courses of large stones and one of timbers. The costs are to be paid by the royal treasury. Also, the gold and silver articles of the house of God, which Nebuchadnezzar took from the temple in Jerusalem and brought to Babylon, are to be returned to their places in the temple in Jerusalem; they are to be deposited in the house of God (Ezra 6:3–5).

History documents the birth, death, and achievements of Cyrus the Great. His name is recorded in the Bible over twenty times. *Encyclopedia Britannica* recognizes that "in 538 [BC] Cyrus granted to the Jews, whom Nebuchadnezzar had transported to Babylonia, the return to Palestine and the rebuilding of Jerusalem and its temple."[29]

It is ironic that the descendants of the very nation instrumental in returning the Jews to Jerusalem during the reign of King Cyrus now wants them "wiped off the map."

Darius I wrested the Persian kingdom from the descendants of Cyrus the Great, but the establishment of his rule was fraught by skirmishes with the surrounding provinces. Darius proved to be quite the tactician. His trusted generals used Darius's small army of Medes and Persians to great advantage and were able to solidify Darius's rule over the entire Persian Empire.

Darius was a forward-thinking ruler whose legal expertise

produced the "ordinance of Good Regulations" used to create a uniform code of law throughout the empire. He created a system of mail transport much like the Pony Express. Darius built a system of roads that stretched for 1,500 miles from Sardis in Turkey to Shustar (the site of Daniel's overnight visit to the lions' den). Darius I was succeeded by his son, Xerxes I—also known as Ahasuerus— the king who took the Jewess Hadassah (better known as Esther) as his queen.

The story of Esther has all the elements of a modern-day love story: A beautiful young Jewish girl torn from her homeland and taken as a captive to Persia, a tyrannical ruler who banished his queen from the royal throne and initiated a search for her successor, and of course, a dastardly villain, Haman. It was he who desired to perpetrate genocide against the Jews:

> Then Haman said to King Xerxes, "There is a certain people dispersed and scattered among the peoples in all the provinces of your kingdom whose customs are different from those of all other people and who do not obey the king's laws; it is not in the king's best interest to tolerate them" (Esther 3:8).

Esther's uncle, Mordecai, challenged the queen to approach the king (a move that, uninvited, could have been punishable by death) and ask for the salvation of her people. In encouraging her to do so, Mordecai confronted Esther with these timeless words:

> For if you remain silent at this time, relief and deliverance for the Jews will arise from another place, but you and your father's family will perish.

And who knows but that you have come to your royal position for such a time as this? (Esther 4:14).

Esther's response to Mordecai is magnificent:

> Go, gather together all the Jews who are in Susa, and fast for me. Do not eat or drink for three days, night or day. I and my maids will fast as you do. When this is done, I will go to the king, even though it is against the law. And if I perish, I perish (Esther 4:16).

With great trepidation, Esther approached Ahasuerus and was granted an audience. The plan for the destruction of the Jews by the foul villain, Haman, was thwarted and Esther's people were allowed to live in peace in Shushan.

Many empires have fallen prey to the march of time. However, in Persia—or Iran—the Arab onslaught produced a cultural mix that was unique. Persia would forever be dramatically influenced by the armies of Mohammad, but so would the conquerors be influenced by their Persian subjects. Arabic became the new language, Islam became the new religion, mosques were built, and Islamic customs became the norm for the people of Persia.

Political correctness is not an invention of modern-day America; it has dictated the actions of people from the beginning of time. For many Iranian nobles, conversion to Islam was a politically correct move that enabled them to keep their vast holdings and coveted social positions.

For others, the impetus for conversion was tax evasion. Their Muslim superiors had levied an exorbitant tax against all non-Muslims, which they wished to avoid. Some Jews living in Iran were forced, on forfeiture of their lives, to convert to Islam. Many, such as the Zoroastrian priests, simply fled the country.

Although the conquest of Iran by the Arab hordes was relatively violence-free, the ensuing struggle for leadership culminated in a bloody and lopsided battle. Hussein ibn Ali, the grandson of the Prophet Mohammad, and forces loyal to his challenger for the role of leader, Caliph Yazid, met on the plains of Karbala—today one of the holiest sites in Iraq. (It was to be a watershed event in Islam, for it was here that Hussein died, and it was here that the irreparable division between the Sunnis and the Shi'a began.)

The Temple of Doom

Shi'a Islam was founded in AD 661 by Ali ibn Abi Talib. It was from his name that Shi'a evolved. It is literally a derivation of *Shi'at Ali*—"partisans of Ali." As a descendant of Mohammad, he was thought to have been the last of the true caliphs. He was wildly popular until he came face-to-face in a battle with the army of the governor of Damascus in AD 661. It is said that the Damascene soldiers attached verses from the Koran to the tips of their spears. When faced with fighting a force hiding behind the words of Mohammad, Ali's army declined to fight. Ali, left only with the option of negotiating with his enemy, sought appeasement. While he escaped death at the hands of his enemy in open combat, Ali was eventually killed by one of his own rabid followers.

When Ali died, the governor of Damascus, Mu'awiya, anointed himself caliph. Ali's son, Hassan, the rightful heir to the caliphate, died under suspicious circumstances, while the next in line of succession, Hussein, agreed to do nothing until Mu'awiya was dead. He was soon disappointed yet again, however, when Mu'awiya's son, Yazid, appropriated the position of caliph, and went to battle against Hussein. The bloody battle of Karbala that erupted resulted in the deaths of Hussein and his entire army. Only Hussein's baby boy survived the carnage and became the hope of reestablishing Ali's claim to the caliphate.

Notable among the various dynasties of Persia were the Safavids who ruled from 1501 to 1736. It was under this dynasty that Shi'a Islam became Iran's official religion. It was also during this time that Persia was united into a single sovereignty that became the bridge to what we now know as Iran.

It was the Afsharid leader, Nadir Shah, who first declared himself the shah of Iran in 1736. He invaded Khandahar in Afghanistan, and two years after assuming the throne in Iran, Nadir Shah overran India. He amassed great wealth, including the seizure of the renowned Peacock Throne and the 105-carat *Koh-i-Noor* (Persian for "mountain of light") diamond, presented to Queen Victoria in 1851 and now part of the celebrated British Crown Jewels. Nadir Shah was a tyrannical ruler; his reign ended with his assassination in 1747.

The Afsharid dynasty was followed by the Zand and Qajar dynasties. In 1906, Iran experienced a constitutional revolution that divided the power of rule between the shah and a parliamentary body called the *Majlis*. The last of the Qajar dynasty rulers, Ahmad Shah Qajar, was overthrown in a coup in 1921, and the Pahlavis—the father and then the son who sat on the Peacock Throne until 1979—taking power as shahs. Ahmad Shah Qajar died in exile in France in 1930.

It was the first Pahlavi, Reza Shah Pahlavi the Great, who in 1935 asked the world to stop referring to his nation as Persia and to use the name Iran instead. *Iran* means "land of the Aryans" and was the name the natives used in referring to their country.[30]

During more than twenty-five centuries of history, Persians have maintained their unique sense of identity. Though they converted to Islam, they have not always followed the accepted views of the religion. To an extent, Zoroastrianism, the religion of the early Persians, colors the Iranian variety of Islam.

Iran is now not only one of the largest countries in the Middle East, but also in the Islamic world. Because of past experiences, Iran has developed a thorny separatism. Invaded during both world wars and later set upon by Iraq, Iran has reason to fear foreign influence.

The borders of Iran remained largely unchanged during the twentieth century, but the desire to recapture the glory of the vast Persian Empire has apparently lain dormant. Perhaps this pragmatism is the driving force behind Iran's seemingly sudden emergence as a budding player in the world's nuclear superpower game.

It was during the reign of the last shah of Iran, Mohammad Reza Pahlavi, that plans were instituted to bring Iran into the nuclear age. Bushehr was to be the site of the first two reactors, and indeed, construction on the site began in 1975. While the shah was still in control, research and development of fissile material production was also initiated. Most of the shah's ambitions ended with the Islamic Revolution of 1979, and for a time, nuclear pursuits were hampered.

Babylon Will Rise Again

In my bestselling book *Beyond Iraq: The Next Move*, I discussed many of the biblical implications of the Second Gulf War, including the fact that Saddam Hussein saw himself as Nebuchadnezzar rein-carnate. It is odd to note that since the publication of that book, Hussein's end was very much like that of Nebuchadnezzar:

> Immediately what had been said about Nebuchad-nezzar was fulfilled. He was driven away from people and ate grass like cattle. His body was drenched with the dew of heaven until his hair grew like the feath-ers of an eagle and his nails like the claws of a bird (Daniel 4:33).

Daniel had just prophesied to Nebuchadnezzar that he was going to go insane, be driven from his kingdom, and end up in the field hiding, looking like a wild animal. Most of what Nebuchadnezzar experienced also happened to Saddam Hussein. On December 13, 2003, US forces found him completely disoriented, hiding in a hole, his hair, beard, and fingernails grown out, and looking like a wild man.

While Hussein's "Babylon" fell with him, the spirit of Babylon identified in the book of Revelation did not. It is important to note that Persia is not mentioned in the book of Revelation, while Babylon—likely the name used to represent the entire region around the ancient city—is used several times as the head of the forces that rise against those represented by the city of Jerusalem—the Jews. In Scripture, Babylon is the seat of Satan's evil domain as much as Jerusalem is the seat of God's righteousness. They symbolize the two alliances that meet against one another in the final battle of Armageddon.

At the same time, however, the book of Ezekiel describes the force that will rise against Israel during the end times with these words, mentioning Persia and others by name:

> The word of the LORD came to me: "Son of man, set your face against Gog, of the land of Magog, the chief prince of Meshech and Tubal; prophesy against him and say: 'This is what the Sovereign LORD says: I am against you, O Gog, chief prince of Meshech and Tubal. . . . Persia [Iran], Cush [other translations have Ethiopia or Sudan—possibly representing African Muslims] and Put [KJV: Libya] . . . [and] the many nations with you. . . . "After many days you will be called to arms. In future years you will invade a land that has recovered from war [Israel's return to existence after WWII?], whose people were gathered from many nations to the mountains of Israel, which had long been desolate. They had been brought out from the nations, and now all of them live in safety. You and all your troops and the many nations with you will go up, advancing like a storm; you will be like a cloud covering the land 'This is what the Sovereign LORD says: On that day thoughts will come into your mind and you will devise an evil scheme. You will say, "I will invade a land of unwalled villages; I will attack a peaceful and unsuspecting people—all of them living without walls and without gates and bars. I will plunder and loot and turn my hand against the resettled ruins and the people gathered from the nations, rich in livestock and goods, living at the center of

the land." . . . "In that day, when my people Israel are living in safety, will you not take notice of it? You will come from your place in the far north, you and many nations with you, all of them riding on horses, a great horde, a mighty army. You will advance against my people Israel like a cloud that covers the land" (Ezekiel 38:1–3, 4–6, 8–12, 14–16).

Upon this assembly of nations against Israel, God declares He will pour out His wrath in what sounds very much like what happened in Hiroshima and Nagasaki:

> When Gog attacks the land of Israel, my hot anger will be aroused, declares the Sovereign LORD. In my zeal and fiery wrath I declare that at that time there shall be a great earthquake in the land of Israel. The fish of the sea, the birds of the air, the beasts of the field, every creature that moves along the ground, and all the people on the face of the earth will tremble at my presence. The mountains will be overturned, the cliffs will crumble and every wall will fall to the ground. . . . I will pour down torrents of rain, hailstones and burning sulfur on him and on his troops and on the many nations with him. And so I will show my greatness and my holiness, and I will make myself known in the sight of many nations. Then they will know that I am the LORD (Ezekiel 38:18–20, 22–23).

Did ancient prophets predict Armageddon would end in a

nuclear holocaust? Many biblical scholars have suggested that it will. Just read the following passages and see what you think:

> Whoever flees at the sound of terror will fall into a pit; whoever climbs out of the pit will be caught in a snare. The floodgates of the heavens are opened; the foundations of the earth shake. The earth is broken up; the earth is split asunder, the earth is thoroughly shaken. The earth reels like a drunkard; it sways like a hut in the wind; so heavy upon it is the guilt of its rebellion that it falls—never to rise again (Isaiah 24:18–20).

> This is the plague with which the LORD will strike all the nations that fought against Jerusalem: Their flesh will rot while they are still standing on their feet, their eyes will rot in their sockets, and their tongues will rot in their mouths (Zechariah 14:12).

> By the same word the present heavens and earth are reserved for fire, being kept for the day of judgment and destruction of ungodly men. . . . But the day of the Lord will come like a thief. The heavens will disappear with a roar; the elements will be destroyed by fire, and the earth and everything in it will be laid bare. Since everything will be destroyed in this way, what kind of people ought you to be? You ought to live holy and godly lives as you look forward to the day of God and speed its coming. That day will bring about the destruction of the heavens by fire, and the elements will melt in the heat. But in keeping with his promise we are looking forward to a new heaven

and a new earth, the home of righteousness. So then, dear friends, since you are looking forward to this, make every effort to be found spotless, blameless and at peace with him (2 Peter 3:7, 10–14).

The True Call of Bible Prophecy

While the exact players in end-time events are not clearly outlined in Scripture, the present situation depicts all of the nations of the earth aligned either with Babylon or Jerusalem, yet we are not without hope. Listen, for a moment, to the words of Jesus:

> See to it that you are not alarmed. Such things must happen, but the end is still to come. . . . The one who stands firm to the end will be saved (Matthew 24:6, 13).

We don't have the prophecies of Scripture so that we can cower and hide. While the Islamofascists are working in a demonic frenzy to bring on Armageddon, Jesus gave us another purpose as we head toward the Tribulation:

> Pray that your flight will not take place in winter or on the Sabbath. For then there will be great distress, unequaled from the beginning of the world until now—and never to be equaled again. If those days had not been cut short, no one would survive, but for the sake of the elect those days will be shortened (Matthew 24:20–22.)

In other words, the severity of those last days—as well as the days in which we now live—depend greatly on the prayers and actions of Christians today. The Bible is not about trying to bring the end of the world as the Islamofascists hope to do, but about bringing salvation and God's love and mercy to a world going increasingly mad. It is not difficult to see who is behind these activities when Jesus plainly told us:

> The thief [the devil] comes only to steal and kill and destroy; I have come that they may have life, and have it to the full (John 10:10).

It is up to Christians to face the present situation in the Middle East with moral clarity, to pray for the peace of Jerusalem, to oppose evil in this world, and pray for justice and righteousness to prevail. It is time for the United States to remember its heritage rooted and grounded in God, recalibrate the people's moral compass of right and wrong to God's way of thinking, and stand beside Israel.

CHAPTER FOUR

Recalibrating America's Moral Compass

Every time the terrorists kill a civilian they win. Every time the terrorists get the democracies to kill a child they win. It's a win/win for the terrorists, it's a lose/lose for the democracies, and it's all because of the asymmetry of morality.

ALAN DERSHOWITZ[31]

We can perhaps forgive them for killing our children, but we can never forgive them for making us kill their children.

GOLDA MEIR[32]

AMERICA IS NOT HATED by Liberal Leftists, appeasement states, and oppressive regimes because it is doing wrong, but because it is doing what is right. The belief of these regimes is that a perfect world includes a weak and anemic America that embraces the perpetrator and castigates the victim. In recent years, the US appears to have taken a slide down the slippery slope of compromise in a futile attempt to placate those who wish to see America decimated. It is imperative that God-fearing Americans quickly unite and fight the spiritual battle for the soul of America. In order to win the battle, men and women of God must stand their ground against the Enemy, backed by the power of God and clothed in the full armor of God. Ephesians 6:12–14a says:

> For our struggle is not against flesh and blood, but against the rulers, against the authorities, against the powers of this dark world and against the spiritual forces of evil in the heavenly realms. Therefore put on the full armor of God, so that when the day of evil comes, you may be able to stand your ground, and after you have done everything, to stand. Stand firm then . . .

When Believers take up the battle cry against the host of fallen angels that were cast to earth along with Satan, the fight is against "spiritual wickedness in high places" (KJV). It is these demonic creatures flooding the world with lack of knowledge, sin, and desolation, and it is these forces that can only be defeated with intercessory prayer.

The foundational promise on which the return of Jesus Christ and all prophecy is contingent is found in Matthew 24:14: "This gospel of the kingdom shall be preached in the whole world as a testimony to all the nations, and then the end will come." This doctrine is taught and followed by more than one billion Christians worldwide who consider themselves evangelical.

The Middle East is the last frontier for the proclamation of the Great Commission, fulfilling the last words of Jesus on earth:

> But you will receive power when the Holy Spirit
> has come upon you; and you shall be My witnesses
> both in Jerusalem, and in all Judea and Samaria, and
> even to the remotest part of the earth (Acts 1:8).

Good versus evil is the doctrine of the Bible from Genesis to the Cross and to the very end of the age. According to an oft-quoted saying by Irish philosopher Edmund Burke, "All that is required for evil to triumph is for good men to do nothing." It was the same doctrine Ronald Reagan used in defeating the so-called "Evil Empire" of the Soviet Union. Yet, while Americans rejoiced over the breakup of the former Soviet Union, Russian President Vladimir Putin has been busily working to resurrect the dried bones of that once-dead empire. At this writing, Russia has invaded parts of the Ukraine in an attempt to re-annex land formerly under Soviet control. Journalist Daniel Greenfield, in an article for *FrontPage Magazine* wrote:

> And entering Crimea is a test . . . . The Western fulcrum is America. Obama drew red lines on Syria and Iran and backed off. What happened next was inevitable. It's also incomprehensible to the Western elites whose religion is diplomacy.
>
> As in Iran and Syria, Obama has passed the Ukraine test with flying colors as his officials distinguished between an invasion and an "uncontested arrival."
>
> They couldn't have done any better if they had issued Putin a map of Kiev.[33]

The challenges issued to the United States by Russia, by ISIL and other terrorist organizations evoke an invitation to return to God or face the consequences of our choices. We must answer the call to wage war against evil and stand in support of Israel.

Why is this necessary for followers of Christ? How is this mission based on the Bible, and how will it birth a Great Awakening in America, and the Middle East, causing these Believers to refocus their passions on confronting the root of all evil?

The question is often asked: How can Christians support a war when Jesus has said, "Love your enemies"? The New Testament clearly states that civil magistrates can wage war against "all enemies, both foreign and domestic." In Romans 13:1–4 we read:

> Every person is to be in subjection to the governing authorities For there is no authority except from God, and those which exist are established by God. Therefore whoever resists authority has opposed the ordinance of God; and they who have opposed will receive condemnation upon themselves. For rulers are not a cause of fear for good behavior, but for evil. Do you want to have no fear of authority? Do what is good and you will have praise from the same; for it is a minister of God to you for good. But if you do what is evil, be afraid; for it does not bear the sword for nothing; for it is a minister of God, an avenger who brings wrath on the one who practices evil.

The Liberal Left hates the America of which Christian presidents have dreamt—that includes Israel, the Bible, and Christians, in general. Christians these days are too often subjected to scorn, ridicule, and discrimination. There is no attack on US culture more deadly than the secular humanists' attack against God in American public life.

The insults and verbal abuse are so severe that anyone who contradicts them is labeled "ignorant, evil, racist, and bigot." The dumbing down of America is well under way, and all in the name of political correctness and the new godless globalism.

The hippies of the 60s have become the establishment against which they once railed. American culture, the media, educational system, courts, arts and sciences, public and private sectors, mainstream Hollywood, public schools, Washington politics, and the judiciary on every level are run by these once-upon-a-time liberals who are self-destructing. America, the noble experiment, is under siege. A tidal wave of evil is sweeping over our nation: the self-injuring, spirit-destroying, conscious-searing practices of pornography, abortion, homosexuality, and drug and alcohol abuse are being supported as they have never been before. There is a vicious moral and spiritual war raging in the hearts and minds of Americans.

The Cost of Denying Evil Exists

At the heart of liberalism is a belief that evil really doesn't exist; people are basically good, and thus individuals can't really be held accountable for the wrong they do. The liberal tactic is that it is better just to talk with people, rather than bringing criminals to justice or fighting to stop those committing crimes against humanity.

The Liberal Left crowd wants God and the Bible driven out of America. Our first president, George Washington, said:

It is impossible to govern the world without God and the Bible. Reason and experience forbid us to expect that morality can prevail in exclusion of religious principle.[34]

John Adams said:

Our Constitution was made only for a moral and religious people. It is wholly inadequate to the government of any other.[35]

Can the liberal, secular humanists' hatred for all things Christian pass Natan Sharansky's "town square test"?

Can a person walk into the middle of the town square and express his or her views without fear of arrest, imprisonment, or physical harm? If he can, then that person is living in a free society. If not, it's a fear society.[36]

The right of a Christian in America to express his or her views without fear of retaliation from liberal organizations is frequently challenged and slowly eroding.

I believe America is under attack by radical Islam because this is a Christian nation. Former president George W. Bush was vilified because he was one of the most devoted Christian presidents in American history, and because he applies Christian principles to every aspect of his life. President Bush has said, "When you turn your heart and your life over to Christ, when you accept Christ as the Savior, it changes your heart; it changes your life. And that's what happened to me."[37]

In his State of the Union Address in 2002, Mr. Bush drew a line in the sand for nations that he considered part of an "axis of evil" threatening the free world. On February 7, 2002, "the president said faith shows the reality of good and the reality of evil."[38]

George W. Bush began his second White House term with his freedom speech, as did the late President Ronald Reagan with his discourse about the threat of evil in the world and the hope of freedom. Reagan quoted John 3:15 (KJV) as his favorite verse: "That whosoever believeth in him should not perish, but have eternal life." It was his favorite, he said, because "having accepted Jesus Christ as my Savior, I have God's promise of eternal life in heaven."

Reagan saw the evil of communism not only as shutting down the churches, but as threatening the eternal salvation of millions of people. He said of freedom:

> Above all, we must realize that no arsenal, or no weapon in the arsenals of the world, is so formidable as the will and moral courage of free men and women. It is a weapon our adversaries in today's world do not have.[39]

Both Ronald Reagan and George W. Bush felt called to become president and worked diligently to stem the tide launched by former president Jimmy Carter. Mother Teresa and I met in Rome, where she told me that she had met with Mr. Reagan in June 1981 following the assassination attempt on his life. She recalled saying to the president, "You have suffered the passion of the Cross and have received grace. There is a purpose to this. Because of your suffering and pain, you will now understand the suffering of the world. This has happened to you at this time because your country and the world need you."

She said Nancy Reagan broke into tears, and Mr. Reagan was deeply moved. Maureen Reagan Revell, the president's daughter, told me that her father repeated the story often and said, "God has spared me for a reason. I will devote the rest of my time here on earth to find out what He intends me to do."

A Prophecy

I had the pleasure of meeting with Ronald Reagan several times at the White House during his presidency. He talked freely about spiritual matters. Shortly after his first inauguration, I was invited to the White House for a private dinner with the Reagan Cabinet and eighty-six of America's top religious leaders, and for the first Middle East national security briefing (on the sale of AWACS to Saudi Arabia).

Bush and Reagan were both greatly influenced by the writings of C. S. Lewis, and especially his book *Mere Christianity*, particularly Book 1, which is entitled "Right and Wrong as a Clue to the Meaning of the Universe." The writings of Alexander Solzhenitsyn were also an influence. Solzhenitsyn addressed the Harvard graduating class in 1978 with a speech entitled "A World Split Apart." He characterized the current conflict for our planet as a physical and spiritual war that has already begun and could not be won without dealing with the forces of evil. His address to the assembly is as relevant today as it was over thirty years ago:

A decline in courage may be the most striking feature that an outside observer notices in the West today. The Western world has lost its civic courage, both as a whole and separately, in each country, in each government, in each political party, and, of course, in the United Nations. Such a decline in courage is particularly noticeable among the ruling and intellectual elites, causing an impression of a loss of courage by the entire society. There are many courageous individuals, but they have no determining influence on public life.

Political and intellectual functionaries exhibit this depression, passivity, and perplexity in their actions and in their statements, and even more so in their self-serving rationales as to how realistic, reasonable, and intellectually and even morally justified it is to base state policies on weakness and cowardice. And the decline in courage, at times attaining what could be termed a lack of manhood, is ironically emphasized by occasional outbursts and inflexibility on the part of those same functionaries when dealing with weak governments and with countries that lack support, or with doomed currents which clearly cannot offer resistance. But they get tongue-tied and paralyzed when they deal with powerful governments and threatening forces, with aggressors and international terrorists.[40]

On January 20, 2005, after praying for guidance on what to choose as his inaugural scripture, George W. Bush placed his hand on his family Bible. He chose the same scripture used by Ronald Reagan at the end of his famous "Evil Empire" speech in Orlando, Florida, on March 8, 1983. President Bush selected Isaiah 40:31 (KJV):

> He giveth power to the faint and to [them that have] no might he increaseth strength. But they that wait upon the LORD shall renew [their] strength; they shall mount up with wings as eagles; they shall run, and not be weary; [and] they shall walk, and not faint.

The real crisis we face today is a spiritual one; at its root, it is a test of moral will and faith. Whittaker Chambers, the man whose own religious conversion made him a witness to one of the terrible traumas of our time, the Hiss-Chambers case, wrote:

> The crisis of the Western world exists to the degree in which it is indifferent to God. It exists to the degree in which the Western world actually shares Communism's materialist vision, is so dazzled by the logic of the materialist interpretation of history, politics and economics, that it fails to grasp that, for it, the only possible answer to the Communist challenge: Faith in God or Faith in Man? is the challenge: Faith in God.[41]

The "Evil Empire" speech delivered by the late President Reagan to the Annual Convention of the National Association of Evangelicals on March 8, 1983, rocked the world. In it he said:

Let us pray for the salvation of all of those who live in that totalitarian darkness. Pray they will discover the joy of knowing God. But until they do, let us be aware that while they preach the supremacy of the State, declare its omnipotence over individual man, and predict its eventual domination of all peoples on the earth, they are the focus of evil in the modern world.

It was C. S. Lewis who, in his unforgettable *Screwtape Letters*, wrote:

The greatest evil is not done now in those sordid 'dens of crime' that Dickens loved to paint. . . . It is conceived and ordered; moved, seconded, carried and minuted in clear, carpeted, warmed, and well-lighted offices, by quiet men with white collars and cut fingernails and smooth-shaven cheeks who do not need to raise their voice. . . . So in your discussions of the nuclear freeze proposals I urge you to beware the temptation of pride—the temptation to blithely declare yourselves above it all and label both sides equally at fault, to ignore the facts of history and the aggressive impulses of an evil empire, to simply call the arms race a giant misunderstanding and thereby remove yourself from the struggle between right and wrong and good and evil . . . I believe we shall rise to the challenge. I believe that communism is another sad, bizarre chapter in human history whose last pages have been written. I believe this because the source of our strength in the quest for human freedom is not material, but spiritual. And because it knows no limitation, it must terrify and ultimately triumph over those who would enslave their fellow man. For in the words of Isaiah, "He giveth power to the faint; and to them that have no might He increased strength. But they that wait upon the Lord shall renew their strength; they shall mount up with wings as eagles; they shall run, and not be weary."[42]

Ronald Reagan's speech impacted the world. Natan Sharansky told me in Jerusalem that he remembers fellow prisoners tapping on the prison walls to communicate the president's message. Lech Walesa, the leader of the Solidarity movement in Poland, said the speech inspired him and millions of others.

A painting entitled *A Charge to Keep* hung in the Oval Office while it was occupied by George W. Bush. It was inspired by a favorite song from Charles Wesley. There is a determined rider ahead of two other riders urging his horse up a steep, narrow path. Words to Wesley's song include:

A charge to keep I have,
a God to glorify,
a never-dying soul to save,
and fit it for the sky.
To serve the present age,
my calling to fulfill;
O may it all my powers engage
to do my Master's will![43]

In December 1998, then Texas Governor George W. Bush flew to Israel. The trip was sponsored by the National Coalition, a Republican-oriented, American lobby group that strongly supported the policies of then Prime Minister Benjamin Netanyahu. Mr. Bush had dinner with Mr. Netanyahu on November 30, as well as meetings with other Israeli leaders. One of the highlights of the trip was a helicopter tour conducted by the foreign minister at the time, the late Ariel Sharon. Bush said to Mr. Sharon, "If you believe the Bible as I do, you know that extraordinary things happen."

When he and Sharon parted company, Mr. Bush shook his hand warmly and said, "You know, Ariel, it is possible that I might be president of the United States, and you the prime minister of Israel." Sharon laughed and said, "It is unlikely that I, such a controversial figure in Israeli politics, would become the prime minister." But Sharon did, in fact, become prime minister in a special election in February 2001. After serving in that capacity for approximately five years, the prime minister suffered a hemorrhagic stroke on January 4, 2006, lapsed into a coma, and spent the next eight years in a coma. Sharon died on January 11, 2014.

CHAPTER FIVE

Only Moral Clarity Will Bring True Peace

*The two most important things that can be done to promote
democracy in the world is first, to bring moral clarity
back to world affairs and second, to link international
policies to the advance of democracy around the globe.*

NATAN SHARANSKY[44]

IN 1991, THE ROYAL PALACE in Madrid was the location
for most of the sessions of the Middle East Peace Conference, which
followed Operation Desert Shield, the first war in Iraq. As I sat in the
palace gallery, I noticed that the Israeli and Arab delegations were
not making eye contact, and when they did, you could see their faces
cloaked in bitterness. There was a spirit of unforgiveness. During
one of the breaks, I met with the Syrian foreign minister and the
Egyptian ambassador.

I turned to the Egyptian ambassador and said, "Why don't you
forgive your brother, as the most famous secretary of state and

prime minister did?" He looked at me, smiled, and said, "It never happened. We've never had such a man." I opened my Bible to the book of Genesis and read him part of the story of Joseph in Egypt, who forgave the brothers who had betrayed him. Unfortunately, my challenge went unanswered.

Benjamin Netanyahu, whom I recommended for his first position in Prime Minister Begin's government in 1982, was shunned by President Clinton on numerous occasions because of Netanyahu's moral clarity and his great admiration for Ronald Reagan. As a member of the National Press Club, I had the occasion to hear Netanyahu speak to that group. He mentioned Ronald Reagan, his policies, and his admiration for him. The members of the NPC laughed in derision.

It is imperative that we know our enemy: the irreconcilable wing of Islam and the evil power that inspires it. Only when God's people see this clearly can we successfully plunder hell to populate heaven.

The basis for defeating the bigotry and despotism of Islamofascism is rooted in our faith in Jehovah God. This battle cannot be won without applying biblical principles. Europe's Leftist elite, like that of the US, have fallen in love with appeasement because they do not believe in evil and thus refuse to confront it.

On September 11, 2001, evil surfaced in America in a way never before seen. Afterward, the nation rallied to confront evil in Afghanistan and Iraq. Since that time, our wounds have healed, our senses have been deadened, and our memories dulled. I believe we are on the brink of the greatest opportunity in history to confront the source of all evil. If we fail, the results will be catastrophic.

The Liberal Left has a difficult time seeing moral issues clearly because most of them reject absolute standards of good and evil, right and wrong. In their world view, man is capable of perfection, human nature is on a path toward enlightenment, and the concept of original sin is primitive.

These same humanists reinvented Yasser Arafat as a peacemaker and gave him the façade of a freedom fighter, not a terrorist. In their eyes, those who blow up Jews are driven to such acts because of injustices. The victims of these crimes are seen as the source of the problem; the perpetrators are seen as innocent and exploited. Those same humanists believe the lie that bad acts must be blamed on society, or psychological or economic circumstances. Moral relativists despise those who grasp the nature of evil. Victims are demonized and murderers are glorified. We saw that in September 1993 when Yasser Arafat was invited to the Clinton White House.

In his State of the Union speech following 9/11 George W. Bush said, "Evil is real, and it must be opposed." President Bush was called "simplistic" because he did not see diversity and tolerance as a reasonable alternative. Liberals demanded that Bush apologize for looking to his God and the Bible for guidance.

Secular humanists make excuses for evil, or, worse, deny its existence or coddle it by refusing to confront the evil. Rather, they feed it. Jesus did not negotiate with evil; He did not sweet-talk it, nor did He compromise with it. True evil is seeing moral issues in shades of gray, rather than in black and white. The reality of evil is disregarded because the Bible is rejected as the gold standard of righteous truth.

The Nazi Party referred to US Ambassador Joseph Kennedy as Germany's best friend in London because of his liberal stance. In the twisted minds of Hitler's followers, the Jews had provoked the war because they intended to destroy the German State. Joseph Goebbels, Germany's Reich Minister of Propaganda during World

War II, wrote: "Each Jew is a sworn enemy of the German people."[45] He believed in the Jewish conspiracy myth called *The Protocols of the Learned Elders of Zion*. To the very end, the Nazis maintained plausible deniability about the grave injustices perpetrated upon the Jews.

If the devil does exist as the Bible says, there is no better proof of it than that those following his agenda seek first to destroy the Jews, and then Christians. It is a lesson we should have learned in World War II, and now face again with radical Islamofascists.

At the Harvard graduation ceremony in 1978, Alexander Solzhenitsyn shocked that august university, and the nation, with his speech, "A World Split Apart." Solzhenitsyn saw the effects of moral decay in America, in the attempts to divorce God from its public squares, and build a wall of separation between Church and State replacing God with the government as the creator of liberties. That having undermined her moral vision, America had lost her courage to confront evil in the world.

Solzhenitsyn noted that while engaged in occasional outbursts in dealing with weak governments, US politicians become paralyzed when dealing with foreign powers and international terrorists. He characterized this ongoing conflict for our planet as a physical and spiritual war that has already begun, and he identified Soviet aggressors as the forces of evil. Solzhenitsyn knew millions of people had been killed in the gulag prison camp system. He himself suffered firsthand:

> How did the West decline from its triumphal march to its present debility? Have there been fatal turns and losses of direction in its development? It does not seem so. The West kept advancing steadily

in accordance with its proclaimed social intentions, hand in hand with a dazzling progress in technology. And all of a sudden it found itself in its present state of weakness.

This means that the mistake must be at the root, at the very foundation of thought in modern times. I refer to the prevailing Western view of the world in modern times. I refer to the prevailing Western view of the world which was born in the Renaissance and has found political expression since the Age of Enlightenment. It became the basis for political and social doctrine and could be called rationalistic humanism or humanistic autonomy: the proclaimed and practiced autonomy of man from any higher force above him.. . . .

The humanistic way of thinking, which had proclaimed itself our guide, did not admit the existence of intrinsic evil in man, nor did it see any task higher than the attainment of happiness on earth. It started modern Western civilization on the dangerous trend of worshiping man and his material needs.[40]

With those few words, Alexander Solzhenitsyn suddenly found himself a pariah. Once lionized by the media, this great man was treated thereafter as though he didn't exist—all because, within the rule book of the intellectual elite, no one who believes in God is to be taken seriously. What's more, the late 1970s was supposed to be an era of détente, a time of lessening tensions. To issue moral judgments about Communism was seen as destructive to all chances for world peace. But Solzhenitsyn was never interested in lessening tensions. He knew that standing for the truth meant confronting the lie—confronting evil.

In his treatise "The Conservative Consensus: Frank Meyer, Barry Goldwater, and the Politics of Fusionism", Lee Edwards, a Distinguished Fellow in Conservative Thought, and Heritage's in-house authority on the US conservative movement, wrote:

> Many [conservatives] consider Reagan's "evil empire" speech the most important of his presidency, a compelling example of what Czech President Vaclav Havel calls "the power of words to change history." When Reagan visited Poland and East Berlin after the collapse of Soviet communism, many former dissidents told him that when he called the Soviet Union an "evil empire," it gave them enormous hope. Finally, they said to each other, America had a leader who "understood the nature of communism."[47]

Reagan was a great admirer of Solzhenitsyn. Reagan agreed with his belief that the struggle between Communist ideology and that of the free world presented a moral conflict. Unlike the Liberal Left, Reagan did not accept the idea that Western democracy and a godless Communism could peacefully coexist. He believed that at some point, confrontation between the two superpowers was a certainty.

Reagan felt that every time relations between the two countries eased, the Soviets took advantage of the opportunity to take three steps forward in their plan for Soviet domination. It was his belief that the entire objective of the Soviet Union was to root out seeds of democracy wherever planted and replace them with the tares of Communism.

The Liberal Left had nothing but contempt for Mr. Reagan's view of Communism. He was labeled a fascist, an extremist, and compared to Joseph McCarthy, the rabid anti-Communist of the late 1940s.

Ronald Reagan said:

> Above all, we must realize that no arsenal or no weapon in the arsenals of the world is so formidable as the will and moral courage of free men and women. It is a weapon our adversaries in today's world do not have. It is a weapon that we as Americans do have. Let that be understood by those who practice terrorism and prey upon their neighbors.[48]

Liberals refused to believe that a totalitarian state was by definition evil in Reagan's day, and they still hold to that perverse ideology today.

Jesus' battle was between darkness and light. He taught us to pray that God deliver us from evil. One hundred million people died in the twentieth century under totalitarian regimes. I am very aware of the Jews who died in the USSR, and in Europe, but that is only part of the heartbreak.

In May 2014, God opened a miraculous door for me to travel to Belarus. It was a truly life-changing experience. I stood on the spot near Vishneva where my great-grandfather perished inside his synagogue. The doors to the synagogue had been nailed shut as Nazi soldiers stood outside and screamed, "Christ killers!" as those inside were burned to death.

My family's story is tragic, but it is far from unique. Nearly one quarter of the Jewish people who were murdered during the Holocaust died in that area of Europe—roughly a million and a half. I stood by the marker that had been erected in the so-called "Valley of Death" and could almost hear the screams of those being buried alive simply because they were Jewish. One lady told me of her experience as a little girl. She had a painfully vivid recollection of Nazi soldiers celebrating the murder of thousands of Jewish people with songs and rejoicing.

I can readily echo the words of President Bush following the 9/11 attacks:

> I know that many Americans at this time have fears. We've learned that America is not immune from attack. We've seen that evil is real. It's hard for us to comprehend the mentality of people that will destroy innocent folks the way they have. Yet, America is equal to this challenge, make no mistake about it. They've roused a mighty giant.[49]

But in the years following the heinous attacks of 9/11, Americans have lost their sense of outrage. Editorial writer Kathleen Parker wrote of this loss:

> Words have a way of seeping into our vocabulary and, through overuse or distortion, soon begin to lose their meaning.
>
> Who could have imagined that the word "beheading" would become commonplace, as though we were discussing a sport or a new product?

"Another American was beheaded yesterday," the newscaster explains. And then, "On a brighter note, a lost little kitten found her way home in a shocking way. We'll tell you about that ... right after this."

Who doesn't love a kitten story? But thus juxtaposed, the beheading, so atrocious and mind-boggling at first, now becomes nearly routine-ish and banal in the way that evil can become....

More beheadings are promised and presumably will continue until we prevail in a battle that is more likely to last decades rather [than] the two or three years that the [Obama] administration has suggested. The worst things imaginable aren't just possible, they're already happening.[50]

Unfortunately, the approach of the Obama administration toward terrorism has been one of appeasement, of the failure to label terrorists for what they are: murderous fanatics. For example, at Fort Hood, Texas, in 2009 Nidal Malik Hasan killed thirteen military personnel and wounded dozens more during a shooting rampage on the military base. Witnesses described Hasan as shouting, "Allah Akbar!" (Allah is greater) before unloading several weapons into unsuspecting bystanders. The president and his staff labeled this heinous crime "workplace violence." Hasan eventually wrote to ISIL leaders requesting that he be allowed to join the Islamic State.

A second such instance occurred in Moore, Oklahoma, in September 2014. Alton Nobel, a food-plant worker who had recently converted to Islam, decapitated a fellow employee in a fit of rage as he, too, allegedly screamed Islamic expressions. His acts have been categorized as "workplace violence" and not an act of terrorism.

Again I ask, "Where is the outrage when US citizens have been slaughtered by homegrown terrorists and it is shrugged off as 'workplace violence'? Has our nation become the frog in the pot of cold water, oblivious to the fire beneath until it is too late? Did Americans elect and then reelect a president so complacent that when the Middle East erupts into flames, we will be forced to give in without a fight?"

CHAPTER SIX

Filling the Void

This new enemy seeks to destroy our freedom and impose its views. We value life; the terrorists ruthlessly destroy it. We value education; the terrorists do not believe women should be educated or should have health care, or should leave their homes. We value the right to speak our minds; for the terrorists, free expression can be grounds for execution. We respect people of all faiths and welcome the free practice of religion; our enemy wants to dictate how to think and how to worship even to their fellow Muslims.

PRESIDENT GEORGE W. BUSH[51]

You withdraw when you win. Phased withdrawal is a way of saying, "Regardless of what the conditions are on the ground, we're going to get out of Dodge."

TONY SNOW[52]
(Late Presidential Spokesman for George W. Bush)

JUST AS NAZI FASCISM rose in the 1930s from the ashes of a powerless, defeated Germany to the point of threatening the world, a new totalitarianism in Islamofascism has arisen that promises an even greater challenge. This fanaticism is the central uniting principle of a world of disgruntled, underprivileged people who desire to bring down the nations that have, according to their distorted doc-trines, exploited them for centuries. It is not a war to take what the West has, but to bring the West down to the level of the conquerors. It is more than Communism ever was, because it has added the zeal only possible through religious fervor; therefore it is a greater threat to the world than any battle in which the United States has engaged.

While the Liberal Left scoffs at the idea that such military wimps as Iran could ever be a threat to our borders or existence as a nation, its adherents seem to forget that if Islamofascists get the bomb, conventional military power will mean little. If the objective is simply to attack and disable the West with little fear of reprisal, there is nothing like having an entire regime with the mentality of a suicide bomber willing to hit the US with a few carefully syn-chronized nuclear attacks. That would be better than an invasion. Iran's Grand Ayatollah Ali Khamenei and his supporters' dream of wiping Israel off the map could be accomplished with one nuclear strike centered on Tel Aviv.

Following the 2008 presidential election of Barack Obama, the course was set to totally withdraw US troops from Iraq. The last combat brigade—the 4th Stryker Brigade, 2nd Infantry Division—withdrew from Iraqi territory and just days later, the president indicated that Operation Iraqi Freedom had drawn to a close. He introduced a second initiative, Operation New Dawn, which was designated as approximately 50,000 remaining US troops serving in an advisory capacity only. The final contingent of US troops left Iraq on December 18, 2011. Conservative political pundits advised against advertising a withdrawal date, but the admonition went unheeded.

Iraqi Prime Minister Nouri al-Maliki and President Obama agreed to continue tough security measures, as well as solid diplomatic and economic bonds between the United States and Iraq, even after withdrawal of US troops. As has been witnessed, those pledges were shattered by the rise of ISIL and its radical Islamic followers.

Former defense secretary and CIA head Leon Panetta has written a book titled *Worthy Fights*. He makes it clear within its pages that the withdrawal was an appalling decision. He writes:

> "[To] me—and many others— . . . withdrawing all our forces would endanger the fragile stability then barely holding Iraq together . . . . Privately, the various leadership factions in Iraq all confided that they wanted some US forces to remain as a bulwark against sectarian violence . . . . We had leverage . . . Under-Secretary of Defense Michèle Flournoy did her best to press that position, which reflected not just my views but also those of the military commanders in the region and the Joint Chiefs. But the President's team at the White House pushed back, and the differences occasionally became heated . . . . To my frustration, the White House coordinated the negotiations but never really led them. Officials there seemed content to endorse an agreement if State and Defense could reach one, but without the President's active advocacy, al-Maliki was allowed to slip away. The deal never materialized.[53]

Have we been so quick to forget the lesson of *The Ugly American*? Perhaps we have, because today the term no longer refers to the hero of that book—a physically ugly but innovative man who went to Southeast Asia to use his inventiveness to raise the standard of living. Instead we use the phrase to refer to a bombastic, egomaniacal consumer of other cultures' resources so many in the world have come to see as the worst of American culture. Despite this, the main lesson of *The Ugly American* was that we lost the war in Vietnam not because of insurmountable odds, but because Washington refused to allow the military on the ground to fight the war without being micromanaged by congressional committees and commissions. Those who called the shots refused to study the Viet Cong and Communists and counteract their tactics. Traditional rules of firepower and the use of military strength to capture territory did little good in the jungle where lines meant nothing and guerilla ambushes were easier than head-to-head clashes. The use of standard infantry techniques from World Wars I and II meant nothing in this chaos, and it is proving to mean even less today in the towns and villages of Iraq and Syria.

Enter ISIL

An old Latin dictum states: "Nature abhors a vacuum." This was proven without question in Iraq when a group of Sunni radicals rushed to fill the void left by the US withdrawal. Like the trapdoor spider with its hidden lair and powerful jaws, ISIL radicals waited patiently for the victim—in this case the entire Middle East—to wander into its snare.

The group that filtered in from Syria was given scant notice by a White House burdened with several debacles: Obamacare, Edward Snowden's release of classified documents from the National Security Agency, and other, lesser issues. ISIL and its agenda were given little attention by the president in an interview with *The New*

Yorker in January 2014. Mr. Obama responded to a question from the interviewer by saying:

> The analogy we use around here sometimes, and I think is accurate, is if a JV team puts on Lakers uniforms, that doesn't make them Kobe Bryant. I think there is a distinction between the capacity and reach of a bin Laden and a network that is actively planning major terrorist plots against the homeland versus jihadists who are engaged in various local power struggles and disputes, often sectarian.[54]

As ISIL began to gobble up more and more land in Iraq and then unleashed its voracious appetite on Syria, Kurdistan, Turkey, and other nearby countries, the White House began to pay a bit more attention. The debate over who was responsible for the lack of attention paid to ISIL heated up after an interview during which Mr. Obama pointed a finger at National Intelligence Director James R. Clapper, Jr. for the lapse. As has too often been the case, there was no acceptance of any responsibility by the president for any miscalculations of the success the terrorist group has experienced and the near-catastrophic breakdown of Iraqi forces. Administration foes jumped on the president's statements by leveling charges that Mr. Obama was again trying to sidestep accountability.

Peter Baker and Eric Schmitt wrote for the *New York Times*:

> A reconstruction of the past year suggests a number of pivotal moments when both the White House and the intelligence community misjudged the Islamic State. Even after the group's fighters

stormed across the border into Iraq at the start of the year to capture the city of Fallujah and parts of Ramadi, the White House considered it a problem that could be contained.

Intelligence agencies were caught off guard by the speed of the extremists' subsequent advance across northern Iraq. And the government as a whole was largely focused on the group as a source of foreign fighters who might pose a terrorism threat when they returned home, not as a force intent on seizing territory.

"I'm not suggesting anyone was asleep at the switch necessarily, but the organization definitely achieved strategic surprise when it rolled into Iraq," said Frederic C. Hof, who previously handled Syria policy for the State Department under Mr. Obama and is now at the Atlantic Council.

"To anyone watching developments in Iraq from mid-2010 and Syria from early 2011, the recovery and rise of ISIS should have been starkly clear," said Charles Lister, a visiting fellow at the Brookings Doha Center in Qater. "The organization itself was also carrying out an explicitly clear step-by-step strategy aimed at engendering the conditions that would feed its accelerated rise."[55]

In December 2013, red flags were raised over the worsening situation of Iraq's armed forces. The US sent an infusion of Hellfire missiles and drones to aid in the curbing of violence in that country. All the while, intelligence sources were forewarning that ISIL was becoming a powerful force in the cities of Fallujah and Ramadi in the northern and western regions of Iraq. Its fanatics, hoisting the dreaded black flag of the nearly obsolete al Qaeda, carried weapons confiscated from the Iraqi army—many of which had been unwittingly supplied by the US— murdered anyone who happened to get in the way of ISIL's forward progress and intimidated those who somehow escaped its destructive assault. Even with that burgeoning threat, scant attention was paid by an administration doggedly unwavering in its decision not to be dragged back into a conflict in Iraq.

In the spring of 2014, al-Maliki swallowed his pride and requested aid from the US, asking for either help with operating drones against ISIL or, barring that, direct intervention by the US military. This came at a time when Mr. Obama was pondering the introduction of a $500 million program to aid Syrian rebels in the fight against Bashar al-Assad. It was clearly difficult for a president who considered US intervention an overreach of its power when used to settle global struggles. By then, though, it was too late.

As inertia gripped the White House, thousands of ISIL Sunni militants streamed across the border between Iraq and Syria, seizing control of Mosul and turning their attention to Kurdistan and Baghdad. According to an Iraqi official, "Tens of thousands of Iraqi soldiers [threw] down their weapons and [ran] away."[56]

With the capture of Mosul, the lights came on in Washington. The president was forced to decide that it might be a good thing to take steps to protect the city of Baghdad. This after thousands had been shot execution-style, crucified, raped, kidnapped, and terrified. It also came to light that there were several Western hostages being held by ISIL. A plan to attempt a rescue failed as the president and his senior aides watched from the White House Situation Room. As

ISIL progressed unhindered across Iraq, it finally became evident that something had to be done to slow its march.

James Wright Foley, a thirty-year-old journalist, was beheaded in August 2014, the first American to face such heinous execution at the hands of ISIL. His death was followed in September by the death of Steven Joel Sotloff, also a victim of beheading. A forty-seven-year-old British aid worker, Alan Henning, and a French tourist and mountaineering guide, Herve Gourdel, were also beheaded by ISIL terrorists. A third US hostage, Peter Kassig, was awaiting execution by his ISIL captors at this writing.

On October 11, 2014, it was revealed that

> Over a three-day period, vengeful fighters shelled, beheaded, crucified and shot hundreds of members of the Shaitat tribe after they dared to rise up against the extremists. By the time the killing stopped, 700 people were dead, activists and survivors say, making this the bloodiest single atrocity committed by the Islamic State in Syria since it declared its existence 18 months ago . . . . Abu Salem and the other men . . . wonder why no one had helped them when their community was under attack. The carnage inflicted on the Shaitat tribe has instilled in the Abu Hamam survivors a loathing for the Islamic State and the warped brand of Islamist politics for which it stands, said Abu Siraj, another of the tribesmen. A former lawyer, he, like most of the men, asked to be identified only by his nom de guerre because he fears

being tracked even to Turkey by the jihadists . . . . "We are tribal people. We will never forget to avenge," said Abu Salem, the commander of the group. "But we will do it by ourselves, in our own way. We won't take any help from anyone."[57]

In January 2015, ISIL militants beheaded two Japanese nationals: Kenji Goto was a journalist who had traveled to Syria to document the stories of individuals in the war-torn country. Haruna Yukawa was a security consultant who hoped to help Japanese companies with safety issues. The terrorists demanded $200 million from Japan in exchange for the two captives.

Jordanian pilot 26-year-old Lt. Muath Al-Kaseasbeh whose F-16 crashed during a bombing mission in December 2014 was also being held by the Muslim extremists. His freedom was tied to the release of Sajida al-Rishawi. She was a failed bomber who had been sentenced to death after an attack in 2005 on a Jordanian hotel which claimed the lives of sixty people.

Jordanian officials were in the midst of completing a deal with ISIL for her release when a video was released detailing the death of Al-Kaseasbeh. He had been caged and burned alive on or about January 3, 2015—weeks before the demands tied to his release. Following that revelation Jordan summarily hanged al-Rishawi and a second terrorist, Ziad al-Karbouly, convicted in 2008 of planning attacks on Jordanians in Iraq.

King Abdullah of Jordan responded to the gruesome execution of the young pilot by saying that ISIL had no affiliation with Islam. On Thursday, February 5, 2015, Jordanian pilots launched a series of airstrikes against the terrorists in Syria and Iraq.

How Willing Are We to Compromise Our Values?

It is as if we learned nothing from fighting two world wars, the Vietnam and Korean Conflicts, and two wars in Iraq. World War I ended with too high a price exacted from the victors—a solution that only laid the foundations for World War II. Had we ended it instead by securing Germany's political future and solidifying its government before withdrawing, World War II might never have happened. Did we depose the Ba'th Party only to let Iraq fall into more dangerous hands? Did we end the rule of the Taliban in Afghanistan only to return it to the merciless tribal warlords who ruled it before them? If we do not replace the iron-fisted regimes with freedom-friendly governments, we will only face bigger problems down the road. The conflict in Afghanistan is ongoing at this writing, with scheduled withdrawal of most US troops by the end of 2014. Only time will tell if that country, too, becomes a vacuum and what evil will then flood into Afghanistan.

Given the severity of the ISIL issue, I can't help but remember a conversation that took place on a September evening in 1980 in Tel Aviv. I sat with former Mossad chief Isser Harel for a discussion about Arab terrorism. As he handed me a cup of hot tea and passed a plate of cookies, I asked, "Do you think terrorism will come to America, and if so, where and why?"

Harel looked at this American visitor and replied, "I fear it will come to you in America. America has the power, but not the will, to fight terrorism. The terrorists have the will, but not the power, to fight America—but all that could change with time. Arab oil money buys more than tents."

What then is the answer to the question: Does the United

States, and more specifically, the Obama administration, have the will to fight terrorism? Townhall.com columnist Walter E. Williams provided this take on the subject:

> If our military tells us that we do have the capacity to defeat the terror threat, then the reason that we don't reflects a lack of willingness. It's that same lack of willingness that led to the deaths of 60 million people during World War II. In 1936, France alone could have stopped Adolf Hitler, but France and its allies knowingly allowed Hitler to rearm, in violation of treaties. When Europeans finally woke up to Hitler's agenda, it was too late. Their nations were conquered. One of the most horrible acts of Nazi Germany was the Holocaust, which cost an estimated 11 million lives. Those innocents lost their lives because of the unwillingness of Europeans to protect themselves against tyranny.[58]

Williams goes on to warn that terrorists have an open door along the southern US border aided by a lack of efforts to control those who leave the country to fight with terror groups in the Middle East. It is horrifying to even consider what it might take to develop sufficient backbone to actually tackle the homeland terrorism issue.

Bringing the War Back Home

In August 2014 a Homeland Security bulletin alerted Americans to the possibility of terror attacks on US soil. In the document, agents warned:

ISIL members and supporters will almost certainly continue to use social media platforms to disseminate their English-language violent extremist messages. Although we remind first responders that content not explicitly calling for violence may be constitutionally protected, we encourage awareness of media advocating violent extremist acts in particular locations or naming particular targets, to increase our ability to identify and disrupt potential Homeland threats. We urge state and local authorities to promptly report suspicious activities related to homeland plotting and individuals interested in traveling to overseas conflict zones, such as Syria or Iraq, to fight with foreign terrorist organizations.[59]

Incredibly, some Westerners have actually traveled to Syria and Iraq to join forces with the vicious and gruesome ISIL murderers. According to US sources, those American citizens who traveled to the Middle East to support the terror organization are thrill seekers, and not terrorists determined to return to the States to wreak havoc on the populace. But, given the actions of the Tsarnaev brothers who were charged with planting bombs in Boston during the Boston Marathon in 2013, it is not difficult to imagine that it could happen.

For example, in October 2014, Michael Zehaf-Bibeau, a thirty-two-year-old Canadian, approached a soldier guarding the National War Memorial in Ottawa and critically wounded the young sentry. Despite efforts to save Cpl. Nathan Cirillo, he died at the scene. Zehaf-Bibeau fled to the Parliament Building, where he was shot to death by Sergeant at Arms Kevin Vickers.

Following the shooting, US officials revealed that Zehaf-Bibeau had crossed the border into the United States at least four times. His last known trip was in 2013. It was through Canada that the 9/11 terrorists also entered the United States.

Intelligence figures reveal that thousands of fighters from foreign countries have linked with ISIL to help establish an extreme Islamic caliphate. Former CIA counterterrorism specialist Aki Peritz, said:

> It's much easier to recruit people—especially those with foreign passports—in Syria than in Pakistan for operations abroad. Given that there are several thousand foreigners in Syria today, it's probably much easier for al Qaeda to spot, assess, develop, recruit, and train willing individuals there than anywhere else in the world.[60]

Brian Michael Jenkins, a senior terrorism expert with the RAND Corporation believes that Khorasan is "scarier" than ISIS . . . because it is focused primarily on attacking the West.[61]

Conservative columnist Charles Krauthammer wrote of the seeming strategy of the Obama administration that appears designed to fail outright. He asks the question:

> As for Syria, what is Obama doing? First, he gives the enemy 12 days of warning about impending air attacks. We end up hitting empty buildings and evacuated training camps . . . . Guerrilla war is a test of wills. Obama's actual objectives - rollback in Iraq, containment in Syria - are not unreasonable.

But they require commitment and determination. In other words, will. You can't just make one speech declaring war, then disappear and go fundraising. The indecisiveness and ambivalence so devastatingly described by both of Obama's previous secretaries of defense, Leon Panetta and Bob Gates, are already beginning to characterize the Syria campaign.

The Iraqis can see it. The Kurds can feel it. The jihadists are counting on it.[62]

We need to get back to winning this battle and make the determination to accept nothing short of clear victory over ISIL and the other terrorist organizations determined to destroy both the US and Israel and to disrupt the entire Middle East. If we don't find the moral clarity to fight this evil until it is soundly defeated, all we will be doing is importing the war to US soil and facing far bloodier conflicts down the road. Is that what we really want?

CHAPTER SEVEN

The Centers of Gravity

There is no way, either to stabilize the situation in Iraq,
or to solve any kind of conflict around us—the Israeli/
Palestinian conflict, all other conflicts—without
dealing today with this Iranian regime. . . . The center
of gravity to deal with the problem today is Iran.

LT. GEN. MOSHE YA'ALON[63]
Israeli Defense Minister

FOR THE AMERICAN PEOPLE in late March and April of 2003, *Operation Iraqi Freedom* seemed a textbook example of what modern warfare could be. In less than six weeks, US-led coalition forces took on Saddam Hussein's defiant regime as an initial step in the War on Terrorism that began in response to the attacks of September 11, 2001. Air raids were surgically precise, losses were at a minimum, civilians were spared as much as possible, and Iraqis celebrated in the streets, toppling statues of the dictator in what was reminiscent of the tearing down of the Berlin Wall.

The seeds of the Second Gulf War were sown in the late 1990s in Somalia. Jihadist forces, under the command of Ayman al-Zawahiri—a suspected instigator of the August 7, 1998, bombings of US embassies in Dar es Salaam, Tanzania, and Nairobi, Kenya—were aided and funded by Iraq through the Sudan. The union was solidified in 1998–1999 with the realization between Saddam Hussein and Osama bin Laden that cooperation was vital in order to humiliate the "Great Satan" of the United States and its "Little Satan" Middle Eastern ally, Israel. While courting bin Laden, Hussein was also paying homage to Yasser Arafat, supporting the Palestinian Authority's terror network by showering monetary awards on the families of suicide bombers who attacked Israel. The plan was to create total disarray in the Middle East, thereby jeopardizing the interests of the US and its regional allies, which also included Saudi Arabia, Egypt, Kuwait, and Jordan.

When terrorists struck at the heart of America on 9/11, what had been only the possibility of war to combat terrorism worldwide became a grim reality. Noting the response to the attacks, Hussein was persuaded that after Afghanistan, Iraq would be first on President Bush's list of terrorist-harboring, terrorist-supporting nations and that an attack was imminent. Hussein began to plot a guerilla defense against a possible US invasion.

The necessity of stopping Saddam Hussein's terror network became even more apparent when the Israelis captured three men trying to cross the Jordan River into the Palestinian Territory in September 2002. Following interrogation, the Israelis learned that the three were graduates of the Hussein-trained Arab Liberation Front. The trio, along with Iraqis and terrorists from other Muslim countries, had received special training by the infamous "Unit 999" commissioned by Hussein and specializing in hijacking, explosives, sabotage, and assassination.

The three infiltrators revealed that others in the unit,

including members of al Qaeda, were "trained in handling chemical weapons and poisons, especially ricin." Following training, they moved to join Ansar al-Islam, a Kurdish wing of bin Laden's al Qaeda. The three had been exported to Israel specifically to target civilian aircraft with shoulder-fired missiles at Tel Aviv's Ben Gurion Airport. They were also ordered to target Americans en route to Iraq.

Clusters of the trainees were dispatched to Turkey, France, and Chechnya. This was later confirmed by Turkish Security Forces who arrested two al Qaeda operatives with instructions to attack the US airbase at Incirlik with chemical weapons.

Armed with intelligence reports such as those indicating that Iraq was supplying WMDs to bin Laden's terrorists, the United States began to put together a coalition to stop Saddam Hussein in Iraq. Since the end of Desert Storm in 1991, Hussein had been defying UN weapons inspectors and the UN Security Council in a game of cat and mouse about Iraq's WMD programs. Iraqi anti-aircraft batteries and missiles had from time to time locked onto and even fired upon coalition fighters running routine missions to enforce the northern and southern no-fly zones that had been set up at the end of the First Gulf War.

No Cooperation from the Arab World

Unlike the coalition formed during the First Iraq War, the Arab world chose to sit on the sidelines of the second engagement. The fear of retaliation by rabidly radical Muslims within their ranks could not be overcome by persuasion or diplomacy. A confrontation with the various terrorist factions operating in the Middle East could well mean internal upheaval, death, and destruction, not to mention the violent overthrow by extremists of existing rulers in a 1979-style Islamic Revolution against moderate Arab states.

Vulnerable Arab countries feared that a US attack on Iraq would prove to be the glue that would cement the various terrorist networks into a cohesive force that would severely punish anyone seen to be cooperating with the US-led coalition. There was a very real fear that, instead of liberating Iraq for democracy, it would become a haven for brutal terrorist groups to plan and execute a takeover of the entire Muslim world. Having successfully run the US out of Lebanon in 1983, terrorist organizations did not tremble in fear at facing allies of the "Great Satan." As we have seen in previous chapters, this very real fear became reality with the rise of the Islamic State and its monstrous followers.

Ripples in the Pool

A long-standing friendship between Hussein's sons and Syria's Bashar al-Assad made him the perfect cohort to assist in hiding Iraq's supply of WMDs. Syria acted as the go-between for the purchase of military equipment for Iraq from Russia, Yemen, and other black market suppliers in Africa. The country's defense minister at the time, Mustafa Tlass, was culpable in the illegal sale of Iraqi oil in order to pay for the various arms purchases.

With Hussein's acquisition list in hand, Syria went shopping for munitions, replacement parts for tanks, planes, antiaircraft artillery, etc. It was not a stretch for Syria to desire to acquire such material, but it was far more revealing when the purchasing agent began to inquire about parts of a Kolchuga radar system manufactured in the Ukraine, or for laser-guided missiles for the Russian-made Kornet, an antitank missile. That raised a few eyebrows. Convoys from Syria to Iraq transported thousands of the Russian-made missiles, as well as several hundred shoulder-fired antiaircraft missiles. Not all of the armaments left their storage facilities in Syria. To protect against US bombing runs, large numbers of parts and munitions stayed behind in the safety of Syria.

Ever defiant, Bashar al-Assad also pursued strategic alliances with the other two members of what President Bush had labeled the "axis of evil"—North Korea, Iraq, and Iran. Even though Iran and Iraq had been bitter enemies in the 1980s, Iran's mullahs placed the perseverance of the region's radical Islamic footprint above any past differences. Rather than culminating in a Western-type democracy as the Obama administration had envisioned, it became a ploy to rid the region of secular governments and replace them with a Sunni-Islam inspired caliphate.

By May 2011, Syrian protesters began lobbying for the removal of Assad as Syrian president. This escalated within months to the formation of the Free Syrian Army. As battles escalated in 2012, the death toll began a dramatic rise, and in early 2013, chemical weapons attacks were authorized against the town of Khan al-Assel in Aleppo, and within months another attack with the nerve agent sarin was launched against Ghouta, Damascus. The Russians negotiated a deal with Assad to remove and destroy all of Assad's chemical weapons. In mid-2014, the UN announced completion of the removal of those weapons, and also released figures indicating that nearly 200,000 people had perished in the Syrian conflict.[64]

But that wasn't the only announcement to cause consternation in the region. The Middle East Review of International Affairs (MERIA) released pictures of Kurds appearing to have been gassed by ISIL troops in July 2014. According to journalist Paul Alster:

That fighting came just one month after Islamic State forces surged through the once-notorious Muthanna compound in Iraq, the massive base where Hussein began producing chemical weapons in the 1980s, which he used to kill thousands of Kurds in Halabja in northern Iraq in 1988. Experts believe the chemical weapons were used on July 12, in the village of Avidko, close to Kobani, the Kurdish town on the Turkish border that is now the scene of fierce fighting between Kurds and Islamic State forces. If Islamic State fighters did indeed gain chemical weapons in Muthanna, it would corroborate a 2007 CIA report that confirmed their presence there. That report was cited when, in June, Islamic State fighters captured the Muthanna facility from Iraqi soldiers and allegedly seized a cache of chemical weapons, including more than 2,500 degraded chemical rockets contaminated with deadly mustard gas. If Islamic State has chemical weapons, they also could have obtained them in Syria, where embattled President Bashar Assad has as many as 16 factories for making deadly chemical weapons, despite pledging to get rid of them under pressure from the West.[65]

Former *New York Post* columnist Arthur Ahlert added:

The latest revelations on the details of Saddam's weapons stockpile, now potentially in the hands of Sunni radicals, affirm the Bush administration's characterization of Iraq as a territory situated in a hotbed of radicalism, flooded with a bevy of highly dangerous weapons and overseen by a criminal rogue regime. Indeed, the WMDs are to say nothing of the Hussein government's nuclear weapons program, also put to a stop by intervention in Iraq . . . . the latest details of Saddam's WMD stockpile—something there can be no doubt that the Secretary of State [John Kerry, former member of the Senate Committee on Foreign Relations] was aware of—exposes yet again the left's great deception on the danger of Hussein and the motivation behind the Iraq war.[66]

With ISIL on the march, it is a direct challenge to the Shi'a populations of Syria, Iraq, and Iran. Would there not be a certain amount of irony if, years after Saddam Hussein's regime had been declared WMD-free, chemical and biological weapons were finally found in Syria in the hands of those terrorist groups? Iraqi general Georges Sada, second in command of the Iraq Air Force who served under Hussein, has stated unequivocally that Saddam's undiscovered cache of WMDs had been transported into Syria for safekeeping. Who could fathom the horror of such weapons falling into the hands of the Islamic State?

Various groups encompass the armed rebels that have taken up weapons against Assad, but are chiefly comprised of the Free Syrian Army, the Islamic Front. Lebanon's terrorist group, Hezbollah, joined forces with Assad in 2013. The rapid growth of ISIL by July 2014 resulted in the Islamic State controlling approximately one-third of Syria, including the majority of its oil and gas production facilities. For anyone with a modicum of knowledge regarding the Middle East, what is happening in Syria is the equivalent of the

Wild West shootout at the OK Corral. The factions at work in the uprising in Syria and the bloodshed in Iraq are neither inconsequential terrorist groups nor are they seeking democracy. Rather, the aim is, as I've stated before, a Sunni-controlled caliphate that eventually swallows the entire Middle East and ultimately the world.

This pertinent bit of information seems to elude the Liberal Left media worldwide. It appears unable to comprehend the truth that Islamic radicals are more than willing to participate in the overthrow of a secular government—not for the purpose of achieving freedom and democracy, but in order to place themselves under the thumb of a far more despotic Islamic regime. As Joe Herring and Dr. Mark Christian wrote in an article for *American Thinker*:

Apprehension of these truths require the West to confront the elephant in the room—the one that political correctness forbids us to address—that being Islam, and its ideology of supremacy.

Terrorism is a tool, not an ideology. "Terrorist" is a functional description of someone who employs this tool in furtherance of their agenda.

The failure in the West to name that agenda is at the root of our failure to defeat it. In the Middle East, that agenda is the re-birth of an Islamic caliphate. In the West, it is a relentless Islamist agenda to mainstream Islamic doctrine in the mind of the average citizen, incrementally positioning Islam as an irreproachable inevitability, declaring any opposition as Islamophobic and anti-religion.[67]

A victorious US coup against Bashar al-Assad was hampered by three major roadblocks: He presented no immediate threat to the US mainland or to US interests abroad; he was backed by Russian strongman and president, Vladimir Putin; and Syria was a proxy of Iran. The danger from Putin waned as Russian troops challenged the Ukraine and the West levied strong sanctions for his meddling in the region. Since Putin already has ties to Assad, it is possible that he could receive a call from Assad to assist in reclaiming areas overrun by ISIL, which would position Russian troops in Syria and northern Iraq. This would create a situation that would pit the US against Russia in the Middle East. Then the question becomes: Not when, but how soon would open clashes follow?

With the need for assistance against ISIL, the US has turned a blind eye to Iran's nuclear ambitions, much to Prime Minister Benjamin Netanyahu's chagrin. He has stated that Western nations must not be blinded to the Iranian leaders' ultimate strategy—wiping both Israel and the US off the map—despite their cooperation with the US-led operation to stop ISIL. Netanyahu reiterated that Iran's nuclear program should not be allowed to go forward under any circumstances. Said the prime minister:

> You don't have to give Iran . . . what they want in the nuclear deal . . . . They're going to fight ISIS anyway. If [Syrian President Bashar] Assad were to demand his chemical weapons back in return for fighting ISIS, he would be laughed out of court . . . . Why do they need centrifuges? They say they need it for civilian nuclear energy. That's not true. Other big countries . . . have civilian nuclear programs but

not one centrifuge. This way, you are giving them the ability to build a nuclear bomb.[68]

The Obama Administration appears to be participating in a very dangerous game in several areas. Journalist David Kupelian wrote of the president's penchant for game-playing in regard to both the Arab Spring and Iran's nuclear ambitions:

> In virtually every conflict in the Middle East, Obama has inexplicably supported the wrong side, from Egypt to Libya, and has inserted himself into the brutal Syrian civil war, providing support for the Muslim Brotherhood and even al-Qaida affiliates. Yet he mysteriously failed to support—in word or deed— the genuine 2011 Iranian revolt when thousands of anti-government protesters called for an end to the terror-sponsoring regime that rules that country. Many were shocked that Obama stood on the side- lines and said nothing when the protesters urgently needed his support in overturning one of the most evil governments on earth.[69]

And in regard to Iran, Kupelian wrote:

> In the short term, both sides appear to win. For sheer optics, Obama gets to act out his narcissis- tic delusions of grandeur and to step in—much like Neville Chamberlain—to grasp "peace in our time" through brilliant diplomacy with Iranian lead- ers. In reality, the real winner is Iran, which wins

the precious time it needs to complete its development of a deployable and deliverable nuclear bomb. Worse, Obama's amateur and naïve "diplomacy" with Iran makes it even harder for Israel—living under an existential threat from an imminently nuclear Iran—to attack that nation's nuclear installations preemptively.[70]

What the Liberal Left refuses to acknowledge is that Middle East politics mirrors Newton's Third Law of Motion: When one body exerts a force on a second body, the second body simultaneously exerts a force equal in magnitude and opposite in direction on the first body. Or to paraphrase Mr. Newton: Every action has an equal and opposite reaction. Everything that happens in the Middle East causes a reaction—whether it's a rocket fired from Lebanon into northern Israel, the massacre of Shi'ite Muslims in Iraq, or the whirr of a centrifuge in Iran. It is imperative that the West learns to anticipate rather than respond. A match has been set to the primer cord in the Middle East. It is certainly now time to sit up and take notice.

CHAPTER EIGHT

The Real Battle Begins

Since the revolution by Khomeini, the view of Iran is to try to spread the Muslim revolution all over the world. To ruin whatever smells democratic, to ruin whatever seems democratic, and on the remnant of those democratic walls to build a new entity— an extreme Islamic regime that will be operated according to the Sharia Law which is the Islam leaders' codex of laws. What they want to see is a new world where Islam is in control, and all entities will be like Iran, meaning they will be controlled and ruled by the ayatollahs, by the spiritual leaders, the clerics.

GENERAL DANI YATOM
Former Head of the Israeli Intelligence Service Mossad
and Chief of Staff under Prime Minister Ehud Barak

THE GLOBAL CRY COULD BE HEARD: Revival is coming to the Middle East! But that was not the kind of revival you and I might have thought about when we heard that word . . . not the tent meetings of our childhood, with their sawdust trails and mourners' benches, or the football stadiums filled to capacity with those who traveled from miles around to hear Dr. Billy Graham. It wasn't even the weekend revival with a special guest speaker or a Christian rock band, or the campmeeting programs that still abound on religious broadcasting networks.

No, this revival is vastly different and infinitely more deadly. It is a revival of the desire inherent in jihadists for a worldwide caliphate (a form of government that draws its authority from Sharia Law), a revival of Islam and its twisted, demon-inspired desire to see every knee bow to Allah and every tongue confess that there is but one god—Allah—and Muhammed is his messenger.

The revival fire that sprang forth in the spring of 2011 was the essence of *jihad*, a holy war waged by Muslims against infidels, and all who disagree with jihadists are infidels regardless of religious affiliation. This hard lesson is being learned by all who deign to oppose ISIL. Perhaps this is a lesson President Barack Obama, ever the Pollyanna, still needs to learn. When invited to address a group of students at the famed St. Xavier's College in Mumbai, India, in November 2010, the president was asked his opinion of jihadists. His answer was most enlightening:

> The phrase *jihad* has a lot of meanings within Islam and is subject to different interpretations. Islam is one of the world's great religions. More than a billion people practise Islam. The overwhelming majority view their obligations to their religion as ones that reaffirm peace, fairness, tolerance. All of us recognize that this great religion in the hands of a few extremists has been distorted to violence, which is never justified. One of the challenges we face is, how do we isolate those who have these distorted notions of religious war? We can all treat each other with respect and mutual dignity. We should try to

live up to universal principles and ideals that Gandhi so fought for. We live in nations of diverse religious beliefs. It's a major challenge in India and around the world. Young people can make a huge impact in reaffirming that you can be a strong observer of your faith, without putting somebody else down or visiting violence on somebody else. I think a lot of these ideas are formed very early and how you respond to each other is going to be as important as any speech that a president makes in encouraging the kind of religious tolerance that is so important, in a world that is getting smaller and smaller. More and more people of different background and different territories and ethnicities are interacting and learning from each other. All of us have to fundamentally reject the notion that violence is the way to mediate our differences.[71]

I can but wonder if the Obama rhetoric based on "hope and change" could ever overcome the wild-eyed radical with his or her hand on the detonator of a backpack filled to capacity with plastic explosives, nails, screws, glass, ball-bearings, and other instruments of torture and death designed to wreak maximum damage on innocent civilians nearby. There is no remorse at the jihadist revival, no repentance, no about-face from hatred and evil toward love and good. There is only revulsion for the Jew, the Christian, and even for the Muslim who dares to disagree. One must bow a knee to Allah or die in the conflagration of the jihadist battle for supremacy on Earth. That is the underlying principal of jihad.

One of the difficulties with so-called revival in the Middle

East is that no one seems to know exactly who the players are. It is difficult to align with the "right" side when the soldiers wear no uniforms and the man or woman or even the child next door—no matter the race or country of origin—could be as much a threat as the fanatic halfway around the world. The lines of terrorism have become so blurred, so ameliorated, that we no longer hear the phrase "war on terror."

Since George W. Bush left office, the definition of the battle in which we daily fight has succumbed to political correctness. We now talk of the "enduring struggle against terrorism and extremism" or the "ongoing struggle." It has also been referred to by the almost romantic appellation "twilight struggle."[72] This is no struggle; it is war. It is a war between two spirits and two books.

Since taking office, President Obama has done everything possible to court the Muslim world—from toning down rhetoric used to refer to the conflict to choosing an Arab network for his very first televised interview. His image was captured as he bowed awkwardly to King Abdullah of Saudi Arabia and then took the administration's dog and pony show to Cairo for a broadcast designed to win over the fanatics who simply want us dead, period.

The current Islamic revival seems to have begun sometime in the 1970s. During that decade the world began to see more overt signs of the growing influence of Islam in countries outside the predominately Muslim nations. It manifested in a resurgence of Islamic culture, dress, division of the sexes, the introduction of Sharia Law, and the inclusion of Islamic terms in general conversation. Another sign of the resurgence of Islam was the increase of attendance during the Hajj—or annual pilgrimage—to Mecca. What had been a relatively small gathering of some 90,000 in 1926 has grown to over 2 million annually.[73] Attendance would be exponentially larger except that many adherents of Islam are too poor to afford the trip to Mecca.

There are those Muslim historians who believe that just as the Christian Church has experienced periods of revival—with men like Martin Luther, John and Charles Wesley, Dwight L. Moody, Billy Sunday, Hudson Taylor, and of course, Azusa Street[74] in Los Angeles in 1906—so the Muslim community experiences waves of revival. Academic Michael Cook noted:

> What is striking about the Islamic world is that, of all the major cultural domains, it seems to have been the least penetrated by irreligion; and in the last few decades, it has been the fundamentalists who have increasingly represented the cutting edge of the culture.[75]

The men credited with keeping the flame alive before the 1970s are hardly household names: Jamal al-Din al-Afghani (who has been called "one of the most influential Muslim reformers of the nineteenth century;"[76]) Hassan al-Banna, founder of the Muslim Brotherhood in 1928; and Rashid Rida. It was Rida who wrote concerning the importance of Sharia Law for the Muslim masses:

> Those Muslim [rulers] who introduce novel laws today and forsake the *Shari'a* enjoined upon them by God . . . They thus abolish supposed distasteful penalties such as cutting off the hands of thieves or stoning adulterers and prostitutes. They replace them with man-made laws and penalties. He who does that has undeniably become an infidel.[77]

Under Sharia Law those who gamble or drink alcohol can be flogged; husbands are permitted to beat their wives for any infraction deemed inappropriate. In cases of an injury, the injured party can demand payment in kind—an eye for an eye, limb for a limb. Regardless of gender, thieves can be punished by having a hand cut off, and highway robbery is punishable by crucifixion or mutilation. Homosexuality is dealt with by execution. Adulterers may be stoned to death or beaten. Anyone who is openly critical of the Quran or Sharia Law are in danger of receiving the death penalty.

Two actions in the 1970s were primarily responsible for the resurgence in Islamic fanaticism. The first was the emergence of the Organization of Petroleum Exporting Countries (OPEC) on the world stage. In 1973, after gaining a major role in the pricing of crude oil, OPEC flexed its oil-gorged muscles and precipitously raised the price of a barrel of oil. It was a means of punishing the U.S for resupplying Israel with weapons during the Yom Kippur War. Though not an attack with guns and explosives, the resulting rise in oil prices rocked global markets and created long lines at gas pumps.

To cope with the rise in oil prices, smaller and more efficient cars were introduced to the consumer. As buyers became more energy conscious, demand decreased and OPEC lost its dominant place atop the world market. OPEC members began to quarrel among themselves, and new suppliers presented a challenge. To counter the rise in alternate energy sources, Saudi Arabia increased its production, thereby pushing the price of crude down.

President Jimmy Carter feverishly tried twice to avoid an energy crisis during his one-term presidency. In July of 1979 the situation exploded and Carter faced a second calamity as OPEC announced additional price increases. US gasoline prices went through the roof, followed by purported shortages nationwide. The result was another series of long lines and short tempers at gas pumps. Gasoline that had sold for $14 per barrel rose to $40 per barrel on the spot market. Prior to that time, the price of OPEC oil had fluctuated between $2.50 per barrel and $14 per barrel.

James R. Schlesinger, Carter's energy secretary, lit a match to an already volatile situation when he reported to Congress that the energy crisis and lack of Iranian oil imports were "prospectively more serious" than the oil embargo enforced by the Arabs in 1973.[78]

The second devastating event that would rock the United States in particular and the world in general was the deposing of the shah, Mohammed Reza Pahlavi, and the return to Iran of the fanatical Shi'a imam, Ayatollah Ruhollah Khomeini.

It is incomprehensible to imagine that Khomeini could so mesmerize the majority of an entire nation with his persuasive rhetoric that the populace would blindly follow him. Khomeini had promised what would be in American political terms "a car in every garage, and a chicken in every pot," and his fellow countrymen believed him. Much like Jimmy Carter, Khomeini championed everything but promised nothing in the way of programs to achieve his ends. Even though he emphasized "change," Khomeini offered no substantive plan to implement change.

Khomeini had been in exile since 1963, first in Turkey and then in Najaf, Iraq. His exile was the direct result of political protests against the rule of the shah. He opposed what he referred to as the "Westoxication"[79] of the monarchy. He ranted against giving Iranian women the right to vote and called for the unification of the Muslim world. Khomeini spent a brief time under arrest in March 1963, but he soon returned to his fiery attacks against the shah. He was arrested again in June of that year and spent two months in prison in Iraq. In October 1963 he urged an embargo on parliamentary elections; that cost him eight months in prison and then deportation.

Moving from Turkey to Najaf, Khomeini found himself in an important center of Shi'a piety. It was there that he established his reputation as an uncompromising opponent of Reza Pahlavi. Khomeini was to forever alter the Western view of Iran and Shi'a Islam, and he would drastically change the future of one young revolutionary, Osama bin Laden, and a future politico, Mahmoud Ahmadinejad.

A 1979 CIA memorandum stated:

> While in Iraq, Khomeini began working closely with the Islamic Terrorist Group *Mujahedeen-e-Khalq* (the People's Strugglers). In late 1972 Khomeini issued a religious declaration, or *fatwa*, that enjoined faithful Shi'a to support the *Mujahedeen* and called for the devout to provide funds for their use. The money was raised from the *ulema* (Muslim scholars trained in Islamic law) and in the bazaars and funneled to Khomeini, who in turn gave it to the terrorists.[80]

The Grand Ayatollah did, indeed, hold the strings of a purse filled with blood money from other Arab sources, including Libya and the PLO.

Two events then took place in Iran, both linked to the shah and both spurring Khomeini and his followers to revenge. These two events would essentially seal the fate of the monarch. First, Ayatollah Hossein Ghaffari, a vocal critic of the shah's regime, was allegedly tortured to death by Pahlavi's security forces. The cleric and Khomeini had corresponded during Khomeini's exile in Najaf; his death only added fuel to the Islamic revolutionary fires already burning in the Grand Ayatollah's bosom.

Second, in October 1977 Khomeini's son Mustafa died of bulimia with heart complications, but antigovernment forces pointed a finger at the shah's secret police, SAVAK, and Mustafa was proclaimed a martyr. This only served to further incite Khomeini's followers against the shah. While there were various groups opposing the shah's regime, i.e., leftists, the People's Mujahedin of Iran (MEK), Communists, and other groups, Khomeini had suddenly become the most notable opponent to Pahlavi's rule.

While the shah made impressive internal changes, young men and women in Iran were swarming to radical Islam. Iran had never before seen anything like this. University students gathered at Islamic study centers to debate the imams of Shi'a Islam. Young women clothed themselves in the *chadors* (long black veils) that had been outlawed by the shah. This new, radical Islam exploded on the campus of Tehran University in October 1977. A group of students calling for the isolation of women on campus rioted, leaving behind a trail of burned-out buses and broken windows.

Khomeini's ability to turn local mosques into cauldrons of revolutionary turmoil was absolutely remarkable given the territorial nature of the mullahs and other ayatollahs. In a move that, in hindsight, was one of the most imprudent decisions by the shah, Pahlavi freed a number of pro-Khomeini mullahs from Iran's prisons in 1978. These disgruntled clerics bent on revenge gladly joined Khomeini's underground and were among the many whose mosques were made available to the radicals.

The network of mosques proved to be much more effective than the efforts of the National Front. Khomeini was slow, methodical, and determined to seek revenge against his adversary, the shah, no matter the time or cost in money or lives. The Grand Ayatollah recruited from the ranks of mid-level mullahs who whipped their followers into rabid, pro-Khomeini militants.

The ayatollah's charisma was especially appealing to the lower classes, the *mostazafin* . . . the dispossessed. They saw him as their savior, the one who would rescue them from their lives of toil. Columbia University professor Ahmad Ashraf wrote of the ayatollah: "Khomeini gave the masses a sense of personal integrity, of collective identity, of historical rootedness, and feelings of pride and superiority."[81]

The Carter Administration opted to join forces with Khomeini's choice for prime minister, Mehdi Bazargan, a weak and ineffective puppet, rather than back the shah's choice, Shaphur Bakhtiar. In less than eight short months, Bazargan would be ousted and Khomeini would then choose as prime minister Mohammad-Ali Rajai. He was a member of the Islamic Republican Party, which had been formed specifically to aid Khomeini in achieving his objective of an Islamic Republic. The Party was disbanded in 1987—mission accomplished. Iran would regress under the oppressive regime of Khomeini until his death in June 1989. But it would not end there; the die had been cast and the country would remain under the thumb of radical Islamic clerics.

CHAPTER NINE

Iran Rises

*In Iran, there is no freedom of the press, no freedom of speech,
no independent judiciary, no free elections. There is no freedom
of religion—not even for Shiites, who are forced by Iran's
theocracy to adhere to one narrow set of official rules.*

ELLIOT ABRAMS[82]

SOME MIGHT BELIEVE the roots of unrest in Iran go back
to the 2009 election that the Green Party felt was stolen from them
by Ayatollah Ali Khamenei and his hand-picked leader, President
Mahmoud Ahmadinejad. Indeed, the dissatisfaction goes much
deeper. Many of Iran's devout Muslims remain faithful followers of
Islam; however, they no longer believe in the late Ruhollah Khomeini's
Islamic Republic; that dream suffered a disheartening death.

Journalist Karim Sadjadpour asked a very pertinent question
in an article for *Foreign Policy*:

> How is it, many wonder, that a system that has
> profoundly underperformed for three decades could
> remain in power?[83]

The answer can be found in the reality that many Iranians are too fearful to enter the fray unless or until they are certain there is a chance for real change.

Following the announcement of 2009 election results, demonstrations erupted when hundreds of thousands took to the streets to protest Ahmadinejad's reelection as fraudulent. There were a number of reasons for the doubt, among them:

> The Interior Ministry announced the first results within an hour of the polls closing and the official result less than a day later. The ministry is supposed to wait three days after voting before it certifies the result, to allow time for disputes to be examined . . . The country uses paper ballots that must be counted by hand—a time-consuming process. But for people to have confidence in those announcements, a country needs an independent electoral commission that acts fairly and transparently . . . there are no independent election observers in Iran.[84]

Demonstrations were quelled by the feared Basij, a paramilitary group loyal to Ahmadinejad. According to news reports, members of the Basij were photographed breaking into homes and shooting live ammunition into the assembled crowds. Hospitals reported a number of gunshot victims brought into emergency facilities. The IRG and Basij were also accused of vandalism and of entering university dorms at night and taking students away.

On February 14, 2011, Iranians again took to the streets in protest of government human rights violations. Two opposition leaders, Mir-Hossein Mousavi and Mehdi Karroubi, were placed under house arrest and denied access to telephones or the Internet. Their homes were blockaded, and they were not allowed visitors.[85] Protesters were met with armed resistance in the major Iranian cities, where residents dared to join in the demonstrations.

In Tehran's Revolution Square, members of the armed forces mounted motorcycles to beat back the protesters. It was reminiscent of the Basij attacking throngs of Iranians following the 2009 elections. Websites for the opposition parties stated that at least one person was killed when security forces opened fire in Hafteh Tir Square, while some were injured and/or detained. Isfahan demonstrators were met with pepper spray and baton-wielding agents of the government.

Despite the attempted uprisings at home, Iran's Shi'a leaders were rejoicing at the potential for a cataclysmic shift in the balance of power among Muslims in the region. Cashing in on the ouster of Mubarak, Iran dispatched two warships to the Suez Canal, where new leaders in Egypt broke a thirty-year ban and allowed passage through the waterway to a port in Syria. As if that weren't monumental enough, it also marked the first time Iranian warships had been allowed to dock at a Saudi Arabian port, Jeddah. Some observers were convinced it was an act of the Saudis kowtowing to a nation with visions of becoming the leader of a worldwide Muslim caliphate.

With the US media focused on events in Libya, it was the perfect time for Iran to flex its muscles, and flex it did. There were a number of notable and alarming accomplishments while the warships were docked in Syria:

> ✧ Iran and Syria formally agreed to cooperate on naval training, including personnel exchange.

✧ In the wake of the collapse of the Egyptian military's efforts to impede arms smuggling into the Gaza Strip, Iran rushed in to build new infrastructure in the Sinai to enable more efficient arms transfers to Hamas.

✧ Russian Defense Minister Anatoly Serdyukov said that Russia decided to fulfill a contractual obligation to complete the transfer of cruise missiles to Syria, despite entreaties by the Israelis not to do so.[86]

The controlling military leaders in Egypt also decided in early April 2011 to extend a hand to Tehran. During the thirty years of Mubarak's controversial regime, he resisted overt contact with Iran. With Ahmadinejad's bold venture into Syrian waters, Egyptian Foreign Minister Nabil Elaraby indicated his country's willingness to reestablish diplomatic ties:

> The Egyptian and Iranian people deserve to have mutual relations reflecting their history and civilization. Egypt is open to all countries, and the aim is to achieve common interests.[87]

Bearing a greeting from Iranian Foreign Minister Ali Akbar Salehi, Amani said the Iranian government welcomed Egypt's proposal to restore ties. The split between the two countries came after the Islamic Revolution and ascendancy of Ayatollah Khomeini, and was exacerbated by Egypt's peace treaty with Israel.

Former Lebanese prime minister Saad Hariri charged Iran with "flagrant intervention" in the affairs of Kuwait, Bahrain, and

Lebanon. Hariri leveled his criticism at the Shi'a majority in Iran and said unequivocally that it was no longer acceptable for the Iranians to interfere in the affairs of Lebanon or other Arab countries. He feared Lebanon would become an Iranian satellite, and could quite easily, were Hezbollah's leaders to decide to do so. That terrorist group is a proxy armed and funded by Iran. Its members total more than the national Lebanese army and have taken delivery on thousands of missiles and rockets imported from Tehran.

It is apparent that Saudi King Abdullah, another long-time US ally, is running scared, fearful for the future of his kingdom, which is in the sights of both Iran and the Islamic State. He has little room to negotiate with either. His monarchy is tightly controlled by Wahhabi mullahs, who refuse to bargain with the Shi'a sect.

Saudi Arabia, the home of Wahhabism, is now in the crosshairs of Islamic State leaders who have been vocal in their criticism of the House of Saud and its hold over the country. There is a wide rift between what ISIL sees as the modernists in Saudi Arabia and its own members.

What might the Islamic State plan for the cradle of Wahhabism in the Middle East? The purpose is to cause a total disintegration of the Kingdom of Saudi Arabia. The plan seems to be a return to the teachings of al-Wahhab and then demand that Wahhabism becomes the sole foundation for Islamic beliefs. What would that entail? Every Muslim would be forced to accept Wahhabism or be slaughtered. All property would revert to ISIL as spoils of war—including that of any family members. Any hesitation or reservation would result in execution.

If the Kingdom of Saudi Arabia were to be overcome by Islamic State zeal, the region would be forever changed—for the worse. The Middle East would become grotesquely distorted in ways we cannot even conceive. The Islamic State is a time-bomb waiting to explode with a hatred for all the trappings of wealth—but, ironically, without which the organization would perish due to lack of funding.

The Islamic State's strategy seems obvious: Steamroll Iraq, Syria, and Jordan, and then target Mecca and Medina. This move, if successful, would bestow validity on ISIL as the new rulers of Saudi Arabia, before moving forward with an attempt to take out Israel, Europe, and the US

Ibn Abd al-Wahhabi, the man responsible for the spread of Wahhabism in Saudi Arabia, wandered the deserts of the region formulating his own version of Islam—one that hearkens back to the days of Mohammad. So strong were his beliefs that al-Wahhab battled any method of worshipping Mohammad, including the practice of making hajj (annual pilgrimage) at his burial site in Medina. This was explained away as conferring deity status on the prophet. That ideology is scorned by other Muslims who express doubt that one can be a practitioner of Islam and not honor the Prophet Mohammad.

It was exactly al-Wahhab's unrealistic, rigid, and disturbing pronouncements that were banned in 1818 by the Ottoman Turks, but which were dramatically revived in the 1920s to assume the shape of the Saudi Arabian empire of today. Ironically it was an official of the British government, Harry St. John Philby, the father of double agent Kim Philby, who became a confidant to Abd al-Aziz. The elder Philby converted to Wahhabism and worked diligently to promote al-Aziz to the position of king following what Philby was certain would be the fall of the Ottoman Empire. The British convert's plan was simple: Win Western support for al-Aziz and bind Saudi policy to that of Britain and the United States—a gambit that succeeded.

Another offshoot of Philby's strategy was that Western ideologues failed to recognize the dangers inherent in Wahhabism and its capability to revert to an initial bloody, inflexible, and harsh state. Seemingly, ISIL is the answer to this restoration.

The US is apparently struggling to catch up with and successfully battle the Islamic radicals and with no workable plan of how to deal with the murdering, beheading fanatics should they gain yet another foothold in the Middle East.

US influence in the region continues to wane moment by moment. Hosni Mubarak in Egypt—gone; his replacement and Muslim Brotherhood member, Mohamed Morsi—gone; Tunisian and Bahraini ties—severely threatened; Yemen cooperation—vanishing; King Abdullah II in Jordan—struggling to maintain control; King Abdullah in Saudi Arabia—deeply concerned; Hamas and Hezbollah—growing like insatiable giants and feeding on war materiel making its way into Lebanon and Gaza from determined outside sources; ISIL—who knows the outcome.

International affairs expert Ali Reza Nader believes:

> I think the Saudis are worried that they're encircled—Iraq, Syria, Lebanon; Yemen is unstable; Bahrain is very uncertain . . . . They worry that the region is ripe for Iranian exploitation. Iran has shown that it is very capable of taking advantage of regional instability.[88]

With upheaval in the area, Iran is clearly trying to flex its muscles in the region—even if it might mean a temporary partnership with the United States to battle ISIL—in order to achieve ascendancy over the Gulf States. The ousting of the Taliban in Afghanistan and

Saddam Hussein in Iraq effectively eliminated two of Iran's biggest enemies, both of whom helped curb the rogue nation's objectives. All Iran's Ali Khamenei has to do is to wait patiently at the borders of both countries and take advantage of any opportunity to make inroads.

Although Shi'ism is not a massive arm of Islam, and Iran's leaders are not spokesmen for all Shi'ites, it does not diminish their shared faith or lessen the feeling that they have been victimized by the Sunni majority. Thus, there is the possibility that the Shi'a in other nations will rally around Iran in hopes of gaining ground in their own quest for power.

Iran's bold attempt to set up a Muslim caliphate is not a foregone conclusion, especially with the ascendancy of the Islamic State. Moreover, there are additional players standing by for an opportunity to exercise their rights to interfere in the politics of Egypt, Tunisia, Yemen, and other Middle East countries in flux.

Never doubt that Iran will take advantage of any and every opportunity to attack either the Great Satan or the Little Satan. Hatred among its leadership for both countries is immense. Those behind the curtain who pull the strings of the figurehead Iranian president have seen that "the regional balance is shifting, in potentially decisive ways, against their American adversary and in favor of the Islamic Republic."[89]

As I mentioned earlier, it is no secret that Iran pours about $1 billion yearly into Lebanon in support of Hezbollah. Another $100 million is tossed Hamas's way, and Islamic Jihad benefits annually to the tune of about $50 million. Funneling funds to terrorists is only one reason why the powers that be in Washington erred dramatically when they refused to back the opposition in Iran in 2009 and again in 2011. They failed to realize that the threat from

Iran is not from the resistance; it is from the element surrounding its leaders who export radical Islamic terrorism to countries around the world.

New Wolf, Old Sheepskin

Hassan Rouhani, elected in 2013 to replace the departing Ahmadinejad, is the more conventional wolf in sheep's clothing who thinks he can hoodwink the world at large. Unfortunately, his ploy seems to be working. Prime Minister Netanyahu said of the new Iranian president:

> I wish we could believe Rouhani's words, but we must focus on Iran's actions. And it's the brazen contrast, this extraordinary contradiction, between Rouhani's words and Iran's actions that is so startling. Rouhani stood at this very [United Nations] podium last week and praised Iranian democracy . . . But the regime that he represents executes political dissidents by the hundreds and jails them by the thousands.[90]

The prime minister went on to state what so many seem to have overlooked or not comprehended: Iran's participation in the Syrian civil war during which so many innocent civilians continue to die; terrorist attacks have been launched by Iranian leaders in twenty-five cities on five continents; and that Iran is actively backing proxies that are intent on destabilizing Lebanon, Yemen, Bahrain, Gaza, and other Middle Eastern countries, and openly target Israel.

Mr. Netanyahu then enumerated all the reasons why Iran and its controlling clerics could not be believed: 1) all Iranian nuclear facilities are hidden deep underground to forestall or negate attacks; 2) facilities for uranium enrichment have been cloaked in secrecy; 3) intercontinental ballistic missiles have been developed with the specific purpose of delivering nuclear warheads that would most certainly reach Israel and could within years reach cities on the Eastern Seaboard of the United States; and 4) Iran's leaders are prepared to subject the populace to crippling economic sanctions in order to keep International Atomic Energy Agency officials from scrutinizing the country's atomic operations. The prime minister had this unalterable summation: Iran's facilities are not for peaceful nuclear pursuits.

Rouhani obviously believes in his trite but effective hale-fellow-well-met strategy. The success of his falsely friendly approach was touted in his 2011 book when he wrote:

> While we were talking to the Europeans in Tehran, . . . we were installing equipment in a plant where they convert Iranian yellow cake to enrichable form . . . by creating a calm environment we were able to complete the work, we were able to complete a crucial part of Iran's nuclear weapons program.[91]

Mr. Netanyahu summed up that theory quite succinctly: "Rouhani thinks he can have his yellowcake and eat it too."[92]

Sadly, it is seemingly working: Mr. Obama is a lame-duck president desperate and shows signs of being willing to do anything to create a legacy for which he will be long remembered. Israel, on the other hand, needs no reminder of what can happen when past lessons are buried under a barrage of bluster. Its people know the price that will be extracted if the fanatical regime in Tehran is allowed to arm itself with atomic weapons.

Of greater concern to Israel were attempts by President Rouhani to persuade the West to lessen sanctions against his country. Talks in Geneva in November 2013 were aimed at doing just that if concrete changes were made to Iran's nuclear program. In January 2014, Rouhani's efforts bore fruit when the European Union released a statement that read in part that the organization had "suspended certain EU restrictive measures against Iran for a period of six months." French leaders were the first to express doubts regarding Iran's long-sought lessening of sanctions in return for a more transparent nuclear program. According to French Foreign Minister Laurent Fabius, Paris could not agree to a "sucker's deal." As evidence, he pointed to the reservations that the Iranians would continue their stealthy march toward securing nuclear arms. The French reticence seemed to indicate that a crack was forming in the Western powers' façade.

Doubts from French leaders were apparently overcome, however, when the interim deal was struck between Iranian Prime Minister Rouhani and the so-called "P5+1 countries" comprised of the United States, France, Russia, China, and France plus Germany. The deal gave Iran six months and $7 billion dollars in sanction relief during which time attempts to reach a final agreement on Iran's future nuclear pursuits would be discussed.

Prime Minister Benjamin Netanyahu said of the deal:

> What was reached last night in Geneva [July 19, 2014] is not a historic agreement, it is a historic mistake. Today the world became a much more dangerous place because the most dangerous regime in the

world made a significant step in obtaining the most dangerous weapons in the world .... I want to clarify that Israel will not let Iran develop nuclear military capability.[93]

Leaders of Muslim countries with largely Sunni populations—Saudi Arabia, Kuwait, the United Arab Emirates, Bahrain, Qatar, Egypt, and Jordan—were coldly silent on the accord reached in Geneva. Chairman Abdullah al-Askar of Saudi Arabia's Shoura Council, a group that advises the Saudi government on policy, said:

> I am afraid Iran will give up something to get something else from the big powers in terms of regional politics—and I'm worrying about giving Iran more space or a freer hand in the region. The government of Iran, month after month, has proven that it has an ugly agenda in the region, and in this regard no one in the region will sleep and assume things are going smoothly.[94]

Unfortunately, with so much done clandestinely in Iran, how could anyone be certain of compliance by Iran's rulers on any agreement? And frankly, why would those clerics, who have no shortage of insolence and audacity, agree to suspend nuclear enrichment for any period of time? Simple: The money to keep their program running has been severely compromised by the sanctions. There is speculation that the $7 billion in sanction relief will not benefit the Iranian people, but will go directly into the coffers of Supreme Leader Ali Khamenei's Revolutionary Guard Corps. Such a lofty sum would purchase a lot of equipment for the various centrifuges in the land of the ayatollahs.

Talk of an agreement between the Iranians and the Russians to "convert the uranium into specialized fuel rods for the Bushehr nuclear power plant"[95] may or may not come to culmination, and there is no guarantee that if it does, the concord would be permanent.

In an article for the *New York Times*, David E. Sanger wrote of a proposal between the two countries to elevate Russia to the role of nuclear caretaker for Iran:

> It places President Vladimir V. Putin at the center of negotiations that may well determine the future of the Middle East, a position he is eager to occupy. "There have been numerous iterations of Iranian-Russian cooperation in the past, and they have not come to fruition," Karim Sadjadpour of the Carnegie Endowment for International Peace said on Sunday. "Often the economics do not make sense. And the Iranians mistrust the Russians almost as much as they mistrust the United States."[96]

Meetings of the P5+1 group in Vienna, Austria, in mid-October 2014 proved to be inconclusive, reported Paul Richter:

> The future of Iran's planned research reactor at Arak is again proving a major sticking point in international talks over Tehran's disputed nuclear program, according to a key negotiator. Western officials fear that the heavy-water reactor, once operational,

could provide a significant supply of plutonium. Plutonium is one of two materials, along with highly enriched uranium, that can fuel a nuclear bomb. Iran says the 40-megawatt Arak reactor is intended to produce isotopes for cancer and other medical treatments. It agreed to halt installation work at Arak late last year as part of an interim deal to buy time for negotiators to reach a broader accord . . . . Russia's chief negotiator said there was "no consensus" among the seven countries on the Arak facility, which is southwest of Tehran.[97]

One thing is certain: If the US hopes to be blessed by God Almighty, her loyalty must be to Israel and not to her enemies; her willingness to act in support of Israel, unwavering. Sadly, no recent occupant of the White House, regardless of party affiliation, seems to understand that biblical precept.

CHAPTER TEN

The World War
Against Terrorism

*I see the threat posed to the United States and Israel as the
beginning of a 100-year war. You can call it World War III.
You can call it the beginning of a new type of warfare. . . . I
would rather not use analogies to World War One and World
War Two . . . this as a new kind of warfare that the West is
clearly disadvantaged by. The asymmetry of morality makes
it very hard for us to fight groups that have no morality.*

ALAN DERSHOWITZ[98]

IN ADDRESSING THE TERRORISM crisis that is gripping
the world and causing entire nations to forget the difficult lessons
learned during World War II, let's look back at the beginning of
2006 in Iraq. While targeting coalition troops and, in particular, the
Americans, a new level of violence began arising between Shi'ites
and Sunnis. On February 22, 2006, two bombs exploded in the Shi'ite

al-Askari mosque in Samarra, severely damaging its golden dome and interior.

The mosque is powerfully significant to Shi'a Muslims because it is the burial place of Ali al-Hadi and his son, Hassan al-Askari, the Tenth and Eleventh Imams. They are the immediate predecessors of the Twelfth or Hidden Imam, Muhammad al-Mahdi, the one known as the *Mahdi* for whom al-Sadr's Mahdi Army is named, who, legend has it, disappeared down a well in Iran in the tenth century and, it was prophesied, would one day return and triumphantly spread Islam to the world. It is believed his apocalyptic return will bring the world under control of a new Muslim caliphate that will lead Islam to world supremacy.

One of those responsible for this bombing had been wearing an Iraqi military uniform. Shi'ites responded by attacking and destroying various Sunni mosques. Several Sunni imams were summarily executed by al-Sadr's Shi'ite militia. Shi'ite mobs in other Iraqi cities stormed jails and executed inmates. In retaliation, groups of Sunnis attacked Shi'ites, dragging them from their vehicles to be murdered. As many of the US-trained and armed Iraqi police force looked on in fear, others had simply joined the assailants. Not even a curfew imposed on Baghdad could stop the slaughter. Bodies were dumped in the streets after having been handcuffed and then shot execution-style. In all, 184 Sunni mosques either lay in rubble or were vandalized, and more than one thousand Shi'ites and Sunnis were murdered.

In the ensuing months, sectarian death squads roamed the Baghdad streets killing thousands. It appeared that some group was trying to sow the seeds of ethnic violence in the hope of starting a civil war.

Descent into Anarchy

With cries that the resistance would not end until the infidels were driven from Iraq, new recruits joined daily. Intelligence sources indicated a new cooperation among heretofore antagonistic factions. Some Shi'ite groups were consorting with Sunni groups; Ba'thist brigades worked alongside the *fedayeen* (Arab guerrillas) to take out coalition troops and bring down American aircraft. The US and coalition forces were caught in the crosshairs of every terrorist organization in operation in Iran, Iraq, and Syria, and could do little to stop the resulting bloodshed. The disorganized Ba'thist forces that fell so rapidly under the initial assault regrouped as guerilla warriors with only one intention: to strike the coalition forces at every turn.

The Muslim world did not see this as a war to curb Saddam Hussein's terror activities, but rather as another attack by "Crusaders" against Islam. According to author Yossef Bodansky, one of the most respected analysts in the Arab world, Abdul Bari Atwan, made a further comparison:

> The US forces have not liberated Iraq; they have humiliated it, occupied it, torn it apart, and subjugated its sons. The United States is now preparing to subjugate the rest of the Arabs in the same way and by the same destructive operation; therefore, it will not meet with anything except resistance and hatred. . . . This means that the aggression will not stop at the borders of Iraq, exactly the same as when Hulagu [a Mongol leader] occupied Baghdad [in the thirteenth century], looted it, enslaved its

inhabitants, and destroyed it as a springboard to occupy the entire region.[99]

To a seriously affronted Muslim world, the infidels—this time American soldiers rather than Mongols—had again ridden into Baghdad to pillage and humiliate the Iraqi people. The late Osama bin Laden issued the call of jihad against US troops. Soon Iran's President Mahmoud Ahmadinejad donned the mantle of Ayatollah Khomeini, took up bin Laden's call, and fostered an Islamic revolution aimed at religious ideologies worldwide, including Sunni Islam, Judaism, and Christianity.

In the rush to prepare for invasion by American and coalition troops, Saddam Hussein set out to cover his tracks and eliminate all threats. In a move designed to prevent coalition forces from interrogating one of the world's most brutal and prolific terrorists, Hussein's elite troops entered an Iraqi upper-class stronghold in Baghdad and assassinated Abu Nidal, along with four of his henchmen. Nidal had been responsible for the deaths of hundreds in terror attacks worldwide. Although Hussein had ordered the murder of Nidal, he was reacting to pressure from Hosni Mubarak in Egypt and Yasser Arafat, who did not want Nidal's secrets exposed to Western scrutiny. With intelligence supplied to Hussein by Russian leader Vladimir Putin, Nidal had received overtures from the CIA and was considering disclosing confidential information in exchange for asylum. Hussein made sure that didn't happen.

Perhaps the biggest challenge for the US was the renewed battle against Saddam's secret weapon: the parallel, underground force trained by North Korea in the art of carrying out a prolonged guerilla war. To provide further safeguards for himself, Hussein established an equivalent government with outposts around Iraq as a firewall against a US invasion. The warriors inside this network were trained to create civil upheaval and insurrection against invading forces. To facilitate the fighters, Hussein engaged China and North Korea to build a series of underground bunkers nearly undetectable from the air. These bunkers were thought to house his stockpile of weapons, including the elusive WMD.

It was no wonder that as Operation Iraqi Freedom advanced, coalition troops found themselves under constant bombardment from a variety of terror cells and networks hard at work to create civil strife. With Syria's help as a backer of terror activities and a shelter for terrorists, as well as an open pipeline for incoming jihadists, it was no wonder the US found it more and more difficult to police Iraq. And, although they had no formal agreement to cooperate, Syria became a recruiting ground for Iran to enlist the aid of Hezbollah fighters in and around Baghdad.

Spurred on by influential ayatollahs whose Friday sermons were filled with hateful anti-US oratory, and the incentives of food and spending money, young Muslims in surrounding Arab countries, Syria, Saudi Arabia, and Palestine, among others, were eager to join the fight to expunge the infidels from Arab land. It didn't hurt the cause that there was also a promise of paradise and seventy-two young virgins should a recruit become a suicide bomber.

One of the most vocal proponents of the rebellion was Moqtada al-Sadr, who made no secret of his ties with Iran. During the height of resistance in July 2003, al-Sadr made a four-day visit to Iran for meetings with senior leaders in Ayatollah Ali Khamenei's office. There he received an appointment as an official emissary of Iran's Ayatollah Kazen Haeri, a leader in the Shi'a community.

Al-Sadr committed to pursue the Iranian plan for Iraq, a theo-cratic government that wed the political and the religious. It was his assignment to denigrate Ayatollah Ali al-Husayni al-Sistani in Iraq, to undertake assassinations, and to foment resistance in any way possible. In return, he would be supplied with expert assistance from Hezbollah and the elite Qods Force of Iran.

Al-Sadr's mentor eased the way for success for his protégé by issuing a *fatwa* (a legal opinion by an Islamic scholar) aimed at Saddam's Ba'th Party members. He decreed that they were open targets for Moqtada's death squads, thus giving him permission to commit murder. Even as al-Sadr received a license to incite rebellion, a decree was issued to Iranian-supported cells to engage British troops near Basra, as they were thought to be easier targets for factions trained in Iran. A group of pro-Iranian militant agita-tors whipped a local group in the city of Majar al-Kabir into a killing frenzy. The result was the mob killing of six members of the Royal Military Police. A second attack targeted the British 1st Battalion of the Parachute Regiment. The third British detachment to come under assault was the crew of a Chinook helicopter attempting to rescue a detail of British soldiers under small arms and grenade fire. Iran determined to do the very thing it had chastised the US for doing: interfering with the government in Iraq.

In July al-Sadr introduced his Mahdi army to the people of Najaf. His announcement was made to a group of followers garbed in shrouds, ostensibly to indicate their readiness to die as martyrs. Their rallying cry was reminiscent of that introduced by Khomeini: "Death to America" and "Death to Israel."

Al-Sadr had at his fingertips a network of terrorists, some from Lebanon, and others from Iran and Syria. Their only purpose was to kill the "invaders" and anyone associated with them. The path of the jihadists was crowded with those willing to be martyred for the resistance.

With so many willing to take on the Americans and the coalition, attacks against the troops escalated daily. The weapons of choice grew more sophisticated: missile launchers and grenades, RPGs and military-grade IEDs.

Civil War

Iraq rapidly descended into anarchy, with various factions warring against each other and against coalition troops. Death squads roamed the streets of Baghdad; Sunnis fought Shi'ites; ayatollahs battled ayatollahs for predominance; and in the background, Iran continued to arm and support groups loyal to Tehran. In bloody street battles, it was hard to differentiate between civilians and rebels. For every two steps forward, it seemed US troops were forced to take three back.

During the occupation, ambushes, suicide bombings, kidnappings, and murders became the order of the day. Roadside bombs using IEDs targeted anyone who happened to get in the way. Suicide bombers attacked coalition checkpoints and other gathering places with regularity.

By the end of 2006, a new name was being given to the IEDs: EFPs—which stands for "explosive-formed penetrators." Unlike regular roadside bombs, EFPs remained intact as they exploded. The steel tubes with curved metal seals formed a kind of super shrapnel that could penetrate a tank's or Humvee's™ armor. The explosion turned the caps into molten jets of metal. Other than keeping a low profile, US troops had little defense against these better-engineered booby traps. Again, evidence suggested these were being smuggled in across the Iranian border.[100]

In my 2006 interview with former CIA director James Woolsey, he said this of Iran's involvement in Iraq:

> Iran is playing a very important role in Iraq by smuggling in improvised explosive devices and the technology for them, by helping militias such as Muqtada al-Sadr's brigades attack Sunni, and troubled survivability of the government in Iraq. Iran has a long border with Iraq. It's been infiltrating money, terrorists, various, I think, operational gear, and weapons for some time. It's one of the biggest problems in Iraq.[101]

As the war progressed, one thing became abundantly clear: Those we were fighting were not a ragtag band of disgruntled Iraqis, but professional, well-armed terrorists.

Enter Iran, Again

As 2006 neared an end, the Islamic radical offensive against American forces escalated. On October 26, in the midst of Ramadan, suicide bombings intensified in the heart of Baghdad. An American Black Hawk helicopter was downed near Tikrit, a first for the terrorists in this conflict.

On October 28, revolutionaries targeted a tank north of Baghdad, shot a Baghdad deputy mayor—an American ally—in the head at a café in Baghdad, struck an Iraqi military police convoy, bombed a shopping area serving Iraqis working for the government, and blew up an American supply train near Fallujah. The attackers didn't stop there. October 30 saw the dawning of another day of intense terror activities: US military patrols were hit, roadside bombs detonated, police stations strafed with gunfire, American bases hit by mortar fire, and an American patrol ambushed. The incidents spilled over into the next day with raids on Americans in Mosul and Abu Ghraib. As October gave way to November, the strikes intensified, both in power and superiority.

Once the terrorists became aware they possessed the capability to bring down a Black Hawk, an all-out campaign to rid the skies of US helicopters and troop transport planes unfolded. With an arsenal of rockets and machine guns, the insurgents were able to hit the engine of a Chinook helicopter. The crash killed sixteen and injured twenty on board. Another assault on a Black Hawk near Tikrit resulted in the deaths of all six crew members. Yet another Black Hawk, hit by machine-gun fire, rolled violently and crashed into a second helicopter, bringing both down. Seventeen were killed and five wounded.

November 2006 saw an increase in the number of strikes and a new round of assassination attempts aimed at those thought to be in collusion with the US Car bombings increased as American patrols were decreased to protect the troops. American commanders instigated new evasive actions designed to safeguard American units, and the terrorists took advantage of the reduction in force.

Meanwhile, Osama bin Laden had not been idle. He was busy setting up training camps in remote locations to provide on-the-job training for insurgents flooding into Iraq. The objective was to establish numerous small cells in a short period of time, equip them with arms and funds, and send them forth to create murder and mayhem at will. The CIA determined that bin Laden had a pool of some 10,000 Saudi radicals ready and willing to join his cause, a situation that could ultimately signal trouble for the House of Saud. Why? A number of bin Laden's commanders had joined him straight from the ranks of important tribes in Saudi Arabia.

However, just as the terrorists had their training network, so did the US Once again the armed forces called on the Israelis, long immersed in combating antiterrorism and urban fighting. The Intifada had served as an excellent training ground for the Israel Defense Forces (IDF). They were, in turn, able to share knowledge acquired in the trenches with US troops. Special combat units were sent to Israel to train, and in return, Israeli commanders were invited to the United States to provide instruction for their US counterparts.

The Israelis were also able to provide information on special operations and knowledge of the particulars of dealing with the kind of social structure the Americans were encountering in Iraq. The US even went so far as to clandestinely import Israeli instructors into Iraq to provide on-the-ground indoctrination.

CHAPTER ELEVEN

Iran's Burgeoning Nuclear Ambitions

It is crystal clear to me that if Arabs put down a draft resolution blaming Israel for the recent earthquake in Iran it would probably have a majority, the US would veto it and Britain and France would abstain.

AMOS OZ, ISRAELI WRITER[102]

AS THE WAR IN IRAQ PLODDED ON, it was revealed that Iran had reentered the race for nuclear power. After the revolution of 1979, Iran's nuclear program was all but defunct. With the overthrow of the shah, Western backing disappeared. Ayatollah Khomeini suspended the nuclear program for a time, calling it "un-Islamic," but it was resumed later with support in training and hardware from North Korea, China, and Russia.

Contractors who had been working with the shah's government cancelled all nuclear contracts including the one to complete work on the Bushehr nuclear plant housing two partially completed reactors. The facility was further decimated in repeated attacks during the Iran–Iraq War of the 1980s. In 1995, Iran engaged Russia to rebuild one of the reactors at Bushehr much to US chagrin, but little evidence existed that Iran's nuclear capabilities would produce anything more than electricity. Then in 2002, Alireza Jafarzadeh, a member of the dissident People's Mujahedin of Iran (also known as *Mujahadeen-e-Khalq* or MEK for short), revealed that Iran had two secret facilities concerned with something more than just powering cities: a partially underground uranium enrichment site at Natanz and a heavy water facility in Arak.

Thus began the cat-and-mouse game outlined in detail in my book *Showdown with Nuclear Iran*. Iran, because of the extremism of its worldview, saw no reason to play things straight with the infidels. Needless to say, this issue came to a head again in the summer of 2006 with two new events.

The first was a package of incentives offered to Iran by the EU3 (Great Britain, France, and Germany) and the United States to stop its uranium enrichment programs. Iran promised a response to this by August 22, 2006. The second was Iranian talks with world leaders that took place in early July before the G8 summit in Russia during July 15–17. At these talks, Iran was told that pressure verifying its nuclear program was peaceful would be a major point of discussion at the summit.

To this, Iran's response was twofold as well. As Israeli Prime Minister Isaac Hertzog related to me:

> Mr. Ali Larijani, who was the head of the National Security Council of Iran, completed his negotiations with Javier Solano, on behalf of the G8 in

Europe, and instead of flying back home, landed in Damascus . . . [on] the morning of the abduction [of two Israeli soldiers on July 12 near the Israel-Lebanon border]. Now tell me if that's a coincidence?[103]

Shortly after those kidnappings, Hezbollah began firing Katyusha rockets into Israel's northern cities. The result was the Israeli–Hezbollah conflict that saw Israel push deeply into Lebanon with the hope of disarming Hezbollah. A UN ceasefire proposal brought hostilities to an end on August 11, 2006, but despite suffering the destruction of most of their rocket launchers and armaments, much of the world's Liberal Left media proclaimed Hezbollah the true winner of the fighting. During this time, the G8 summit had met and adjourned, and the press was paying little attention to Iran and its uranium enrichment. On July 31, however, the UN Security Council set an August 31 deadline for Iran to stop enrichment activities or face sanctions. The warning was toothless, and the deadline came and went with no further action.

The second was Iran's response to the UE3 and US incentive program on August 22, which was basically a long document saying they would gladly return to the negotiating table, but refused to stop their enrichment activities, which had, of course, been the prerequisite set forth in the incentive plan for negotiations to resume. On August 31, then president Ahmadinejad boldly stated via Iranian television, "They should know that the Iranian nation will not yield to pressure and will not let its rights be trampled on."[104] On October 23, he further announced, "The enemies, resorting to propaganda, want to block us from achieving (nuclear technology) . . . But they should know that today, the capability of our nation has multiplied tenfold over the same period last year."[105] Then on October 27, an Iranian spokesperson announced that it had doubled its nuclear enrichment capabilities. "We are injecting gas into the second cascade, which we installed two weeks ago," the unidentified official reported.[106] An Iranian official also announced that Iran would add 3,000 new centrifuges to the facilities at Natanz by March 2007 of the type a BBC expert said could be used to enrich uranium to weapons grade.[107]

Obviously Iran still has displayed no intentions of stopping its nuclear pursuits just because we've asked them nicely and repeatedly. Their refusals were finally bearing fruit as the West decided to ease sanctions for a period—a move surely seen as weakness on the part of Western nations and the United States.

According to all sources, Iran is very close to its determined plan of possessing nuclear weapons capabilities. Pakistan, North Korea, and even Russia can be thanked for the advances in nuclear technology enjoyed by this rogue nation bent on the destruction of the Great Satan (United States) and the Little Satan (Israel).

While the world's eyes were turned toward Israel and Lebanon in the summer of 2006, Iran's nuclear pursuits slipped under the radar of world leaders. One can but wonder how much additional technological progress was made by the scientists at the enrichment facilities scattered across Iran as Hezbollah lobbed shrapnel-laden missiles into the midst of Israeli cities.

Of course, the estimates of when Iran might possess the technical capabilities to produce a nuclear device have ranged from the end of 2006 to the prognostications of Director of National Intelligence John Negroponte. He told BBC Radio's *Today* program that "Tehran could have a nuclear bomb ready between 2010 and 2015."[108]

Iran's Proxy Wars

Despite the kidnappings and missile attacks in the summer of 2006, it was much earlier—in 1983—that I realized how serious Iran's threat is. A little past 6:00 a.m. in Beirut I was standing on a beachhead along the beautiful Mediterranean talking with a group of US Marines.

The troops, stationed at Beirut International Airport, were just beginning a new day. One marine sentry at the airport gate looked up to see a big yellow Mercedes truck barreling down on the security gate. The sentry reportedly stated that the driver of the truck smiled at him as he crashed through the gates. The truck was on a course for the lobby of the barracks. The sentries, armed only with loaded pistols, were unable to stop the speeding vehicle.

The Mercedes carried explosives equal to six tons of TNT. The driver rammed into the lower floor of the barracks, which discharged his deadly cargo. The explosion was so great that the four-story building pancaked floor by floor into a heap of rubble. Many of the 241 dead were not killed by the blast itself, but were crushed beneath the cinder-block building as it fell.

Not since the first day of the Tet Offensive in Vietnam (January 31, 1968) when 243 were killed had America recorded such a deadly one-day toll on its military. It remained the deadliest post–World War II attack on Americans overseas until the World Trade Center and Pentagon attacks of September 11, 2001.[109]

In order for the "Great Satan" to be eradicated so that an Islamic divine culture might emerge, violence is condoned. It was Iran's proxy in Lebanon, Hezbollah—the *Party of Allah*—that attacked the United States' 8th Battalion of Marine in their barracks in Lebanon in 1983.

Little did I know at the time that Iran would push America out of Lebanon through its terrorist tactics and orchestrate a scenario so diabolical that the president of the United States would provide protection for the world's then most fearsome terrorist organization, the PLO. More than 10,000 of Yasser Arafat's terrorists were allowed to board ships for Tunisia as Israeli General Ariel Sharon was told to stand down. This was despite the fact that he and his forces had Yasser Arafat in their crosshairs with a chance to severely cripple terrorism for years to come. Instead, victory was snatched from them and the terrorists profited. Israel has since suffered the consequences in the form of repeated attacks by Iran's proxy suicide bombers and Katyusha rocket attacks. In the years since the fight in Lebanon in the 1980s, the US has done little but encourage the use of such terrorist tactics over and over again. We shake our fists, but in the end withdraw before any real victory.

Today, Iran stands all the stronger for our lack of resolve and inability to truly curb the ambitions of its leader. Harvard law professor Alan Dershowitz had this to say about Iran's threat:

> One of the reasons I personally was against the war in Iraq—for me it was a very close question, but I came out against it—was because I thought it would divert attention from Iran, which posed a much more serious threat because religious extremism is always more dangerous than secular extremism. I also worried about the rule of unintended consequences—that the tyranny of Saddam Hussein would be replaced by a tyranny of radical Islamists—and unfortunately those fears have come to fruition.[110]

Yes, Iran is serious—deadly serious. Its leaders' intentions can neither be taken for granted nor minimized simply because a group such as ISIL has captured the media's attention. Iran seeks converts to its fanatical lifestyle from every nation, not just among the Arabs. Remember after all, Iranians are not Arabs, but Persians. Theirs is not a racial war, but a religious one. Iran wants nothing more than that every knee on earth should bow to Allah, and that there should be no real peace in the world until the world submits to Islam.

It is hard to believe in our politically correct society today when talk of religion in government is so looked down upon, but we are facing a religious zeal that is like nothing we have ever seen. Perhaps the founder of the Islamic Revolution, Ayatollah Ruhollah Musavi Khomeini, said it best: "I say let Iran go up in smoke, provided Islam emerges triumphant in the rest of the world." Intolerance is the order of the day in radical Islam; Christians, Jews and, indeed, Muslims who disagree are considered infidels, less than dogs. How long will it be before Iran entertains the snake of ISIL and allows access to its nuclear enrichment program? What horrors would that unleash on an unsuspecting world?

Persecution of non-Muslims in Iran has long been a fact of life, a report presented in October 2014 by the UN's Special Rapporteur on the situation of human rights in the Islamic Republic of Iran, Ahmed Shaheed, details the intolerance experienced by its religious minorities. According to the information submitted by Shaheed:

> At least 49 Protestant Christians are currently
> detained, many for involvement in informal house
> churches. In April 2014, security forces raided an

Easter service in a private home in southern Tehran
and detained six individuals.[111]

During his campaign for president, candidate Rouhani notably
promised:

> All ethnicities, all religions, even religious minori-
> ties, must feel justice. Long live citizenship rights.[112]

According to Dwight Bashir, deputy director of policy and
research at the US Commission on International Religious Freedom:

> The state of freedom of religion and belief in Iran
> is not improving, it is deteriorating.[113]

The Islamization of Palestine was orchestrated through Iran.
Palestinians were secular nationalists, not Islamic fundamental-
ists, before Iran's influence held sway. It was the Iranian mullahs
who indoctrinated the children of Palestine with the dogma of the
Islamic Revolution, and persuaded them to become human bombs.
A by-product of the radical Muslim influence has been the decline
of a Christian presence in the Palestinian Territory.

Hamas, which controls the Palestinian Territory today, is a
pawn of Iran, getting much of its financial support and weapons
from Tehran, as is Hezbollah in Lebanon with its ten thousand
missiles. The world saw Iran's true intentions the day Israelis intercepted a Palestinian ship, the *Karine-A*, in the Red Sea on January 4,
2002. The ship was loaded with Katyusha rockets with a maximum
range of twelve miles as well as assault rifles, antitank missiles,
mines, ammunition, and explosives. Most of the weapons were

Iranian, and all were bound for Iran's proxies entrenched in Gaza and Lebanon.

Iran poses a grave nuclear threat, not only to the region, but to the world. Peaceful Muslims worldwide are slowly being hijacked by the more radical elements. Iran is becoming a central player in the Shi'ite versus Sunni sects of Islam. Iran's leaders rejoiced when, under the tutelage of Ayatollah Khomeini, the US Embassy in Tehran was overrun and Americans were held hostage for 444 days. The jubilation continued when Iranian proxies in Lebanon struck a deadly blow to the aforementioned marine compound that resulted in the US packing its bags and going home. Iran focused on Iraq with every intention of driving coalition troops out of that country just as it did in Lebanon, thus creating a unified Shi'a state from the Persian Gulf to the borders of Syria, and eventually, beyond. Meanwhile, to the west, Israel stands by watching quietly and preparing to defend herself against any and all threats.

The fact is: The real danger is Iran, which will likely soon possess nuclear arms capabilities, an accomplishment few in the world—and especially Israel—are willing to let happen peacefully. So, as the diplomatic struggle to end Iran's nuclear agenda grows increasingly fruitless, Israel's elite troops practice for an assault on Iran's underground sites. Helicopters, F-15s, snipers, and trained bomb-carrying dogs have drilled for months in preparation to halt Iran's ability to use nuclear weapons to wipe Israel "off the map."

The "point of no return" for Israel will come when Iran has within its grasp the ability to produce a nuclear weapon—the point at which Iran has finally overcome technical difficulties in refining natural uranium to include roughly four percent uranium-235. Once that point is reached, Iran's scientists merely need to repeat the process enough times to produce the purity of uranium-235, considered weapons grade—something that would be made much easier with the 3,000-plus centrifuges Iran has reportedly installed.

If diplomacy with Iran to stop its refinement of nuclear materials continues to prove futile, the inevitability of an Israeli strike on key development facilities in Iran looms ever closer. Such an attack could set the stage for every nation in between—Israel, Lebanon, Syria, Jordan, Saudi Arabia, Iraq, Kuwait, and Iran—to become the battle-grounds for World War III that France, Great Britain, Russia, and Germany were in World War II. Certainly if Israel is forced to attack, the skirmish we saw between Hamas in Gaza and Israel in 2014 will seem like children shooting off bottle rockets in comparison.

Israel has reiterated that it will not allow "atomic ayatollahs" to point their nuclear weapons at Jerusalem. That fear is multiplied by America's nightmare that nuclear weapons will fall into the hands of ISIL or Iranian-sponsored terror squads. For this reason, America continues to seek ways to diplomatically persuade Iran to abandon its nuclear program, but the clock is on Iran's side. The longer Tehran stalls, the closer it gets to the capability needed to produce weapons-grade uranium—a point which the West seems content to allow Iran to reach, unless, of course, we are all willing to convert to Iran's form of Islam at the barrel of a nuclear silo. While the United States and Europe might possibly delay too long, Israel simply cannot.

Still others sit idly by, some more interested than others. The moderate states of Jordan, Saudi Arabia, Egypt, and Kuwait are anxious for peace in the region, and realize they would also be targets of a nuclear Iran because of their friendliness with the West. North Korea pushes forward with its own nuclear program and missile tests, flexing its muscles threateningly toward the Far East and the world. War and genocide rage along ethnoreligious lines in Sudan where hundreds of thousands have died. Meanwhile, the Taliban is doing everything it can to reemerge in Afghanistan in skirmishes that draw little attention.

A Critical Year

The 1960s produced a television series called *Lost in Space*. While much of that series may have been forgettable, except to today's cult following, one catchphrase resurfaces from time to time. One of the characters was a child named Will Robinson. His companion was a robot whose attitude toward young Will was always protective. When threatened with peril, the robot would intone, "Danger, Will Robinson! Danger!" While the robot could warn of danger, Will was the one responsible to take proper evasive action to protect himself and/or his family.

Today, we in America are being warned repeatedly about the danger we face from ISIL and from Iran's headlong rush to acquire nuclear weapons. Once that occurs, and even if it suffers a setback immediately afterward, Iran can always proceed to produce nuclear weapons in secret later, because its nuclear scientists will already have the knowledge of how to do so. Iran must never be allowed to reach this point in its nuclear research.

Many have cried, "Danger, America, danger!" And, like young Will Robinson, the decision to act to protect our nation and our families is ours to make, the plan ours to execute. The safety of future generations is in our hands. The questions now are: What will we do with this deadly knowledge? How much time do we have to act? Do we have the resolve to win the war on terror regardless of what it takes? Or do we allow ourselves to be swallowed up in the tsunami of terrorism that is certain to invade the shores of America if the Islamofascists are not stopped?

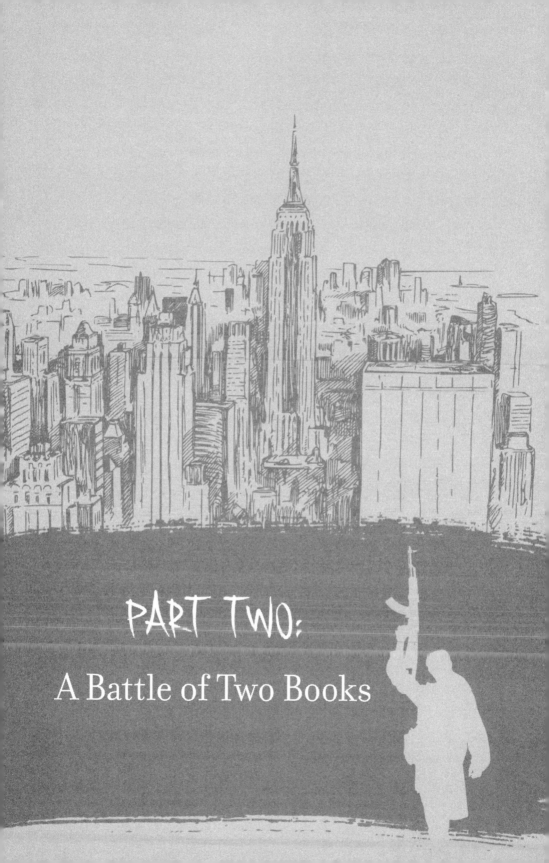

PART TWO:

A Battle of Two Books

CHAPTER TWELVE

Fumbling Our Ally, Iran

Ayatollah Khomeini will "eventually be hailed as a saint."
UN AMBASSADOR ANDREW YOUNG

Khomeini is a "Gandhi-like" figure.
WILLIAM SULLIVAN
US Ambassador to Iran

HOW DID IRAN become one of the leading global terror centers? I've written a bit about the take-over of the country by the Ayatollah Khomeini, but let's take another giant step back and look at some things that transpired before he came to power.

Though unrest had been bubbling under the surface in Iran, it began to boil over during the lavish 2,500th anniversary celebration of the founding of the Persian Empire from the time of Cyrus the Great. With its 200 million-dollar price tag, it was the single most breathtaking display of how seemingly out of touch the shah was with the people of Iran. Many mark it as the beginning of the end of his reign. The occasion succinctly symbolized the Western leanings of the shah, which so infuriated the Shi'a Muslim majority of Iran, few of whom gained any benefit from the millions collected from Iran's oil revenues. It fueled the Iranians' hatred of him all the more when they saw hundreds of millions spent on foreigners for the three-day anniversary celebration.

The oil boom of 1974 did nothing to alleviate the problem either; instead of Iran again becoming the great civilization Shah Pahlavi promised Iranians it would become through his progressive programs, Iranians experienced alarming inflation and could only sit and watch as the gap between rich and poor grew all the more exaggerated. The black market thrived as bureaucracy, bottlenecks, shortages, and inflation hampered legitimate businesses. Meanwhile, tens of thousands of jobs went to foreign workers. Many of these were to help operate the expensive, high-tech US military equipment the shah bought to bolster his army as he dreamed of becoming a world power.

One of the organizing forces in this growing dissatisfaction with the shah's reign—and one that was greatly underestimated—was Ayatollah Ruhollah Khomeini. He had been exiled in 1964 for his opposition to the shah's White Revolution, a series of reforms to modernize Iran, including voting rights for women, land reforms abolishing feudalism, changes in the laws to allow the election of religious minorities, and civil code changes giving women legal equality in marital issues, a move that would break up property owned by some Shi'a clergy.

Khomeini began his career as a respected, but minor, religious figure in the Iranian city of Qom. After he went public with his criticisms and personal attacks against the shah, he was arrested on June 5, 1963. A three-day protest riot broke out and ended with Khomeini being kept under house arrest for eight months then released, but only to attack the Pahlavi government again. In November of 1964, he was arrested a second time and deported to Turkey to live in exile. He was later allowed to move to Iraq, where he spent the next thirteen years of his life. In 1978, Khomeini ran afoul of Iraq's then vice president Saddam Hussein and was forced to flee. From Iraq, the ayatollah traveled to Neauphle-le-Château, France.

During those years, Khomeini refused to be silent and continued to exert influence in Iran by building a formidable support network through the power of the spoken word. His weapon of choice at the time was not the sword, the gun, or the suicide bomber; it was simply cassette tapes of his recorded sermons. The tapes were smuggled into Iran by pilgrims returning to the holy city of Najaf in Iraq. The tapes were duplicated over and over and passed among the masses that were eager to see the shah deposed. Khomeini, among others, fueled Muslims' disdain for what was called *Gharbzadegi*, "the plague of Western Culture," and teachers like him found many willing to embrace the more leftist interpretations of the Shi'a faith. Khomeini's influence grew as the Pahlavi dynasty waned. At the same time, the United States became a symbol of the West that mullahs and clerics felt was corrupting Iran because of the shah's close ties and obsequiousness to it.

Democracy Undermined

It is worth noting here that the shah was not seen as a Western puppet only because of his friendliness with the United States, but because of the 1953 coup by the US and Great Britain that first propelled him into a position of power. During the first half of the twentieth century, Iran became increasingly important on the international stage because of the discovery of oil there under the Qajar dynasty in 1908. As industrialization gripped the globe, the discovery of this coveted commodity would prove to be one of Iran's greatest bargaining chips on the world market, both in the twentieth and twenty-first centuries.

In 1921, Reza Khan, Pahlavi's father (also known as Reza Pahlavi and later as Reza Shah), a military leader, staged a coup against the Qajar ruler. He marched his troops into Tehran and seized the capital virtually unopposed. His demand that the government resign was met, and his cohort, Seyyed Zia'eddin Tabatabaee, was declared prime minister of Iran. Reza Khan was named commander of the army and took the name Reza Khan Sardar Sepah.

In 1923, Reza Khan was officially named prime minister by Ahmad Shah Qajar before Qajar was exiled to Europe. The *Majlis* (members of the Iranian Parliament) declared Reza Khan the shah of Persia on December 12, 1925. His son, Mohammad Reza Pahlavi—the man Khomeini would help depose in 1979—was named crown prince.

It was at that time Reza Khan adopted the title of Reza Shah, and he ruled Iran for sixteen more years. His accomplishments were many: Under his leadership, the Trans-Iranian Railway from Tehran to the Caspian and Persian seas was completed; the education system was improved and its budget rose from $100,000 to $12 million. To encourage studies, he exempted secondary school students from military service. He founded Tehran's university in 1934[115] and many others in the years following. Reza Shah also sought to diminish the power and influence of traditional religious schools. He instituted a law of uniform dress which made European-style attire mandatory for every man, with the exception of religious students who were required to take a government examination before they could exercise this exemption. Numerous Iranian students received European educations because of his progressive programs.

During most of this time, the world at large still referred to the lands governed by Reza Shah as Persia, which came from the Greek name *Persis*. On March 21, 1935, the shah requested that the public worldwide henceforth use "Iran" as the official name of the nation.

World War II brought a change in leadership for Iran, but not a change in the ruling house. Fearing that Reza Shah's refusal to allow British troops to be stationed in Iran would lead to an alliance with Nazi Germany, the UK and the USSR joined hands to force Reza Shah to abdicate the Peacock Throne. His son, Mohammad Reza Pahlavi, assumed the throne on September 16, 1941. Reza Shah went into exile first to the island of Mauritius, then to Johannesburg, South Africa. He died there in 1944.

Mohammad Reza Shah Pahlavi began his reign apparently with every intention of following the dictates of a constitutional monarchy (the form of democratic government in Great Britain and the form Iran had assumed in 1906). Though he was the monarch, the shah took a hands-off approach to domestic politics and generally yielded to the wishes of the Iranian Parliament. Pahlavi predominately occupied himself with the affairs of state and either openly defied the prime ministers or impeded the legislative process in such matters. Prone to indecision, however, Pahlavi relied more on manipulation than on leadership. He concentrated on reviving the army and ensuring that it would remain under royal control as the monarchy's main power base.

In 1951 a strong rival to Pahlavi's power emerged when Mohammed Mossadegh, a nationalist, was elected prime minister of Iran. In spite of Pahlavi's British connections, Mossadegh secured the votes necessary in Parliament to nationalize the

British-controlled Anglo-Iranian Oil Company (AIOC) in what became known as the Abadan Crisis. This cut off British profits from and control of Middle Eastern oil. In response, Great Britain decided to depose Mossadegh and his cabinet, thus solidifying Pahlavi's power. When they asked Harry Truman to help with the coup in 1951, he refused, but when they asked Dwight Eisenhower shortly after his election in 1953 for US support and help in their plans, Ike agreed.

So it was that a military coup (codenamed "Operation Ajax") headed by former minister of the interior and retired army general Fazlollah Zahedi, with covert support by British Intelligence and the CIA, finally forced Mossadegh from office on August 19, 1953. Zahedi became the new prime minister, authority was pulled from the democratically elected wing of the government and redeposited in the throne of the shah, and Mossadegh was tried for treason. In return, the shah agreed to let an international consortium of forty percent British, forty percent American, fourteen percent Dutch, and six percent French companies run Iranian oil production for the next twenty-five years. Profits were to be split fifty-fifty with Iran, but Iran was never allowed to audit the books to see if this had been done fairly, nor were any Iranians allowed to be on the board of directors of any of these companies. It was at this time that the Anglo-Iranian Oil Company became the British Petroleum Company (BP), one of the root companies of British Petroleum today.

It was the first time in history that the United States had helped to undermine a democratic government—a decision we would pay for in 1979 and, some might argue, are still paying for today, when the US made another very costly mistake in turning its back on the shah it had initially brought to power.

Enter Jimmy Carter

When Jimmy Carter entered the political fray that was the 1976 presidential campaign, America was still riding the liberal wave of anti-Vietnam emotion. In fact, a group labeling itself the Institute for Policy Studies (IPS) was determined to inject liberal politics into every arena. Their network included many of what were labeled "alternative media outlets." The IPS-controlled Liberal Left was determined that Democratic front-runner Jimmy Carter would adopt the platform written by Marcus Raskin, one of the founders of IPS. Raskin and his henchmen were able to wrest a promise from Carter that he would, if elected president, cut spending by the military and contest the production of the B-1 bomber, among other things.

Iran was an early bone of contention among Carter's staff selections. In truth, Carter's transition team asked for an in-depth report on Iran even before he assumed the reins of government. In reevaluating the Carter presidency, John Dumbrell wrote that Walter Mondale and his aide, David Aaron, had links to the Iranian resistance based in the US They were persuaded that the shah was not entitled to rule Iran and determined he needed to be restrained. Others in Mondale's periphery simply wanted the ruler removed from the throne. According to Congressman David Bower, "opportunists in the State Department were trying to out-Carter Carter."[116] Once in office, the president's Liberal Left supporters felt justified in redoubling efforts to remove the shah from the Peacock Throne.

When James Earl Carter took office in January 1977, he inherited the well-ingrained policies of Richard Nixon and Henry Kissinger. During the five years preceding Carter's inauguration, the shah had purchased some $10 billion in US military materiel. Nixon and

Kissinger had set in motion an agenda for the next several decades. The US government's presence in the Persian Gulf region and its supply of oil from that area were contingent on the goodwill of the shah. The US looked to the shah for the economic survival of Western industry, and the shah relied on the US for the arms and assistance to implement his vision for Iran's future. Failure on the part of either entity could cause unimagined economic and political upheaval.

In the mid-1970s, the shah had morphed from an insecure young leader to one who was fully in control of the bureaucracy in Iran, who was working to bring the country into the twentieth century, and who was not looking for advice or direction, not even from his mentor, the United States government. When Jimmy Carter arrived in Washington, D.C., he was the recipient of the years-earlier Richard Nixon–Henry Kissinger arms sales policies that placed the security of one of the world's richest regions in the hands of a monarch whose determination to bring social and economic change to Iran did not take into account the smoldering fires of Islamic unrest.

The shah had enjoyed a prolonged political association with the Republican administrations of Richard Nixon and Gerald Ford. He was understandably wary of Carter, whose campaign platform stressed both human rights issues and reduced arms sales. This was a major concern, as the shah's regime had been criticized for the actions of its secret police, the SAVAK, and had a long-standing relationship with US arms suppliers.

Pahlavi's personal confidant, Asadollah Alam, illustrated his prescience by writing in his diary about the shah's concerns over Carter's election, "who knows what sort of calamity he [Carter] may unleash on the world?"[117] In September of 1976, Alam met with Uri

Lubrani, Israel's representative in Iran, and asked for his assistance to help improve the shah's image with the American people.

In that same year that Jimmy Carter was inaugurated, Islamist leader Ali Shariati died and a huge potential rival to Ayatollah Khomeini was removed, thus solidifying Khomeini's support in Iran. In October of that year, Khomeini's son Mostafa died of what was apparently a heart attack, but anti-government forces pointed the finger at SAVAK for the death, and Mostafa was proclaimed a martyr. While there were various factions opposing the shah's regime—leftists, the People's Mujahedin of Iran, Communists, and other groups—Khomeini had suddenly become the most popular opponent to Pahlavi's rule.

At the same time, with the hope of improving the US image as the benevolent superpower to the post-Vietnam world, Jimmy Carter created a special Office of Human Rights, and the shah emerged high on the agency's list of leaders to monitor. Washington put pressure on Pahlavi to relax his control and allow more political freedom. This prompted the release of more than three hundred political prisoners, saw censorship relaxed, and the court system overhauled, which had the unforeseen side effect of allowing greater freedom for opposition groups to meet and organize.

Carter's Secretary of State Cyrus Vance was the first in the administration to visit Iran. Vance was in the country for a meeting of CENTO, the Central Treaty Organization, to discuss security in the region. While traveling with Vance, an "unidentified spokesperson" for the State Department leaked the information that the US was pleased with the shah's human rights efforts and was therefore willing to sell him AWACS aircraft.[118] In July, President Carter informed Congress that it was his objective to sell seven AWACS planes to Iran. After months of congressional wrangling and intense debate, the sale was approved. The final package included an additional $1.1 billion in spare parts and instruction.

While the shah's internal changes were making an impression on Carter, young men and women in Iran were swarming to radical Islam. Historically, Iran had never seen anything like this. University students gathered at Islamic study centers to debate the imams of Shi'a Islam. Young women clothed themselves in the *chadors* (long black veils) that had been outlawed by the shah. This new, radical Islam exploded on the campus of Tehran University in October 1977. A group of students calling for the isolation of women on campus rioted, leaving behind a trail of burned-out buses and broken windows.

While the ultimate aims of different groups opposing the shah varied greatly—some wanting a return to constitutional monarchy, others a socialist/communist government, and the imams and clerics championing an Islamic Republic—Khomeini artfully united these groups against the shah by avoiding the specifics of what would happen beyond toppling the Peacock Throne. As a result, opposition groups that would normally have been contending with one another instead grew more unified—a remarkable feat by Khomeini that accelerated the revolution and later proved to be a deadly mistake for all but the Islamists.

Carter, Pahlavi, and Khomeini

In her memoir, *An Enduring Love*, Farah Pahlavi, wife of the late shah of Iran, wrote of her impressions of the Carter presidential campaign:

> During the whole of his campaign, Jimmy Carter had proclaimed the theme of human rights, the

freedom of the people, which in reality has to be treated with caution, taking the economic and cultural context of each country into account. The Iranian opposition saw an ally in Carter for future struggles, and the rush of demands (on the Shah) in the spring of 1977 would doubtless not have been so great had another man been elected to the White House.[119]

On November 15, 1977, the shah and Empress Farah flew to the US for a visit with President Carter and the First Lady in Washington. As the two couples stood on the south lawn of the White House, they were met by hundreds—some say thousands—of Iranian students who had congregated in Lafayette Square. (At that time, the US boasted an Iranian student population of over 60,000.) In a move to control the crowd, Washington police lobbed tear gas canisters into their midst. Unfortunately, the tear gas blew across the White House lawn and into the eyes of the Carters and their visiting dignitaries. With faces streaming tears, the Carters were forced to cut their greetings short and retreat into the White House.

The two men were to meet again about six weeks later in Tehran. President Carter had been in the Middle East to promote a peace plan between Israel and her neighbors. He and Rosalynn planned a brief visit to Tehran to spend New Year's Eve with the shah and Empress Farah. Before leaving the States, Carter was presented with a declaration signed by a number of well-known Iranian activists. Rather than present the declaration to Pahlavi, Carter rose to the occasion and toasted the shah with:

> Iran, under the great leadership of the Shah, is an
> island of stability in one of the more troubled areas of

the world. This is a great tribute to you, Your Majesty, and to your leadership, and to the respect, admiration, and love which your people give to you.[120]

With these words, Jimmy Carter reinforced the pro-shah stance that had long been American policy. However, in just months, Iran would be gripped by bloody riots as the shah struggled to quell the radical Islamists and other groups bent on deposing him.

During Ramadan in August 1978, large demonstrations erupted all across Iran. Curfews were imposed in some cities following days of mass rioting. The city of Abadan was the site of a grizzly mass murder said to have been staged by Islamic radicals. The doors of a theater hosting an Iranian film were barred while the building was torched; 477 people died in the conflagration. The shah's attempts to suppress the rioting were rejected by enemies and supporters alike. His enemies saw it as a weak attempt at appeasement, and his supporters just saw it as weakness, period.

While the shah was desperately trying to regain control in Iran, Ruhollah Khomeini had been in Iraq fomenting revolution. In his book *The Spirit of Allah: Khomeini and the Islamic Revolution*, Amir Taheri wrote of the charges that Khomeini's underground network leveled at the shah. He was randomly accused of being a womanizer, a homosexual, a Jewish convert, a drug addict, and a Catholic. He was also labeled the "American Shah" and "Israel's Shah." Even the Empress Farah did not escape Khomeini's twisted defamation. She was maligned as an adulteress and incredibly linked to none other than Jimmy Carter.[121]

Khomeini's rhetoric was designed to incite fear in the lower classes in Iran—the have-nots who were forced to do without while witnessing the overindulgence of the upper classes. It trumpeted what was seen as the shah's collusion with Israel and the United States. The intellectuals, the political vanguard in Iran, initially took a wait-and-see attitude, but it was not long before they joined forces with the oppressed and poverty-stricken who took to the streets to protest the shah's policies. With the help of PLO-supplied weapons, trained terrorists, and the murders of Iranian demonstrators as a means to incite the mobs in the streets, the mayhem spread. No wonder Yasser Arafat was hailed as a friend by Khomeini after he seized control of Iran. (Arafat's reward was the gift of the Israeli Embassy in Tehran with a PLO flag flying overhead.)

Things were only beginning their downward spiral—a situation that would soon affect not only Iran, but Iraq and the entire Middle East.

CHAPTER THIRTEEN

The Rise of Islamofascism

What is Islamofascism? Islamofascism is radical Islam combined with undemocratic institutions in such a fashion that it creates a threat to the neighborhood, and in concentric circle fashion. A threat to the extent to which Iran develops a missile envelope that goes outward, and all of a sudden it begins to encapsulate the American-European allies [in the Middle East] and eventually [sets its aims on] the United States itself.

PROFESSOR RAYMOND TANTER [122]

IN THE LATTER YEARS of the twentieth century and the onset of the twenty-first, several Muslim countries claimed numerous residents who were considered to be secular practitioners of Islam. These included Iran and Turkey, along with many inhabitants of Cairo and other cosmopolitan cities in the Middle East. Thanks in part to Jimmy Carter's stint in the White House and events in Iran, these areas are now nurseries for crazed clerics bellowing forth hate-filled tirades at every opportunity. Let's take a look back at the relevant events in the Carter Administration that brought us to this place in world history.

In November 1978, Carter appointed George Ball, an under-secretary of state in the Kennedy and Johnson administrations, to study the situation in Iran and make policy recommendations. Ball's eighteen-page communiqué was strongly critical of Nixon's Iranian policies. He inferred that the rule of the shah was at an end and encouraged Carter to begin dialogue with Ayatollah Khomeini.

It was also in November that Ambassador William Sullivan telegraphed the White House to report that the shah's support was rapidly eroding, including that of the military. Sullivan encouraged the administration to adopt a transition policy that would support a takeover by the military and the mullahs. In his report, Sullivan called Khomeini a "Gandhi-like" personage, a moderate, and a centrist who would not personally involve himself in the politics of Iran.[123] James Bill, a leading expert on Iran, proclaimed in a *Newsweek* interview on February 12, 1979, that "Khomeini is not a mad *mujtahid* [high-ranking clergyman] . . . but a man of impeccable integrity and honesty."[124] Somehow, these learned men had totally missed the fact that Khomeini and his fellow militants viewed the revolution as a struggle between an oppressed Iran and the "Great Satan" superpower of the United States.

Carter's national security advisor, Zbigniew Brzezinski, counseled the president to reject George Ball's report, although Ball likened the shah's regime to that of "Humpty Dumpty" in the sense that it was irreparable. Brzezinski's counsel was that Carter should dispatch a high-level military liaison to Iran in support of that country's armed forces. Carter chose General Robert "Dutch" Huyser, deputy commander-in-chief of the US European Command under Alexander Haig. Huyser's personal interaction with Iranian military leaders for over a decade made him the obvious choice. It was the shah who expressed to Huyser his concerns that he would alienate President Carter by not moving quickly enough to institute sweeping human rights changes to appease the administration.

In Huyser's own words, he was charged by President Carter to convey [President Carter's] concern and assurances to the senior military leaders at this most critical time. It was of vital importance to both the Iranian people and the US government that Iran have a strong, stable government which would remain friendly to the United States. The Iranian military was the key to the situation.[125]

In my book *Showdown with Nuclear Iran*, I wrote of a meeting I had later with Robert Huyser:

> Huyser was a man of principle and moral clarity and believed that his mission was to support Prime Minister Shapour Bakhtiar and Iran's generals. Carter promised that the US would protect and provide all assets needed to shore up the government, which was increasingly endangered by violent protests against the regime of the Shah, Mohammed Reza Pahlavi. Despite a history of support going back to World War II, Carter had no desire to see a pro-Shah regime in power. The comparison made sense to a point: the Ayatollah opposed the Shah, who had a terrible record of human rights abuses. But that's where the comparison breaks down. Gandhi was nonviolent. The Ayatollah was anything but.[126]

In Huyser's assessment of the situation in Iran, he opined that the United States should have learned the importance of the "need to stand by one's friends." He felt that by abandoning the shah, a long-time partner in the region, the US had "lost a close and sturdy ally which could have provided stability for Western interests in the Persian Gulf." General Huyser said of the Carter administration:

> The administration obviously did not understand the Iranian culture, nor the conditions that prevailed in the last few months of the Shah's reign. I believe that Washington should have recognized the seriousness of the situation early in 1978. If the real intent was to support the existing government, much could have been done to bolster the Shah's lagging confidence and resolve . . . [127]
>
> The President could have publicly condemned Khomeini for his interference. He could have solicited the support of our allies, and in conjunction with them he could have given material support to the Bakhtiar government.[128]

Unfortunately for the US, these were not all the ills suffered as a result of electing the Georgian peanut farmer to the presidency. History will ultimately define Carter's White House years by

- ✧ the Soviet's invasion of Afghanistan (Carter's response was to boycott the 1980 Olympics in Moscow) and the birth of Osama bin Laden's terror organization;

- ✧ recession, high inflation, high (21.5 percent) interest rates, long gas lines and rationing;

- ✧ the fall of the shah of Iran, the inception of the Islamic Revolution, and the rise of Islamic fundamentalism;

- ✧ the loss of US stature worldwide;

- ✧ the American hostage crisis that ultimately cost him reelection;

- ✧ extreme micromanagement;

- ✧ the alienation of Congress;

- ✧ South Korea stripped of US missiles and Carter's offer to remove all troops;

- ✧ reduction of the defense budget by $6 million;

- ✧ emasculation of the CIA by cutting 820 intelligence jobs;[129]

- ✧ praise of such heinous dictators as Tito, Ceausescu, Ortega, and following his presidency, Kim il-Sung of North Korea;

- ✧ the rise of Marxism in Nicaragua;

- ✧ the relinquishing of control of the Panama Canal to a dictator. (Hutchison Whampoa, Ltd., a front for the Chinese military, which now controls entrance and egress points at either end of the canal.)

An American Ally Deposed through Neglect

As the defiance against the shah's regime grew, Iran's Prime Minister Shapour Bakhtiar persuaded the monarch and his family to leave the country. Ostensibly, Bakhtiar's plan was to try to pour

oil on Iran's troubled waters. He disbanded SAVAK, freed all political prisoners, and allowed the shah's nemesis, Ayatollah Ruhollah
Khomeini, to return to Iran.

In February 1979, Khomeini boarded an Air France flight to
return to Tehran. Barely off of the plane in his return the cleric
voiced his opposition to Prime Minister Shapour Bakhtiar's government pledging, "I will kick their teeth in." He appointed his own
competing interim prime minister and defied any to oppose him,
stating that such an act would be a "revolt against God."[130] On March
30 and 31, a popular vote nationwide endorsed the establishment of
an Islamic Republic. With that, he became Supreme Leader (*Vali-e
Faqih*). On April 1, 1979, the greatest April Fools' joke of all time was
played on the people of Iran: Khomeini proclaimed the "first day of
God's government," and established himself as the Grand Ayatollah.
He awarded himself the title of "Imam" (the highest religious rank
in Shi'a Islam). The events following that proclamation have had a
lasting effect not only on Iran, but on the entire Middle East and
the rest of the world.

The newly crowned Grand Ayatollah had showed the rest of
his Arab brethren how to unify secular, social, and religious groups
in their hatred for the shah and the US; he used it as a political
and military tool to overthrow the government. Once back in Iran,
Khomeini coldly rewarded those who had supported his revolution with a swiftness and brutality that even SAVAK couldn't
have mustered.

A killing spree followed, with former officials of the shah's
government targeted, as well as those who had been looking for
something other than an Islamic Republic with Khomeini as its
supreme leader for life. Even fleeing Iran wasn't enough. In the
decade following the Islamic Revolution of Iran, at least sixty-three

Iranians abroad were killed or wounded, including the man who had allowed Khomeini to return, former prime minister Shapour Bakhtiar. In the months following the coup, dozens of newspapers and magazines opposing Khomeini's government were shut down, and a "cultural revolution" began as universities were closed for two years to cleanse them of Western influence. Thousands in the government and military lost positions because they were seen as too Western leaning. Many groups were classified as outsiders and became targets of the very government by which help had been provided to pave the way to power.

Carter Tries to Make Friends with a Viper

The Carter Administration scrambled to assure the new regime that the US would maintain diplomatic ties with Iran. Even as that message was being relayed to the ambassador in Tehran, the embassy was besieged on February 14, 1980, by a mob of Islamic militants, many wearing headpieces identifying them as Palestinian *fedayeen*. This was further proof of Khomeini's reach in the Islamic world. Rather than return fire on the intruders, Ambassador Sullivan surrendered the embassy after a scramble to destroy sensitive electronic devices and classified documents. In the midst of the chaos that followed, Khomeini's personal representative, Ibrahim Yazdi, arrived in the embassy. Yazdi and another mullah were able to turn the crowd back, thus insuring the safety of the occupants of the embassy.

At this juncture, the ambassador attempted to reassure Khomeini that the US had accepted the inevitability of the uprising and would not intervene in Iranian affairs. However, the US

Embassy was seen as a den of spies gathered to overthrow Iran as it had done in 1953. As a result, extremists saw it as a target that needed clearing out in order to protect the fledgling Islamic Republic rather than a voice to be trusted.

Khomeini could not have defeated the shah of Iran on issues that interested the mullahs alone. Either the Iranian or US armed forces could easily have taken out the rebel forces, but Carter knew little of the effective use of military power—even given that he had no will to use it—and viewed Khomeini as more of a religious holy man in a grassroots revolution than the founding father of modern terrorism. Thus the US failed to act on behalf of its longtime ally, the shah. At the same time the Iranian national armed forces chose a stance of neutrality "in order to prevent further disorder and bloodshed,"[131] so it did not act either. With the declaration that the military would remain impartial in the struggle, Khomeini realized his dream: Iran was his, and the process of total Islamization could begin.

The shah of Iran left his country a broken and ailing man, his body wracked by cancer. His first stop was a visit to his good friend Anwar el-Sadat in Egypt. From there he moved briefly to Morocco, then to the Bahamas, and then Mexico. Despite his long association as a key United States ally, the shah was initially denied entry into the US However, as his cancer— non-Hodgkin's lymphoma—grew worse and he needed more sophisticated medical treatment, the door finally opened for him to enter the United States on October 22, 1979.

Before departing Mexico City for New York, the shah wrote in his personal journal:

Clearly, I was a very sick man. . . . Nine months had

passed since I left Iran, months of pain, shock, despair,
and reflection. My heart bled at what I saw happening
in my country. Every day reports had come of murder,
bloodshed, and summary executions. . . . All these horrors were part of Khomeini's systematic destruction
of the social fabric I had woven for my nation. . . . And
not a word of protest from American human rights
advocates who had been so vocal in denouncing my
"tyrannical" regime . . . the United States and most
Western countries had adopted a double standard for
international morality: anything Marxist, no matter
how bloody and base, is acceptable.[132]

An Embassy Under Siege

It was not necessarily the shah's arrival in New York that sparked
what would later become known as the "Second Revolution." It was,
rather, a string of innocent contacts from well-wishers that would
incite the hostile take-over of the US Embassy mere weeks later. A
videotape of the shah receiving such visitors as Henry Kissinger,
David Rockefeller, several former Iranian officials, and other dignitaries was shown in Iran.

For those Iranians who were paranoid that the shah might
attempt to return, this was proof of the duplicity shared by both
the shah and Washington. Coupled with reports of counter-revo-
lutionary forces taking up residence in Iraq and in Iran, little else
was needed to fuel the fires of another anti-American backlash.
Khomeini's new regime soon began to suspect the US of plotting to
deprive them of the fruits of their victory and the desire to restore
American influence in Iran in a new form.[133]

On November 4, 1979, a group of student dissidents who had adopted the appellation "Imam's Disciples" entered the US Embassy in Tehran for the second time, again with little resistance. Although Khomeini denied any knowledge of the impending takeover of the US Embassy, it was likely his vitriolic anti-American oratory that gave the mob of some three to five hundred young Iranians the impetus to seize the compound. Khomeini had denounced the government as the "Great Satan" and "Enemies of Islam."[134] Khomeini's ploy was to cast the US as evil and himself as the defender of righteousness.

When the dust settled, sixty-six American hostages were in the hands of their Iranian captors. Their captivity would last 444 days. The jailers were instructed not to release their prisoners until the shah was sent back to Tehran to stand trial and the billions of dollars he had allegedly appropriated from the people of Iran be returned.

Carter never understood. Khomeini said, "The West who killed God and buried Him is teaching the rest of the world to do so," and went so far as to openly accuse the US of being the fountain of the entire world's evil. When the head of the French Secret Service, the Count of Maranche, suggested to Carter in 1980 that Khomeini be kidnapped, and then bartered for an exchange with the hostages, the president was indignant. "One cannot do that to a holy man," he told the French super-spy.[135] In fact, the Carter-appointed ambassador to the UN, Andrew Young, asserted that the ayatollah would "eventually be hailed as a saint."[136] It was Young who proudly identified with the Iranian militants, because it reminded him of the Civil Rights struggles in the US

Public support and sympathy for Jimmy Carter sharply eroded as time passed and he remained indecisive on how to handle the hostage crisis. Negotiations, both overt and covert, were not productive, and there were no indications that the captors were relenting. Finally in April 1980, Carter approved a risky mission of extraction by helicopter. The plan was doomed almost from the start. Three of the helicopters vital to the plan malfunctioned; eight servicemen lost their lives and three were wounded when on takeoff their chopper crashed into a C-130 transport plane. The aborted attempt only added fuel—and video footage—to the Iranians' gleeful assertion that the "Great Satan" was impotent—a toothless tiger.

In a renewed effort to secure the release of the hostages before newly elected president Ronald Reagan would take office, the Carter Administration entered into negotiations with the Iranians to release assets frozen by the US government when the embassy was overrun and the hostages taken. US Deputy Secretary of State Warren Christopher and a small contingent of State and Treasury Department officials flew to Algiers for face-to-face negotiations with an Algerian team representing the Khomeini government. When a final agreement was reached, the Carter Administration relinquished $7.977 billion to the Iranians. According to one source, the transfer required fourteen banks and the participation of five nations acting concurrently.

Although negotiations continued into the wee hours of January 20, 1980, Carter's efforts to secure the release of the hostages on his watch remained fruitless. In fact, an ABC television crew documented Carter's futile "all-night effort to bring the hostages home before the end of his term."[137]

President Harry S Truman's desk in the Oval Office sported a sign that read, "The buck stops here." Perhaps, the same could have been said of Jimmy Carter's involvement in fomenting the Islamic Revolution. It was truly the birth of the Islamofascism ideology we fight today in the War on Terror.

President Carter excelled in other areas but was always at a distinct disadvantage when confronted with American foreign policy, having been a Washington outsider before being elected president. Jimmy Carter's intelligence did not disguise the fact that he could not fully assimilate or truly understand the situation in Iran.

CHAPTER FOURTEEN

Jimmy Carter's Liberal Legacy

More and more, Democrats are starting to worry that they have a more um, colorful version of Jimmy Carter on their hands. Obama acts cool as a proverbial cucumber but that awful '70s show seems frightfully close to a rerun.

ERIC ALTERMAN[138],
American Historian

JIMMY CARTER had originally crept into the White House with a campaign emphasis on the word *faith*. It was a theme that appealed both to conservative Christians and liberal Democrats disenchanted with the Johnson and Nixon White House years. This tactic gave Carter a slight edge with the American public, and that—coupled with his popularity in the South—won the election. He may have pulled the wool over the eyes of Southern conservatives, but it wasn't long before he divorced himself from their influence, and since leaving office he has broken with his Southern Baptist tradition, as well.

In fact, Carter said of one-time supporter, Rev. Jerry Falwell, "in a very Christian way, as far as I'm concerned, he can go to hell."[139]

It apparently was no surprise to Southern Baptist Theological Seminary President R. Albert Mohler, Jr., who wrote in the *Atlanta Journal-Constitution*:

> The former president actually began distancing himself from the Southern Baptist Convention years ago. . . . On issues ranging from homosexuality and abortion to the nature of the Gospel and the authority of Scripture, the former president is out of step with the majority of Southern Baptists . . . the theological divide between Carter and mainstream Southern Baptists is vast.[140]

The Carter presidency can, perhaps, be summed up with two words: wretched ineptitude. America's thirty-ninth president was of the overly inflated ego that was chiefly responsible for Carter's early alienation of Congress, and in fact, from his own Democratic Party. House Speaker Thomas "Tip" O'Neill was shunned as early as Carter's Inaugural dinner when he found his table on the far fringes of the event. Ned Rice of the *National Review* described Carter as "the Barney Fife of American presidents: alternatively bumbling, then petrified, then egomaniacal, then back to bumbling, and so on for four long, surreal years. One of history's true buffoons."[141] It is interesting to note that 1976 was a banner year for future presidential hopefuls: Carter was elected president, William Jefferson Clinton became attorney general in Arkansas, and Albert Gore won a place in the Tennessee House of Representatives.

Carter's government might best have been classified by the word *pacifism*, an ideology that was clearly expressed in his choice of Cabinet members. His appointment of Cyrus Vance as secretary of state should have sounded the alarm through the halls of Congress and it clearly set the stage for a dovish administration. (Vance resigned in protest of the aborted hostage rescue attempt.) Henry Kissinger said of the Carter Administration:

> [It] has managed the extraordinary feat of having, at one and the same time, the worst relations with our allies, the worst relations with our adversaries, and the most serious upheavals in the developing world since the end of the Second World War.[142]

Carter all but ignored congressional suggestions regarding appointments to various posts and continued to select suspected pacifists to populate upper-level posts.

Many of those who were recruited to implement Carter's newly adopted globalism policies were selected from the George McGovern fringe. Some were tagged "the Mondale Mafia" after Carter's vice president, Walter Mondale. In fact, a number of Carter appointees including Anthony Lake, Richard Holbrooke, and Jessica Tuchman went on to serve in the Clinton White House. During the early days of the Carter Administration, the triumvirate of Cyrus Vance, Zbigniew Brzezinski, and UN Ambassador Andrew Young had comparable input into foreign policy decisions.

The agenda, as put forth by Carter's Liberal Leftist advisors, embraced what came to be called *regionalism*. It eschewed military intervention in favor of social reform and human rights issues. Historian Jerel A. Rosati wrote, "The Carter administration attempted to promote a new system of world order based upon international stability, peace, and justice."[143] To the detriment of future generations, Iran became the test case for Carter's prototype.

As author Joshua Muravchik wrote in an article for *Commentary*:

> There is little doubt, in sum, that the electorate was right in 1980 when it judged Carter to have been among our worst Presidents. It is even more certain that history will judge him to have been our very worst ex-President.[144]

Carter's legacy of liberalism has had a definite and continuing impact, not only on the Democratic Party of Barack Obama, Hillary Rodham Clinton, and John Kerry, but on the world as a whole. It is a universalism, one-size-fits-all approach. Jimmy Carter became all things to all people in order to try to impress all. He became a champion of human rights, and by so doing, introduced the world to one of the most heinous regimes in history: the new Islamic Republic of Iran. He climbed into bed, figuratively, with Yasser Arafat and the PLO in order to establish a legacy as a "peace-keeper." Far from protecting US foreign policy interests, Carter made whatever concessions he deemed necessary to be seen as the president of peace.

Had Jimmy Carter adopted a slightly more hawkish stance and been more prone to protect US interests overseas—and certainly in Iran—the world could well be a safer place today. The fall of the shah of Iran opened the door to the rise of Islamic radicalism in Iran and throughout the Arab and Muslim countries. It also led to the assassination of Anwar Sadat in Egypt. This is not the footprint of a peace-keeper.

Carter's belief that every crisis could be resolved with diplomacy—and nothing but diplomacy—permeates today's Democratic Party. Unfortunately, Mr. Carter was wrong then and is still wrong today. There are times when evil must be openly confronted and defeated. Without a strong military backup with a proven track record of victories, diplomacy can be meaningless. As Theodore Roosevelt put it, "Speak softly and carry a big stick."

In his book *Failing the Crystal Ball Test*, Ofira Seliktar says of the situation with Iran:

> Although the Carter administration bears the lion's share for the policy failure, the role of Congress in the Iranian debacle should not be overlooked . . . the Democratically controlled congress was responsible for turning many of the [Carter] imperatives into applied policy, most notably in the realm of foreign aid, military sales, human rights, and intelligence . . . leftist and liberal members of Congress strove to put the United States on the "right" side of history. To do so, they had to stop American anticommunist interventions around the world and terminate relations with right-wing authoritarian regimes, many of which faced leftist insurgencies.[145]

While Jimmy Carter has done good things in his life, most notably his association with Habitat for Humanity, his foreign policy decisions as president of the United States led to more turmoil in just about every region where he attempted to intervene. Carter seemed to think that it was enough to talk people into a stupor, and then entice them with treaties and incentives.

Mr. Carter and his fellow pacifists have yet to understand the impossibility of reasoning with the unreasonable. It is never advisable to sell one's soul to the devil in order to keep him at bay. Sooner or later, evil demands the supreme sacrifice and will achieve its goals, not through compromise, but through terror and coercion. This is one lesson James Earl Carter never learned, and one that, it seems, President Obama has likewise failed to grasp. The long-term effect of Obama's policies on the United States is becoming increasingly apparent.

Mr. Carter's connections with Yasser Arafat and the PLO are legendary. It was through Carter's machinations that the late Palestinian godfather of world terrorism was knighted with the Nobel Peace Prize. It is general knowledge that the Carter Center, a nongovernmental organization adjacent to the Jimmy Carter Presidential Library and Museum, is underwritten by funds from Palestinian sources. Perhaps that is why he described the PLO in such glowing terms as "a loosely associated umbrella of organizations bound together by common goals, but it comprises many groups eager to use diverse means to reach these goals."[146] How benevolent! It sounds nothing like the organization responsible for the Intifada against Jews and the murder of hundreds of innocent civilians.

Although Yasser Arafat has departed the earth, Carter continues to court the good will of terrorists, madmen, and leftists, all the while to this day openly criticizing both Bush administrations to any and all who would listen. Perhaps it was a reflection of Jimmy Carter's own divisiveness that caused the chair of the Nobel awarding committee to use the presentation ceremony as an opportunity to criticize the George W. Bush Administration.

Conversely, and to his credit, when Mr. Bush left office and was asked about certain Obama Administration decisions, he replied:

> I'm not going to second-guess our president. I understand how tough the job is. To have a former president bloviating and second-guessing is, I don't think, good for the presidency or the country.[147]

It was not long after leaving office that the world would begin to see Carter's real legacy. As early as 1984, he was suggesting that Russian Ambassador Anatoly Dobrynin support Ronald Reagan's opponent, Walter Mondale, in the upcoming presidential election. In 1986, Carter defied restrictions imposed on Syria for the attempted bombing of a US airliner by filing a false travel plan before departing for Damascus. Obviously, he felt that he was, somehow, exempt from the laws of the land that governs other US travelers. His actions made it apparent to all that he supported al-Assad's regime, and as such, he was treated in Syria to a hero's welcome.

Mr. Carter also felt it incumbent as an ex-president to write a letter to the regimes in Syria, Saudi Arabia, and Egypt, asking them to stall the invasion of Iraq in 2003.

However, it was Bill Clinton who elevated Carter to the role of infallible elder statesman. With Clinton's approval, the former president traveled to North Korea for discussions on that nation's nuclear ambitions. One reporter wrote that Carter agreed to give North Korea "500,000 metric tons of oil, tons of grain, and a light-water nuclear reactor. . . . The unverifiable agreement Carter designed allowed North Korea to develop as many as half-a-dozen nuclear weapons—which he now blames on George W. Bush."[148]

The former president's interference with foreign policy did not end there. He wrote a speech for Yasser Arafat and certified the "election" of Venezuela's Castro clone, Hugo Chavez. In a trip to Cuba in 2002, the erudite Mr. Carter called UN Ambassador John Bolton a liar for daring to insinuate that Castro was developing biological weapons, reports of which, by the way, first surfaced during the Clinton Administration. Knowing these things, it is difficult to understand how James Earl Carter, the man from Plains, Georgia, was awarded the Nobel Peace Prize in 2002.

In his 2007 book, *Palestine Peace, Not Apartheid*, the former president equates Israel's battle to combat terrorism within its borders to that of the hateful South African practice of apartheid. The reader is hard put to find mentions in this book of any actual instances of the dreadful terrorism suffered by the Israelis. It says little about the fact that Israel has given away land in failed attempts to achieve peace with its neighbors, or the ensuing missile attacks and kidnappings initiated from the very land that was given away. Apparently, Mr. Carter has also forgotten Munich and the massacre of the Israeli Olympic team or the murder of Leon Klinghoffer aboard the *Achille Lauro*, among other such atrocities committed in the name of Palestinian liberation. In fact, throughout the book, he champions the PLO and denigrates Israel.

Among the inequities in Mr. Carter's discourse is

- ✧ the deliberate misrepresentation that Israel was the aggressor in the 1967 war;

- ✧ a failure to reveal the threat against Israel that precipitated the destruction of Iraq's nuclear reactor at Osirak in 1980;

✧ the exoneration of Yasser Arafat for walking
out of the peace talks with Ehud Barak.

He, like so many others, gives no credit to Israel for decades of attempts to establish a peaceful relationship with the Palestinian Authority, and in fact faults them for the ills of the region.

Harvard law professor Alan Dershowitz had this to say about Iran's threat:

> It's obvious that Carter just doesn't like Israel or Israelis. . . . He admits that he did not like Menachem Begin. . . . He has little good to say about any Israelis—except those few who agree with him . . . he apparently got along swimmingly with the very secular Syrian mass-murderer Hafez al-Assad. . . . He and his wife Rosalynn also had a fine time with the equally secular Yasir Arafat—a man who has the blood of hundreds of Americans and Israelis on his hands.[149]

Palestine: Peace Not Apartheid is an outrageous misrepresentation of events in the Middle East, but certainly no more outrageous than his leftist manipulation of events in Iran. As recounted earlier, Carter did everything in his power to weaken the shah and prop up Khomeini. Mr. Carter has remained consistent since that time—consistently wrong. He articulates the world view of the Liberal Left.

Jimmy Carter has taken credit for being the architect of peace between Egypt and Israel. He can, indeed, take the credit, but he is not the one directly responsible; it was Menachem Begin. Begin and I had many discussions about the meetings at Camp

David and matters relating to Anwar Sadat. Begin told me that the idea to pursue an accord with Egypt came to him while on a visit to Romania. The prime minister said he mentioned to Nicolae Ceauşescu that he would like to have direct talks with Sadat. This was not an unusual move for Begin. In his first pronouncement as prime minister of Israel, he called on Arab leaders to meet him at their earliest opportunity.

Later, when Sadat visited Romania, Ceauşescu told him of Begin's wish to meet with him. According to the prime minister, an exchange of views took place there, and then later between the two men. Ceauşescu confirmed his role when he remarked in a speech in Bucharest that year that he had acted for the settlement of the Middle East peace issues through negotiations. Sadat used a public occasion to indicate that for the sake of peace, he would be ready even to travel to Israel to speak to the people of Israel from the rostrum of the Knesset.

Immediately, Begin countered by inviting the Egyptian leader to Jerusalem. He extended the invitation in a speech to a delegation of members of the American Congress Armed Forces Special Committee touring the Middle East, which was proceeding to Cairo the next day. When he heard that Sadat later told the same committee he had not received an official invitation, the Israeli prime minister immediately broadcast a special appeal in English directly to the Egyptian people; he followed that with a formal invitation transmitted through the American ambassador.

In a copy of his speech to the people of Egypt appealing to Anwar Sadat to meet with him, Begin said:

Citizens of Egypt, this is the first time that I

address you directly, but it is not the first time I think and speak of you. You are our neighbors and will always be. For the last twenty-nine years, the tragic and completely unnecessary conflict continued between your country and ours. Since the time when the government of King Farouk ordered to invade our land, Eretz Yisrael, in order to strangle our newly restored freedom and democracy, four major wars have taken place between you and us. Much blood was shed on both sides, many families were orphaned and grieved in Egypt and in Israel . . . you should know we have come back to the land of our forefathers. It is we who established independence in our land for all generations to come. We wish you well; in fact, there is no reason whatsoever for hostilities between our people . . . your president said two days ago that he was ready to come to Jerusalem to our Knesset in order to prevent one Egyptian soldier from being wounded. I have already welcomed this statement, and it will be a pleasure to welcome and receive your president with the traditional hospitality you and we have inherited from our common father, Abraham.

I, for my part, will be ready to come to your capital, Cairo, for the same purpose: No more war, but peace, real peace, forever. (Taken from the private papers of Mike Evans.)

I asked Prime Minister Begin if he was really that eager to go to Egypt. With a smile and a twinkle in his eye, he replied, "Yes,

I would really like to see the pyramids. After all, our ancestors built them. But I will assure the Egyptians that we will not ask for compensation."

For years, Mr. Carter has accepted the accolades of those who thought him to be directly responsible for the meetings between Sadat and Begin. Mr. Carter's perception is his reality; he apparently really believes he was the instigator of the Peace Accords between Egypt and Israel. That same perception permeates his book *Palestine: Peace Not Apartheid*.

Jimmy Carter is, in truth, one of the few ex-presidents to openly and maliciously attack a sitting US president. His spiteful comments frequently rival those of any of the self-appointed spokespersons for the Liberal Left, all of whom are "world citizens" loyal to no particular nation. The former president cautions against a strong, unilateral policy in the Middle East. He seems to favor any world political group that is anti-US. It was this Carter ideology that so pleased the Nobel Peace Prize committee. However, it does absolutely nothing to strengthen US ties worldwide.

On August 15, 2006, Carter was interviewed by *Der Spiegel* magazine. It was yet another opportunity for him to spew his hateful rhetoric against President George W. Bush. But then, the American public was becoming accustomed to the Liberal Left's attacks from the likes of John Kerry, Al Gore, and of course, Howard Dean. Carter not only attacked the president, in 2006 during his interview, he castigated Israel for their "massive bombing of the entire nation of Lebanon. What happened is that Israel is holding almost 10,000 prisoners, so when the militants in Lebanon or in Gaza take one or two soldiers, Israel looks upon this as a justification for an attack on the civilian population of Lebanon and Gaza. I do not think that's justified, no."[150]

Mr. Carter seemed to have conveniently forgotten that Hezbollah (a terrorist organization) invaded Israel, killed eight Israeli soldiers, and *then* kidnapped two others. It seems also to have escaped his attention that the prisoners being held by Israel were *terrorists* with one agenda—to kill innocent Jewish civilians.

Apparently, as a card-carrying member of the Liberal Left, Mr. Carter sides with the enemy of the United States at every available opportunity. In her book *Treason*, Ann Coulter writes:

> Liberals unreservedly call all conservatives fascists, racists, and enemies of civil liberties . . . malign the flag, ban the Pledge, and hold cocktail parties for America's enemies. . . . Liberals attack their country and then go into a . . . panic if anyone criticizes them. . . . Every once in a while, their tempers get the best of them and . . . liberals say what they really mean. . . . Their own words damn them as hating America.[151]

She further defines liberals by saying:

> Liberals demand that the nation treat enemies like friends and friends like enemies. We must lift sanctions, cancel embargoes, pull out our troops, reason with our adversaries, and absolutely never wage war—unless the French say it's okay. . . . Democratic senators, congressmen, and ex-presidents are always popping up in countries hostile to the United States— Cuba, Nicaragua, North Korea, Iraq—hobnobbing with foreign despots who hate America.[152]

Publisher William Loeb said of the Carter presidency, "Reelecting President Carter would be the equivalent of giving the Captain of the Titanic an award as Sailor of the Year."[153]

There has long been a general consensus, especially among conservatives, that Jimmy Carter was the worst president in US history. For the past twenty-five years, Carter has behaved badly toward his successors. Sadly, there has been no outcry regarding his boorishness. His acerbic tirades against Reagan and the two presidents Bush—in front of foreign audiences, yet—have been insolent and discourteous, to say the least. Still there are those who overlook his behavior simply because he has worked with Habitat for Humanity.

Many of Carter's pronouncements have been misleading, and in some instances totally erroneous. He made the protection of "human rights" the basis of his entire presidency (and its afterlife). Carter saw change sweeping over the world. In *Our Endangered Virtues*, Carter wrote of his desire to see "democratization" spreading into areas worldwide. The only thing that spread during Carter's administration was hatred for all things Western, *especially* all things Western. His domestic policy gaffes were only equaled, and possibly surpassed, by his foreign policy blunders.

President Jimmy Carter left office scorned by political liberals and conservatives alike. Syndicated columnist R. Emmett Tyrrell, Jr. summed up Jimmy Carter's White House years like this:

> . . . in social policy he was strictly New Age liberal. He even expressed a belief in UFOs. . . . In foreign policy he was a pompous procrastinator, lecturing Americans on their "inordinate fear of Communism." . . .

Carter began his political career welcoming the support of the Ku Klux Klan. He adjusted his appeal to the dominant forces in the Democratic Party of the 1970s. . . . He is another howler voice in the chorus of the Angry Left . . . [154]

In his post-White House years, James Earl Carter is still a pompous howler bent on blackening the US wherever he's allowed to travel as an ambassador of "goodwill." It is perhaps telling that Carter's name and picture are conspicuous by their absence at national functions of the Democratic Party.

Exporting the Islamic Revolution

Soon after seizing power, Ayatollah Ruhollah Khomeini began to realize that he had no use for Iraq's Ba'thist-led government. Having taken refuge in Najaf after being expelled from Iran, Khomeini had seen firsthand Saddam Hussein's repression of the Shi'ite Muslims in that country. To add insult to injury, Hussein had deported Khomeini at the request of the shah in 1978 just as his influence was growing in Iraq.

So it was that Khomeini encouraged the Shi'ites across the border to remove Saddam from power and establish an Islamic Republic like that in Iran. In response, Hussein had the Grand Ayatollah Muhammad Baqir al-Sadr arrested, his sister raped and murdered in front of him, and then al-Sadr himself brutally killed. Five days later, Hussein declared war on Iran.

The bombing of Iranian airfields and military outposts in September 1980 signaled the beginning of that war. While Hussein's initial raid into Iran resulted in the capture of territory that included the port city of Khorramshahr and oil facilities in Abadan, it soon became apparent that Iran had the advantage. Iran's population was concentrated far from the border with Iraq, while the majority of Iraqis lived near Iran's eastern border, easy prey for air attacks.

Throughout the war, both Hussein and Khomeini continued attempts to incite the inhabitants of the other's country to rebel—Hussein, the Sunnis in Iran; Khomeini, the Shi'ites in Iraq. Few from either group seemed willing to submit to the pressure, however.

As the war dragged on and trained military personnel dwindled in Iran, Khomeini induced young Iranians to volunteer for suicide missions. He conscriped youngsters as early as twelve years old and employed them as living minesweepers. The children were manacled together, each given a red plastic key with which to hypothetically open the gates of paradise. Then they marched off across the fields to clear the way. Untold numbers died.

Hussein could raise only disinterested Shi'ite conscripts and Kurds with no interest in fighting against Iran. When the Iraqi military became severely depleted in 1983, Saddam brought out his prodigious supply of chemical weapons, including mustard gas. It was one of several nerve agents used by Saddam during the war.

The US, for the most part, stood on the sidelines as the two countries battled for supremacy in the region. Under Ronald Reagan's administration, Donald Rumsfeld was appointed special emissary to Iraq. In meetings with Hussein, Rumsfeld explored Iraq and American hostility toward both Iran and Syria but failed to confront Hussein's use of chemical weapons. He did discuss that fact with Saddam's Deputy Prime Minister Tariq Aziz, but not with the dictator. It was a clear signal that the Reagan Administration would not pursue justice for Iraq's use of chemical weapons against its enemy. In fact, the administration actually opposed a UN resolution that condemned Hussein's use of such weapons.

Reagan had a valid reason for supporting Iraq during the war with Iran: a victorious Iran would result in it controlling the oil reserves of both countries, as well as the Persian Gulf. It would present an unparalleled opportunity for Khomeini's Islamic Revolution to spread. There was also the very real possibility that the Reagan Administration actually saw Hussein as both a political and economic ally in the Middle East.

In the mid-1980s, however, the Reagan Administration did a sudden about-face and began a clandestine program to arm Iran. The resulting Iran-Contra scandal sent Reaganites scrambling to repair the damage and caused a further tilt toward Hussein's regime in Iraq. In May 1987, the USS *Stark* was hit by two missiles fired from an Iraqi warplane. The two *Exocet* missiles killed thirty-seven American sailors. The administration tacitly accepted Iraq's explanation that the attack was an accident.

In March 1988, Iraqi planes dropped canisters thought to contain mustard gas and two nerve agents, tabun and sarin, over the Kurdish city of Halabja, which at the time was held by Iranian troops. Accustomed to taking shelter underground from Iranian warplanes, the families in Halabja took refuge in basements across the city. What they could not know was that the gas would seek the lowest places in the city. Basements literally became death chambers for those seeking asylum. It is estimated that more than five thousand residents of Halabja perished as the gas spread throughout the city, and from the complications of inhaling the fatal concoction.

The US Senate reacted to the horror that was Halabja by passing the Prevention of Genocide Act. The House, however, passed an emasculated version of the Senate proposal. The administration, still believing that Hussein might become a viable ally in the region, was prone to overlook this and similar acts that killed the Kurds in northern Iraq.

The Iran–Iraq War would last more than eight years with neither side ever really gaining much of an advantage. Millions of Iraqis and Iranians died in the conflagration, at least two million were injured, and the two nations spent a combined total of over $1 trillion. The war was ever a stalemate, neither side being able to defeat the other, nor being able to agree with the other on conditions for a truce. The war between the two neighboring nations was a war of ideologies and divergent civilizations. Hussein saw himself as the Arab leader who would defeat the Persians; Khomeini saw it as an opportunity to export his Islamic Revolution across the border to the Shi'ites in Iraq, and then beyond to other Arab countries. Though this dream for Khomeini would prove unattainable during his lifetime, it has never died.

With the horrific events of 9/11, identifying the enemy has become all but impossible, but essential with any battle. Today's terrorists are largely unidentifiable, because the men and women who carry the fight into cities and streets wear no uniform, have no identifying marks, and look and talk exactly like the neighbor next door—except for the hatred hidden in the heart. So how can we define the conflict and draw battle lines? We must determine what is right and what is wrong, what is acceptable and what is unacceptable. Sometimes that means stepping outside the bounds of political correctness in order to stop the evil that threatens not only the Middle East but the entire world.

CHAPTER FIFTEEN

The Nuclear Bomb of Islam

The Iran crisis is serious because the clock is ticking. Iran is trying to develop a complete nuclear fuel cycle, going from uranium mining to converting the uranium ore to uranium gas compressing that gas into yellow cake and then creating a feed stock which can be enriched . . . into nuclear fuel which would go into a bomb. Marry that fuel with a delivery system like a missile and you have a threat not only to Israel and Saudi Arabia, but probably to portions of Southern Europe.

PROFESSOR RAYMOND TANTER [155]

TODAY, IRAN IS WELL ON its way to becoming a nuclear power, and its targets are none other than what the Ayatollah Khomeini first dubbed the "Great Satan," America, and the "Little Satan," Israel. In the words of James Woolsey, former CIA director, the extremist arm of Islam consists of "theocratic, totalitarian, and anti-Semitic, genocidal fanatics."[156]

With the exception of the two attacks on the World Trade Center in 1993 and 2001, America has, thus far, escaped the barrage of suicide bombers that has long plagued Israel—but for how long? While the current leaders in Iran might see the "dirty bomb" approach as being the most effective against the US, Israel, on the other hand, is well within range of the country's missiles—any one of which could be armed with a nuclear warhead that would wreak untold devastation on the tiny nation of Israel.

And which nations will step into the fray and take the initiative to call a halt to Iran's nuclear objectives? France? Germany? Spain? Great Britain? We simply cannot depend on our so-called Western allies to face down the likes of Ayatollah Ali Khamenei and his minions. Our only real ally in this Middle East mess is Israel, a tiny David in the midst of countless Goliaths. How long will Israel sit by and allow the giant—in this case Iran—to hurl epithets across the barren desert before she reaches into her arsenal and fells this deadly antagonist?

Not long enough to allow Iran to arm itself with nuclear weapons, that seems certain.

At one time, it appeared more and more likely that the US, not Israel, would be the one to go it alone in order to stop the snowballing process of nuclear enrichment in Iran—but in recent months, the US has moved closer and closer to some sort of ill-fated accord with the clerics in Iran.

Even as American and European diplomatic sources try new and improved ways to dissuade Iran's nuclear ambitions, Israel has been forced to prepare for the worst: the need to attack Iran's nuclear facilities just as she took out Iraq's Osirak plant in 1981.

Is such a thing really a possibility? As one Israeli security source said, "If all efforts to persuade Iran to drop its plans to produce nuclear weapons should fail, the US administration will authorize Israel to attack..."[157] But will that happen under Mr. Obama's watch, or will Israel be thrown to the wolves yet again?

The nuclear site at Bushehr is only one of a number of nuclear-based facilities scattered throughout Iran. Some are so deeply buried that it would be virtually impossible to penetrate. These include sites such as Saghand, Ardekan, and what will probably be Israel's first target: Natanz, an enrichment facility.

The obstacles to a successful attack by Israel are enormous and daunting. Israeli planes would have to overfly Turkey; US coordination would be absolutely necessary. Retaliatory assaults would be swift and certain; and the targets are many—strategists number them around 1,000—with perhaps not all yet identified. Israel's F-15 pilots, however, are ready should the signal be given. And, while the mission may be hazardous, Israel's leaders know they must act to preserve the tiny nation, just as was done at Osirik. In September 2012 in a clandestine military exercise dubbed "Operation Orchard," eight Israeli fighter jets dropped 17 tons of explosives on the Syrian site, destroying it.[158]

Israel will not permit its existence to be jeopardized, especially by regimes that have never remained quiet about their desire to give Israel's land to the Palestinians,[159] and to eradicate the tiny nation's people.

The Greatest Equalizer

In 1945, after months of agonizing fighting in the Pacific Theatre, US President Harry S Truman finally issued orders to drop two atomic bombs on Japan in an attempt to bring an end to World War II. On August 6, "Little Boy" fell on Hiroshima with a payload whose explosive power was equivalent to 15,000 tons of TNT. Three days later, "Fat Man" was released over Nagasaki and carried a 23-kiloton (23,000-ton) punch. Approximately 130,000 people were instantly vaporized and more than 340,000 would later die from the effects of radiation caused by those two blasts.

J. Robert Oppenheimer had been absolutely correct. While witnessing the first nuclear test at Alamogordo, New Mexico, on July 16, 1945, he was reminded of a line from the *Bhagavad Gita*, the Hindu scripture: "Now I am become Death, the destroyer of worlds."[160]

In their book, *Endgame*, Lt. General Thomas McInerney and Major General Paul Vallely had this to say when discussing the threat of weapons of mass destructions being used in a terrorist attack:

> Many of the scenarios about terrorism concern "weapons of mass destruction," otherwise known as nuclear, chemical, and biological weapons. . . . As grave as the threats posed by biological and chemical weapons are, however, they are not as grave as that posed by nuclear weapons. . . . A biological attack would not destroy the infrastructure that our country depends upon. Telephone lines would be working. Electricity would be generated and transmitted. Highways and railroads would remain open. Computer networks would remain functioning. However frightening a biological attack might be in theory, it is unlikely to achieve much in fact . . . .
>
> Even if terrorist groups were given chemical weapons from the arsenal of a country, there is no guarantee that they would be able to transport them safely to the target cities or gather them in sufficient

quantities to kill and injure large numbers of people . . . .

Chemical weapons, like biological weapons, do
not destroy buildings or bridges or any other vital
infrastructure or interfere seriously in the operation
of the government.

From a military perspective, therefore, using
nuclear weapons just makes more sense. Mounting a
terrorist operation using weapons of mass destruction would be expensive, even if the most expensive
item the weapons themselves—were "donated" by
Iran or North Korea. If would be extremely wasteful
for the Web of Terror to expend immense manpower
on an operation that would not deliver a crushing
blow to the United States.[161]

Today even a relatively small atom bomb—say 20 kilotons,
roughly the explosive power of that which was dropped on Nagasaki,
though now capable of being transported in a much more compact
container—would kill hundreds of thousands almost instantly and
many more would die from radiation exposure in the days following. Millions more would suffer the effects of the blast for the
rest of their lives. Were such a bomb strategically placed—say in the
US Library of Congress, for example—the blast would destroy the
Capitol Building and the Supreme Court Building as well as a great
number of governmental office buildings including the Department
of Health and Human Services—the very office that would have
otherwise organized the rescue and emergency care operations for
just such an attack. Thousands of key government officials would

die in a split second. When the attacks of 9/11 took place the entire US economy shuddered—what would happen after a nuclear attack on Washington? Or what if the attack hit Wall Street instead? Or even both?

According to former CIA director James Woolsey:

> Hassan Abbasi—I believe his name is—a chief of strategy for Ahmadinejad—said sometime . . . that there were twenty-nine sites in America and the West that if they were destroyed—and he knew how to destroy them—they would "bring the Anglo-Saxons to their knees." And that once that was done, nobody else would fight.[162]

In a meeting with Harvard Law Professor Alan Dershowitz in 2006, I asked about Iran's threat to the United States. Dr. Dershowitz told me:

> Iran is a major, major threat to the United States. Iran, if it's not stopped, will get a nuclear bomb, and it will use that nuclear bomb to blackmail America and other countries. . . . A nuclear weapon whether used, or hung as the sword of Damocles, changes the entire structure and balance of power. . . .
>
> You can deter people who don't want to die, but many of Iran's leaders welcome death. They are part of the culture of death. They see life on earth as only a segue to Paradise with their seventy-two virgins, or whatever the rewards are going to be. . . . It's very

hard to deter a culture that welcomes death, so Iran would be a great threat to the United States.

As Tom Friedman once said, "If terrorists are not stopped in the Middle East, they're coming to a theater near you," and they're coming to the United States, to Europe . . . [even] western European countries are vulnerable to an Iranian nuclear threat.[163]

Prime minister of Israel Benjamin Netanyahu had this to say:

Up until now, nuclear weapons have been in the hands of responsible regimes. You have one regime, one bizarre regime that apparently has them now in North Korea. [However,] there aren't a billion North Koreans that people seek to inspire into a religious war. That's what Iran could do. It could inspire the 200 million Shi'ites. That's what they intend to do, inspire them into a religious war, first against other Muslims, then against the West. . . . It is important to understand that they could impose a direct threat to Europe and to the United States and to Israel, obviously. They don't hide it. They don't even hide the fact that they intend to take on the West.[164]

In June 2002, following the destruction of the twin World Trade Towers in New York City, Suleiman Abu Gheith, bin Laden's press secretary and son-in-law, made a terrifying announcement on a defunct Internet site: "We have the right," boasted Abu Gheith, "to kill four million Americans—two million of them children—

and to exile twice as many and wound and cripple hundreds of thousands."[165] In the perverted and warped minds of these fanatics, the four million represented the number that needed to be killed to balance the scales. In effect, Abu Gheith was saying that America was responsible for the deaths of four million Muslims. The number would be equal to four thousand nine hundred 9/11 attacks.[166]

When Tom Ridge, secretary of Homeland Security under President George W. Bush, was asked to define his greatest nightmare, he replied, "Nuclear."[167]

The Suicide Regime

Iran is certainly not constrained by what, during the Cold War of the twentieth century, was called the MAD deterrent, or "mutually assured destruction." The theory behind this policy was that each superpower engaged in the Cold War—i.e., Russia and the United States—was sufficiently armed to each destroy the other several times over in the event of an attack. The outcome of such an event would bring about the near total destruction of both countries and, by extension, the world.

This theory was directly responsible for the nuclear arms race that was unleashed during the late 1940s, and lasted through the mid-1980s. Both nations had sufficient incentive not to engage in a direct nuclear conflict; both were content to employ proxy wars around the world. Could it have been this "proxy war" concept that gave Iran the idea of stationing groups such as Hezbollah and Hamas in Lebanon and Gaza, and to send proxies into Iraq to foment upheaval in that country?

Perhaps the most pressing question after all is not when will Iran have the bomb? Rather, will its leaders be deterred by "mutually assured destruction"? Or does Iran's leaders, like Khomeini, believe: "Let Iran go up in smoke, provided Islam emerges triumphant in the rest of the world"?[168]

General Yossi Peled, the commander of Israel's northern divisions in the recent fighting between Israel and Hezbollah, said this about Iran having nuclear weapons:

> If this moment comes that Iran has nuclear ability, let's say they decide to make a move in the Middle East to free it from the bad influence of the West. They would take [on] Egypt, Israel, Lebanon—it's against the interests of the Western world and against the US. Don't you think it will limit the reaction of the US? Everything will change. I wish to be wrong, but I don't feel so.
>
> The second point is that they think in a different way than you and me and most of the Western world. Maybe they will be ready to sacrifice half of the Islamic world to destroy half of the Western world. It's possible because they think a different way, have a different religion, live according to a different mentality. And already, they are strong enough to convince their people it is okay to sacrifice a million to achieve control.[169]

Professor Raymond Tanter, a National Security advisor under Reagan/Bush and one of the founders of the Iran Policy Committee, saw that the Islamofascist extremism and nuclear weapons is a mix the West truly can't sit by and let happen:

What difference does it make if an Islamofascist regime gets nuclear weapons? It would be a huge boost to the government of Iran in terms of its . . . diplomatic ability to coerce the neighbors; it would accelerate the arms race in the Middle East where Saudi Arabia, Egypt, and Israel will either acquire or make explicit their nuclear weapons. The threat from Iran is a huge destabilizing factor in US-European relations.

So what then is the nation prepared to do? I say go ahead and try diplomacy but realize that when you are dealing with an Islamofascist regime, diplomacy is unlikely to work. Why not? Because the Islamofascist regime is not a normal regime where you make cost benefit calculations, where you make proposals and counter-proposals, [where] you make compromises. This regime doesn't negotiate in the same manner that a western government would negotiate. Hence you should try diplomacy, but be prepared for diplomatic failure and have options other than military options. That's what I call regime change; by empowering the Iranian people through their opposition groups.[170]

The power of Khomeini's radical Islamic belief system brainwashing the mind of every Islamic fanatic has never been more apparent than in the various attacks that have killed American marines, sailors, and troops in Iraq, as well as in the stolen lives of innocent bystanders, even fellow Muslims. The Iranian-backed death squads in Iraq have no compunction about blowing themselves up in crowded marketplaces, outside schools, or in busy city centers, all the while shouting, *"Allah akbar!"*—"Allah is supreme!"

According to former Palestinian terrorist Walid Shoebat:

> When somebody reaches to the tyranny of Islamic Fundamentalism, people don't matter, just like Hitler. The people do not matter. They're just elements to establish a goal. With Islamic Fundamentalism and Nazism, two things are very similar. The end justifies the means, and there is no respect for borders.[171]

Apparently in the fanatical Islam mind-set, it is okay to kill Muslim brothers, for they will attain heaven; the hated infidels will, they think, go to their reward in hell. For the radical jihadists, the end justifies the murders of innocent Muslim passersby because, after all, they will attain their reward that much sooner. Sadly, young Iranian students have been literally brainwashed by textbooks studied in their schools. The youngsters are taught that to sacrifice themselves as martyrs for the "cause" is the ultimate goal, and that they must be ready at all times for the opportunity to attain that goal.

John R. Bolton, then under secretary for arms control and international security, said in August 2004:

> What we ask for is not much—only what is necessary to protect our security and to prevent Iran from developing nuclear weapons and other WMD. All that Iran must do is to abide by the treaties it has signed banning weapons of mass destruction and stop its program to develop ballistic missiles.

We cannot let Iran, a leading sponsor of international terrorism, acquire nuclear weapons and the means to deliver them to Europe, most of central Asia, and the Middle East, or beyond.[172]

Without serious, concerted, immediate intervention by the international community, however, Iran will reach that goal.

CHAPTER SIXTEEN

The Rise of the Mahdi

*The belief of a returning Mahdi, or 12th imam, is a defining
doctrine within the most populous group of Shiite Muslims
(known as the "Twelvers") . . . believe that the 12th imam
will emerge from hiding during a time of world chaos to bring
order and exalt Shiite believers to their rightful place.*

ROBERT MORLEY, COLUMNIST[173]

WHEN THE PROPHET MOHAMMAD died in AD 632, he
left a political organization that was entirely centered upon him. He
was both the political and military leader, as well as the source of
all revelation for converts to Islam. Prior to his passing, no working
model of government had been established, and no line of succession
was implemented to select his heir. The result was much like what we
see today . . . sometimes violent disagreements among Mohammad's
followers, and especially between the emerging Shi'a and Sunni sects.

It was finally determined that Mohammad's father-in-law, Abu
Bakr, would be the anointed one, the Caliph, or "Successor." The
earliest caliphs, then, were relatives of Mohammad himself. His

first four successors were called the patriarchal Caliphs of Islam. Abu Bakr ruled for two years and was followed by 'Umar. His legatee was 'Uthman, who had the questionable distinction of being the first caliph killed by his fellow Muslims. But 'Uthman held a greater and more lasting accomplishment: he compiled the Quran into a book of printed text. Prior to this achievement, the religious tenets and prayers of Mohammad's followers had been oral only, memorized, and then recited by its adherents.

After the First World War, the Ottoman Empire was no more. It was

> . . . partitioned, creating the modern Arab World (Algeria, Bahrain, Comoros, Egypt, Djibouti, Iraq, Kuwait, Lebanon, Libya, Morocco, Oman, Qatar, Saudi Arabia, etc.) and the Republic of Turkey . . . The remnants of this majestic empire still remain as architectural relics and cultural influences in these regions—they remind us of the fact that splendor and glory never really die.[174]

The institution of the caliphate was abolished in 1924 by Mustafa Kemal Ataturk, the first president of the Turkish Republic. Powers of the caliphate were transferred to the Grand National Assembly (parliament) of Turkey, and the title has since been inactive. The last caliph of Islam had the lengthy title of "His Imperial Majesty the Caliph Abdülmecid II, The Commander of the Faithful and Shadow of God on Earth."[175] He reigned from November 19, 1922, to March 3, 1924. In spite of sporadic efforts to impart new life into the idea of a caliphate—by Sharif Husayn of Mecca after World War I and by King Faruq of Egypt at the beginning of World War II—the tradition waned during the twentieth century.

Since the fanatical Islamic Revolution in Iran in 1979, talk of restoring the caliphate has taken on new meaning. One global Islamist movement, *Hizb at-Tahrir* (the Liberation Party), "has kept this idea alive intellectually for over fifty years by publishing tracts on the subject."[176] Constituents in the organization contend that a condition for growing the spiritual, political, social, and economic strength of the Muslim community is the reinstatement of the caliphate.

The Shi'a battalions of Twelvers in Iran eagerly await the resurrection of the Mahdi, whom they believe to be a direct descendant of Muhammed. This belief is now spreading into the Sunni Muslim culture. It is tied to bitterness and anger against the economy, against brutal and authoritarian governments, and of course, against Israel, the West, and all Christians and Jews wherever they are to be found. The United States in particular and the world in general had best be well prepared when this new caliphate under the Mahdi emerges and makes its entrance onto the world stage. It is currently being upstaged by the Islamic State, but don't be foolhardy and count it out quite yet.

When the Ayatollah Ruhollah Khomeini returned to Iran in 1979 following the overthrow of the shah, there were many who thought the Mahdi—that elusive descendant of Mohammad—had returned to take his rightful place. Khomeini's charisma was especially appealing to the lower classes, the *mostazafin* . . . the dispossessed. In their hysterical longing for the return of the Mahdi, the risen one who would free the masses from privation, discrimination, and tyranny, some claimed to have seen the ayatollah's face in the moon.[177] This would certainly be consistent with the Persian penchant for superstition, numerology, and dependence on "omens, symbols, prophecies, and revelations."[178]

When the vehicle carrying Khomeini left the airport for down-town Tehran, the roads were lined with nearly two million Shi'a Muslims screaming, *"al-Muntazar!"* The Grand Ayatollah was quick to deny that he was "al-Muntazar," one of the names given to the "Hidden Imam." In other words, many thought Khomeini was the awakened Mahdi. Khomeini did, however, explain to his followers that he was the forerunner, the one who had come to open the way for the Hidden Imam to make his reappearance—a modern-day Christian version of John the Baptist.

Al-Mahdi, who is said to have disappeared down a well at the age of five, was the Twelfth Imam in the line of Ali. Refusing to believe he was dead, his followers—sometimes called Twelvers—imbued him with timelessness. They declared him to be merely "hidden," or in a state of occultation, and that at some future date he would suddenly reappear to establish an Islamic caliphate worldwide. The Twelver's eschatology, however, proved problematic; it espoused an apocalyptic upheaval in order for the Hidden Imam to ascend to his rightful place of leadership. These Twelvers championed the tenet that every individual, regardless of his religious belief, would one day bow to Islam—or die. As the self-proclaimed forerunner of the Mahdi, the spirit of the Grand Ayatollah Khomeini lives on in Iran.

The *ummah*, or community of Islam worldwide, is comprised of Sunni and Shi'a Muslims. The two different sects evolved following the death of Mohammad. The Sunnis readily accepted Mohammad's father-in-law as his successor; Shi'a Muslims demanded their leader be a direct descendant of Mohammad. This personage is known to the Shi'a as "Ali"; hence the designation "The Party of Ali."

Through the ages additional subdivisions in the Shi'a sect, all led by recognized descendants of Mohammed, have pitted one group against the other. Their individual designations are derived from the number of the imam that they follow; thus Iran is comprised mainly of followers of the Twelfth, or the Hidden Imam. He succeeded Al-Hassan al-Askari, who died in 874 AD. The Hidden Imam is known by several names, which translate to "expected one," the "hidden one," and of course, Mahdi (promised one). His mystique is enhanced by the legend that the young successor in the lineage of Mohammad was hidden because he was unaccepted by the majority of Muslims. He will apparently be kept in seclusion until the day he emerges to reunite Muslims, conquer the world, and establish an Islamic caliphate.

Shi'ite Muslims believe that the Twelfth Imam will emerge from his hidden location at his second coming, but first, they believe the world will go through great calamities and upheavals. This apocalypse will set the conditions for the Mahdi's return. Perhaps some even see the rise of ISIL as a precursor or one of the great upheavals through which Islam must go before the return of the Mahdi.

Are most people aware that devotees of the Mahdi will do anything to ensure that the world is made ready for the second coming of a false messiah—even if it requires manufacturing an apocalyptic event to ensure a rush to Armageddon?

When he was invited to speak at the United Nations in October 2005, former Iranian president Mahmoud Ahmadinejad called upon Allah to quickly usher in the reemergence of the Twelfth or Hidden Imam at the conclusion of his discourse. Afterward, the fanatical leader claimed that while he spoke to that august body, he was surrounded by a halo of light. Mr. Ahmadinejad later regaled a local ayatollah in Tehran with the story of how "the leaders of the world" stared at him during the time he spoke. He further claimed that they were unable to blink or turn away, as though some unseen force held them in a trancelike state:

The last day when I was speaking before the (U.N. General) Assembly, one of our group told me when I started to say, "In the name of God the Almighty, the Merciful," he saw a light around me, and I was placed inside this aura, and I felt it myself. I felt the atmosphere suddenly change, and for those 27 or 28 minutes the leaders of the world did not blink. When I say they did not bat an eyelid, I am not exaggerating, because I was looking at them and they were rapt.[179]

Ahmadinejad ended his speech to the UN Assembly with this prayer:

From the beginning of time, humanity has longed for the day when justice, peace, equality, and compassion envelop the world. All of us can contribute to the establishment of such a world. When that day comes, the ultimate promise of Divine religions will be fulfilled with the emergence of a perfect human being who is heir to all prophets and pious men. He will lead the world to justice and absolute peace.

O mighty Lord, I pray to you to hasten the emergence of your last repository, the promised one, that perfect and pure human being, the one that will fill this world with justice and peace.[180]

Secular diplomats find it hard to believe that today any political leader would be driven by religious views. This shortsightedness blinds many.

I am reminded of the 1993 bombing of the World Trade Center

that had been planned and organized by Sheikh Omar Abdel Rahman.

The FBI eventually found forty-seven boxes of Rahman's terrorist literature. In an unbelievable display of moral blindness, the agents marked the tops of the boxes, "Irrelevant religious stuff." It seems the very reason for the attacks and failing to connect them to the worldwide Islamic fundamentalist movement that had fueled it was totally dismissed.

This is still true today as the uninitiated smirk and think it is just a bunch of religious foolishness, but Twelvers are deadly serious. Not only do they believe it, but the tens of thousands of mullahs controlling ancient Persia believe it. Restoring the caliphate with the Mahdi as its caliph is their supposed mission from Allah—and Twelvers will go to any lengths to accomplish it, including sending their children out as suicide bombers.

The theology being taught by the Twelvers in *madrassas* (schools) in Iran is designed to promote the idealistic views of suicide bombers:

- ✧ If a suicide bomber commits an act of martyrdom, he/she will feel neither pain nor fear.

- ✧ The suicide bomber believes he/she will not die; all souls go into the ground awaiting the resurrection except the souls of martyrs. They go directly into paradise.

- ✧ Once in paradise, a crown of glory with the jewel of the wealth of the world is placed on the head of the martyr.

✧ They believe the martyr will be given not
one mansion, but 72 mansions. The mansions will be inhabited by 72 black-eyed
virgins (incorruptible). The martyr is taught
that he/she will be invited to a wedding.

✧ Another teaching is that the shedding of the
blood of the martyr will atone for the sins
of seventy of the martyr's relatives, thus
exempting him/her from the horrors of hell.

The belief in this Hidden Imam is so compelling that it could
easily spawn a nuclear attack on Israel and/or the United States
in order to precipitate an apocalyptic event, a means to an end.
Initially, threats seemed merely the idle ranting of Islamofascists;
but when armed with the capability to produce nuclear weapons,
Iran will become a menace with which to be reckoned.

In the minds of Islamofascists, an atomic bomb in Tel Aviv
would usher in the Mahdi, and all the world's *dhemmis* (Jews and
Christians) would instantly be converted to Islam and would bow
in obeisance to Allah. The Hidden Imam, according to Iran's constitution and upon his unveiling, will assume leadership in the
Islamic Republic. All will acquiesce to his authority in what is
essentially an end-time paradigm based on what some call the
Muslim messiah.

The belief that the second coming of the Mahdi will be
prompted by an apocalyptic event is extremely dangerous. Note
that this apocalypse of death and destruction in the Islamic prophecies *precedes* the Mahdi's return. Anyone seeking to fulfill the
Islamic prophecies could decide that a nuclear attack on Israel
or on US interests in Europe is predestined. The resulting chaos

might result in a nuclear retaliation by Israel, by the United States, or both.

In an exclusive interview with Prime Minister Benjamin Netanyahu, I asked him to assess the Iranian threat. He replied:

> Iran is an outlaw state. It fans terrorism and militancy worldwide. It is now organizing the rocketing of civilians in Israel . . . And [Iran] is preparing to be able to launch atomic warheads into an enormous radius. It's not just targeting Israel. If [Iran] only wanted Israel, it would not build those long-range rockets that can now pretty much cover every European capital and soon will cover the US It is precisely this mad ideology that people underrate.[181]

Were an apocalypse needed to set the stage for the return of the Mahdi, those who desire to see a caliphate established would have no reservations about instigating an all-out nuclear attack against Israel—and perhaps anyone else that might get in the way. Israel and the free world should be very alarmed. The question has become: With the rise of the Islamic State, is the stage being set for the production to come?

It is no secret that Iran, an enemy of Israel and the West, and a supporter of the Palestinians, is actively working to get other Arab countries to abandon their cooperation with the United States and Israel. That is one reason the unrest that has gripped the Middle East brings such a critical situation. President Barack Obama must refrain from treating Israel and its prime minister with contempt and from yoking Israel with the burdensome task of making peace, while demanding nothing of the Palestinians. It is highly possible that when the dust has finally settled in Syria and Iraq and other countries surrounding Israel, the tiny Jewish state will be the only friend the US has left in the Middle East.

In an article in the *Washington Post*, journalist Jennifer Rubin wrote revealingly of President Obama's stance with Israel and the Palestinians:

> We can therefore see that Obama's words are entirely at odds with the conduct of the parties in the region. He either chooses to misrepresent the facts or he is blinded by unremitting hostility to Israel. In any event, he indulges the PA's intransigence despite replete evidence that this only worsens the divide between the parties. The inescapable takeaway is that Obama lacks real affection for the Jewish state and when things fail intends to blame Israel.[182]

The groundwork for an attack on Israel was laid by Mahmoud Ahmadinejad as he spewed his hate-filled rhetoric at every opportunity. He said, repeatedly, that Israel should be wiped "off the map"; that the Holocaust is a myth perpetrated by the Jewish people as a justification to give them Palestine; and that the Jews should be relocated to a colony in Europe, or perhaps Alaska.

Israel's sworn enemies would not hesitate to launch an attack to obliterate Israel, even if it meant taking out the Palestinians, too. Of course, such an attack would mean immediate counterstrikes by Israel that would decimate Iran. And while that might give the Palestinians and perhaps even the Iranian population pause for thought, such tactics would be viewed as the ultimate in martyrdom, and thus the ultimate in self-glory. The indoctrination of the martyr complex has become so ingrained in the radical Islamic psyche that human life has no value except in how the person dies; not even the lives of wives and children, mothers and fathers, or friends and neighbors matter compared to the chance to go out in a glorious explosive strike at the infidels.

It was the Ayatollah Khomeini who said:

> I am decisively announcing to the whole world that if the world-devourers [all infidels, i.e., anyone that dared to disagree with him] wish to stand against our religion, we will stand against their whole world and will not cease until the annihilation of all of them. Either we all become free, or we will go to the greater freedom, which is martyrdom. Either we shake one another's hands in joy at the victory of Islam in the world, or all of us will turn to eternal life and martyrdom. In both cases, victory and success are ours.[183]

With this in mind, the tactic of mutually assured destruction is not a restraint that will work with the current leader, Ayatollah Khamenei, the actual power in Iran, and his cronies.

The current ruling mullahs fully believe that Allah has preordained their success; they are determined to tread the path they feel he has laid out for them. And they believe that they will triumph, establishing an Islamic caliphate worldwide; every knee bowing to Islam, and with every Christian and Jew enslaved.

When the Ayatollah Khomeini made his triumphant return to Tehran in 1979, the religious fanatics were convinced they would win. Why? They saw the US as weak. They saw her as having the weapons, but not the will, not the determination, not the resolve to carry out a prolonged war of attrition. The Grand Ayatollah reiterated the belief that the United States lacked the fervor necessary to challenge the Islamic Revolution that was willing to fight for centuries if necessary to reach its aims.

Khomeini laid out the plan: eradicate the nation of Israel; rid the Middle East of the Jews. He convinced his compatriots that the elimination of Israel was a divine edict from Allah's mouth to Khomeini's ear. He, and then his successors, concluded that, when push comes to shove, the United States and its Western allies would abandon Israel rather than go to war on her behalf.

While Khomeini was a hero to the likes of Ahmadinejad, he was actually mentored by Ayatollah Mohammad Taghi Mesbah Yazdi, the man who today is director of the Imam Khomeini Education and Research Institute in Qom. He is also a member of the Iranian Assembly of Experts. Reputedly, the hard-liner Yazdi believes, "If anyone insults the Islamic sanctities, Islam has permitted for his blood to be spilled, no court needed either." [184]

CHAPTER SEVENTEEN

How Possible Is a Terrorist Nuclear Attack?

Human society is based on reciprocity. If you remove reciprocity, justice becomes a lie. A person walking somewhere on a street has the right to live only because and only to the extent that he acknowledges my right to live. But, if he wishes to kill me, to my mind he forfeits his right to exist—and this also applies to nations. Otherwise, the world would become a racing area for vicious predators, where not only the weakest would be devoured, but the best.

ZE'EV JABOTINSKY, ZIONIST LEADER [185]

IN 1999, AS I WAS READING the chapter on the opening of the scrolls in the book of Revelation, I became inspired to write a novel, *The Jerusalem Scroll*. In chapter eight of the novel, I described a meeting in the Soviet Union between the Russian Mafia and an Islamic terrorist organization. The purpose of the meeting: The Islamic terrorist organization was negotiating the purchase of suitcase nuclear bombs:

"Both of us know the United States is the Great Satan," Khaled continued. Remove these obstructionists and we can eradicate the Zionists instantly. In one great sweep, our armies will dispatch these pests." He gestured as if swinging a sword in the air. "Of course, your help is essential for our victory, my brother."

"Yes. Yes." Ivan's smile never changed. He held a Cuban cigar between his thumb and index finder and kept popping it into the black forest above his fat lower lip. The former KGB agent chewed his cigar, but said nothing more.

"We would have no problem transporting the bomb south through Afghanistan and then into Iran," Khaled continued. "Our friend, Osama bin Laden, has already made his facilities in the Kandahar region available to us." He crossed his arms over his chest confidently. "No problem anywhere along the way." He laughed. "The CIA trained and armed his people to fight you in Afghanistan. Now we both win. It's payback time."

The bomb was to be purchased for twenty million dollars.

Avraham studied the man across from him. Tanned, graying, slightly overweight, the prime minister had more determination and sheer guts than one might have thought. Avraham would have to reevaluate his opinion of the leader.

"The gravity of this policy ought to cause the

Western nations to be a bit more temperate toward us and a great deal more supportive of our position."

For a moment Avraham pondered his response. The right words were everything in a conversation of this magnitude. "What if, God forbid, one of those bombs went off in New York City or Los Angeles? I'd think there would be a radical change in perspective." He shook his head.[186]

Unfortunately, just such a scenario seems all too likely today for terrorists to instigate and all too easy for them to pull off.

When Osama bin Laden left the Sudan at the insistence of the United States in 1996, he arrived in Jalalabad on a Hercules C-130 cargo plane specifically outfitted for him. One hundred fifty al Qaeda associates, his children, and wives accompanied him. Bin Laden would soon transition from being a multimillionaire to a billionaire.

He was not the wealthy terrorist that most people later pictured him to be in 1996. The Saudi government revoked his citizenship and froze his assets in 1994. He was in desperate need of a new source of revenue. In 1997, the poppy harvest in Afghanistan had sold 3,276 tons of raw opium, and revenues began to pour into the coffers of al Qaeda at a rate estimated to be between $5 and $16 billion per year.[187]

Bin Laden's cut was somewhere between $500 million to $1 billion per year. His decision to secure suitcase nuclear bombs and nuclear technology from the Russian Mafia cost bin Laden $30 million in cash and two tons of refined heroin.[188]

It is plausible to launch a suitcase-sized nuclear device with a grenade or rocket launcher. These weapons of terrorism could also be triggered in shopping malls, theaters, or sports stadiums in metropolitan areas. The death toll would be astronomical.

In 1998, more than seven hundred reports of nuclear material sales were received at the Russian Defense Ministry. These materials were reportedly being sold to various buyers within and outside the Russian borders.[189]

In November 2001, bin Laden granted an interview to Pakistani editor Hamid Mir. Mir pointedly asked if bin Laden had obtained nuclear devices. Bin Laden responded, "It is not difficult, not if you have contacts in Russia and with other militant groups. They are available for $10 to $20 million." Ayman Muhammad Rabī Al-Zawahiri, bin Laden's chief strategist, interposed, "If you go to BBC reports, you will find that thirty nuclear weapons are missing from Russia's nuclear arsenal. We have links with Russia's underworld channels."[190]

Terrorism and Social Networking

The advent of social networking has introduced another prolific source for the recruitment of terrorists. Tom Osborne with the FBI Counterterrorism Internet Targeting Unit said:

> Social networking sites certainly can and do provide a means to bring like-minded individuals together, whether it is . . . for radicalization, recruitment, or other terrorism objectives.[191]

Britain's *Telegraph* newspaper reported in 2008 that one terrorist posted a message to other jihadists:

> We have already had great success in raiding *YouTube* and the next target is to invade *Facebook*. If American politicians like Barack Obama can use it to win an election, we can use it to take over the world.[192]

While the social network does have rules aimed at barring content that endorses organizations that promote terror, some have managed to stay under the radar of *Facebook* watchdogs. One such organization is a faction that calls itself *Jihad in the way of God*. According to Osborne:

> The Internet is the virtual base that al Qaeda must use, since many of their physical bases do not exist anymore. [The Internet provides] a sense of security and anonymity ... from the relative security of your home computer.[193]

Evan Kohlmann of Flashpoint Global Partners, a security consulting firm based in New York City, delivered a sobering speech on the frightening aspects of social networking. He informed his audience:

> The online network for these guys is more important than nationality, tribe or ethnicity. These connections are becoming the glue that ties terrorist networks together .... These are not places you would consider hotbeds of terrorism, but that's the reality ... Ultimately it comes down to analysts who are smart enough to pick apart the nuggets.[194]

Policing outlawed subject matter is no simple chore, given the number of members dedicated to the use of various social networks. The enormity of the ranks of network users provides a certain amount of anonymity from regulators. One *Facebook* employee explained that maintaining a balance between freedom of expression and a safe social networking site is a delicate tightrope walk. Louis E. Grever, the executive assistant director for the FBI's Science and Technology Branch, says:

> We have detected the use of social networking and multimedia websites by terrorists and have confirmed that they are using those forums for recruiting, communications, and the distribution of propaganda . . . We would hesitate to name specific sites or outlets for fear that they may move away from a specific site or service or alter their tradecraft if they think we have some capability to monitor their activity.[195]

According to Grever, the task of capturing transmissions on the various websites is monumental:

> We work with communications service providers to affect lawful electronic surveillance here domestically. We are not always successful in collecting all the data we have the lawful authority to collect.[196]

Social networking was utilized by Osama bin Laden to lure recruits from the United States to al Qaeda training facilities throughout the Middle East, and especially in Yemen. It allowed the mastermind of the 9/11 attacks to spread his tentacles around the globe and ensnare the dispossessed into the fold. For example, Mohamed Osman Mohamud, a Somalia native who planned an attack during the annual Christmas tree lighting in Portland, Oregon, was an Internet recruit.[197]

YouTube is being used to post Islamic State recruitment videos aimed at attracting and recruiting impressionable young women as brides for its members:

> ISIS is known for using compelling, and usually false, propaganda videos on social media to recruit young westerners to their cause. They promise adventure, safety and an ideal Islamic state, which can appeal to young idealists.... Why, when Islamic fundamentalism has so little respect for women, is ISIS actively recruiting them?
>
> ISIS is carefully recruiting young women because they have found women fighters are useful for controlling other women. As ISIS takes over an area they institute harsh codes of behavior and dress for women. For example, ISIS requires women wear a full niqab veil to almost completely hide their faces and women are not allowed to walk outside without a male escort. Finding women who buy into the rules and are willing to police others is essential for repressing dissent. Of course, women are also being recruited to support and marry ISIS soldiers....
> Dr. Erin Saltman researches radicalization and estimates that one tenth of foreign recruits for ISIS are women. Saltman theorizes that women are drawn to

the image of a Muslim utopia, that they perceive a need to protect Islam from hostile global forces, and that they are caught up in the romance of a moral purpose and may see jihadists as heroes fighting for a good cause.[198]

With the use of the Internet and the diligence of US intelligence and investigative services, it had become more difficult for the likes of bin Laden to plan and execute terror plots on American soil. When he was killed by a US Navy SEAL team and his computer, cell phones, and technical devices were confiscated, the world finally knew how he had communicated:

> Holed up in his walled compound in northeast Pakistan with no phone or Internet capabilities, bin Laden would type a message on his computer without an Internet connection, then save it using a thumb-sized flash drive. He then passed the flash drive to a trusted courier, who would head for a distant Internet café.
>
> At that location, the courier would plug the memory drive into a computer, copy bin Laden's message into an email, and send it. Reversing the process, the courier would copy any incoming email to the flash drive and return to the compound, where bin Laden would read his messages offline.
>
> ...Navy SEALs hauled away roughly 100 flash memory drives after they killed bin Laden, and officials said they appear to archive the back-and-forth

communication between bin Laden and his associates around the world.[199]

Bin Laden's death has not stopped jihadists from continuing to search out plans for assembling improvised explosive devices, exchange strategies for implementing attacks, disseminate propaganda, and solicit funds to support their criminal activities.

There is no more fruitful and abundant ground to be found for fanatical Islamic organizations than *YouTube*, *Facebook* and *Twitter*. It is a recruiter's dream.

An American Hiroshima?

One month after terrorists flew fuel-laden passenger jets into the World Trade Center and the Pentagon, President Bush was presented with an even more diabolical scenario. George Tenet, CIA director, informed the president at the Daily Intelligence Briefing that "Dragonfire," a CIA agent, relayed information that al Qaeda operatives were in possession of a ten-kiloton nuclear bomb, apparently stolen from the Russian arsenal. "Dragonfire" was convinced that the nuclear device was not only on American soil, but was, in fact, in New York City:

> "'It was brutal," a US official told *Time*. It was also highly classified and closely guarded. Under the aegis of the White House's Counterterrorism Security Group, part of the National Security Council, the suspected nuke was kept secret so as not to panic the people of New York. Senior FBI officials were not in

the loop. Former mayor Rudolph Giuliani says he was never told about the threat. In the end, the investigators found nothing and concluded that Dragonfire's information was false. But few of them slept better. They had made a chilling realization: if terrorists did manage to smuggle a nuclear weapon into the city, there was almost nothing anyone could do about it.[200]

Why is the thought of a terrorist organization possessing a nuclear weapon so frightening? America's entire nuclear defense has always been based upon the premise of MAD (mutually assured destruction), or the hope of intercepting intercontinental ballistic missiles in flight through something like the "Star Wars" program of defense satellites. (Israel currently has the Iron Dome missile defense system that successfully targets incoming rockets launched from the confines of its Arab neighbors' land.) No country with nuclear weapons would dare attack America because they know immediate, retaliatory annihilation would result. However, a terrorist organization with no physical address, no telephone number, and no zip code would have no fear of such retaliation.

During the Dragonfire incident, President Bush's first order was to Vice President Dick Cheney. He was dispatched from Washington, D.C., to an unnamed site. Cheney would spend several weeks at the secret location. The president's second order was to a group of Nuclear Emergency Support Team specialists (NEST). They were sent to New York City to hunt for the suspected weapon. (The operation was so top secret that no one, not even Rudolph Giuliani, mayor of New York City, was notified.) In another development, the CIA Counterterrorism Center had intercepted dialogue on al Qaeda channels. However, little concrete information was provided that might have prevented the September 11 attacks in the United States.

The defining thought about a nuclear terrorist attack in the United States is that only about five percent of the ten million cargo containers entering US ports each year are thoroughly inspected.

The serious threat of a Muslim country with access to a nuclear weapon is a valid concern. The truth: Pakistan, a Muslim country, already possesses approximately fifty nuclear weapons, as well as materials for making at least that many more.

American military minds are deeply concerned about a nuclear attack in America. And Warren Buffet, well-known financier, says, "It will happen. It's inevitable. I don't see any way that it won't happen."[201]

Not if—but when.

CHAPTER EIGHTEEN

The Battle for the
Soul of America

We cannot just allow [our moral values] to be frittered away
because we're unwilling to defend them. This, I think, is absolutely
critical . . . our moral values will sustain us. Our values as a
civilization, our religious values, will sustain us because they
are civil values; they are tolerant values, and this, it seems to
me, is the kind of thing that will enable all of us to pull together
and sustain whatever efforts it takes to resist this attack on us

MORT ZUCKERMAN[202]
Editor-in-Chief of *US News & World Report*
and publisher/owner of the New York Daily News

THE BATTLE FOR THE SOUL of America became strikingly
apparent with three horrifying attacks in the 1960s: the assassinations of John F. Kennedy, Robert Kennedy, and Martin Luther King,
Jr. The murders of these three men were as devastating to that generation as was the bombing of Pearl Harbor on December 7, 1941, or
the attack on the Pentagon and the World Trade Center Towers on
September 11, 2001.

Just as the attack on Pearl Harbor plunged the US into a global fight for freedom, so the murders of those three men signaled the end of the age of innocence that had long been enjoyed by the American people. Almost overnight, we went from *I Love Lucy, Leave it to Beaver,* and *Father Knows Best* to Woodstock and the proclamation by German philosopher Friedrich Nietzsche that God was dead. Social revolution that initially seemed harmless—the Beatles, Mick Jagger and his Rolling Stones—was soon followed by the introduction of the LSD craze and hard drugs. The sexual revolution introduced more relaxed attitudes regarding promiscuous sex, open homosexuality, and the legalization of abortion. Soon a full-frontal assault was launched against traditional family values and an American culture steeped in the tenets of the Bible.

The Bible says, "You will know the truth, and the truth will set you free" (John 8:32). Rather than creating freedom, the social revolution of the 1960s enslaved. People became addicted to drugs, sex, pornography, and bizarre philosophical/spiritual beliefs. Values based on Judeo-Christian mores were left behind as the New Age generation turned to Eastern religions and its search for answers to life's biggest questions. Ouija boards supposedly provided insight for the searcher, Satanism saw a rise in practitioners, and we were subjected to the likes of Charles Manson and his demonic cult with a morbid fascination.

Appetites dictated actions, and nothing was sacred any longer. Homosexuals emerged from their closets and began to parade their perversion for the world to see. Not content to expose their sins to light, various gay and lesbian organizations sprang up demanding their "constitutional right" to foist their lifestyles on an unsuspecting public. The apostle Paul in his letter to the Romans said it this way:

In the same way the men also abandoned natural relations with women and were inflamed with lust for one another. Men committed shameful acts with other men, and received in themselves the due penalty for their perversion.

Furthermore, just as they did not think it worthwhile to retain the knowledge of God, so God gave them over to a depraved mind, so that they do what ought not to be done. . . . Although they know God's righteous decree that those who do such things deserve death, they not only continue to do these very things but also approve of those who practice them (Romans 1:27_28, 32).

Our politically correct society today, rather than taking a stand against the homosexual lifestyle, either turns a blind eye with an attitude that it "doesn't affect me," or has bought into the "victimization theory" that being gay is genetic, and there's nothing that can be done about it. Gays, lesbians, and transgenders have labeled themselves a persecuted minority, worthy of particular protection and treatment in their view. They contend that "gay rights" means the gay community has been mistreated and deprived of the fundamental liberties enjoyed by other Americans.

In order to gain acceptance for a perverted lifestyle, gay activists have claimed at various times that Eleanor Roosevelt, Walt Whitman, and even Jesus Christ and the apostle Paul were gay. According to Marshall Kirk and Hunter Madsen in their textbook on gay acceptance:

Famous historical figures are considered especially

useful to us: . . . first, they are . . . dead as a doornail, hence are in no position to deny the truth and sue for libel.[203]

Another tactic used by groups that wish to intimidate and terrorize their detractors is to associate opposition with the infamous Adolf Hitler and his Nazi regime. Said Kirk and Madsen:

> Most contemporary hate groups on the Religious Right will bitterly resent the implied connection between homo-hatred and Nazi Fascism.[204]

This is not about truth; it's about blatant exploitation to advance an agenda: same-sex marriage, openly gay teachers in our public schools, and the acceptance of homosexuality as a normal, "alternative" lifestyle. Did you ever think you would see an openly homosexual movie nominated for an Oscar; homosexual liaisons openly portrayed on television; children's programs teaching that sometimes families have two moms or two dads? If you doubt that, monitor more closely what your children watch.

Nowadays, right is wrong, and wrong is right. Those who oppose the homosexual lifestyle and agenda are labeled "hate-mongers." The truth has been changed into a lie that will ultimately plunge those who embrace it down the slippery slope to hell. The push for gay rights will not end until every opponent is humiliated and quieted.

"Behold, I Stand at the Door . . . "

Most can remember the classic painting of Jesus standing outside a door waiting to be allowed entry. That poignant portrayal of Christ on the outside, wanting to fellowship with His creation is never more powerful than it is today. Prayer has been banished from schools; suits have been filed to force Congress to remove "under God" from the *Pledge of Allegiance*; displays of the Ten Commandments have been removed from public buildings; the motto "in God we trust" is in danger of deletion from our currency. Teachers have been forbidden even to carry a personal Bible in view of students, Christian literature has been excised from library shelves, religious Christmas carols have been banned from school programs, "spring break" has replaced the Easter vacation, and Christmas vacation has become "winter recess."

We can but ask ourselves: Are we better off today than we were in 1963 when, following a suit filed by Madelyn Murray O'Hare, the US Supreme Court in an eight-to-one decision voted to ban "coercive" prayer and Bible-reading from public schools in America? Are our schools safer? Are fewer kids on drugs? Are fewer kids engaged in promiscuous sex? Are fewer crimes committed by school-age children?

Battle after battle has slowly stripped Christians in America of their rights. On July 19, 2004, after a lengthy fight, a 5,300-pound monument of the Ten Commandments was removed from the Alabama courthouse rotunda. Judge Roy O. Moore, who had championed the cry to leave the monument in place, was removed from office—all in the guise of the separation of church and state. The American courts that espouse such movements as "gay rights," "abortion rights," and even "animal rights" are now pursuing the right to be godless. I wrote in *The American Prophecies*:

> We have rejected the foundation of our culture that has traditionally held us together—God and the Holy

Scriptures—and as our culture drifts away from that center, we . . . no longer hear His voice. As a nation, our innocence is being drowned. Things are falling apart. In our halls of justice, in our pulpits, and in the political arenas, those who would speak for God not only lack the conviction to be effective, they are being systematically silenced because of a perverted interpretation of "separation of church and state." First Amendment rights are denied to those who would speak for God, while those who fight for self, special interest, and immorality are passionately intense . . . as the "spirit of the world" takes over. . . . We have witnessed this spirit being more active in our world than ever before through the "isms" of fascism, Nazism, communism, and terrorism—the greatest threats to human liberty we have ever faced.[205]

When the first Continental Congress set out to write the document that would govern the fledgling United States, not one time did our founding fathers adopt the words "separation of church and state." It's not there! Read it for yourself:

Congress shall make no law respecting the establishment of religion, or prohibiting the free exercise thereof.[206]

In the twenty-first century, the courts of our land protect perversion while chastising the Church. The writers of the

Constitution would likely be amazed at the interpretation of the document over which they shed blood, sweat, and tears, and appalled at the lack of moral clarity in America today. The men who approved the purchase of Bibles with congressional funds, the men who regularly called for national days of prayer and fasting, the men who appointed Senate chaplains, would mourn the path down which succeeding Congresses and Supreme Courts have taken this once-proud nation.

John Lennon proclaimed that the Beatles were more popular than Jesus. *Time* magazine reporter John T. Elson wrote, "There is an acute feeling that the churches on Sunday are preaching about the existence of a God who is nowhere visible in their daily lives,"[207] and questioned the dedication of professing Christians. According to Elson's article, God has been replaced by science, and the Church has become "secularized."

With the lack of moral clarity in the secularized church, is there any wonder that this malaise has spread to the governing bodies of the nation? The bedrock foundation of the faith of our fathers has been replaced with shifting sands. The sacrifices of those who have gone before, from the War of Independence that birthed this nation to the War on Terror birthed on 9/11, have been diminished. The blood of dead soldiers, patriots from the past, cries to us from battlefields around the world. These men and women sacrificed all to ensure freedom for all. Perhaps Dr. James Dobson summed it up most succinctly when he admonished:

> We're at a pivotal point in the history of this country. Be a participant. Don't sit on the sidelines while our basic freedoms are lost.[208]

Darkness Descends

I vividly remember the horrifying pictures of New York City following the World Trade Center attack on 9/11. Clouds of black smoke and debris rushed through the cement canyons of that vibrant city, leaving death and destruction in their wake. The vision of people jumping from windows of the burning and collapsing buildings rather than face a certain and gruesome death inside the towers will be forever etched in my mind.

Natural disasters in recent years have produced equally nightmarish memories—the wall of water, the tsunami that devastated parts of South Asia in December 2004; Hurricane Katrina that ravaged the Gulf Coast in August 2005. But none can compare with the amoral blanket of darkness that has settled over America. We see it in movies, television, magazines, and on billboards; we hear it in music that seems to possess the listener; we shoot it into our veins, smoke it in a pipe, or down it from a bottle. It's the epitome of evil.

The "anything goes" sexual revolution of the 1960s was fueled by such "scientific studies" as the Kinsey Report—a man who was said to have sexually abused children in the name of science—and fed by the likes of Hugh Hefner's "Playboy philosophy." The advent of the Internet has only served to make the sexual revolution more readily available.

Internet pornography is a $57 billion industry worldwide, $12 billion in the US alone. According to *Internet Filter Review*, "US porn revenue exceeds the combined revenues of ABC, NBC, and CBS."[209] The average age of a child exposed to pornography on the Internet is eleven years old, and a staggering ninety percent of eight- to sixteen-year-olds have viewed pornography online.

Another favorite pastime of the morally decadent is to try to bring God down to their level. Taking the constitutional edict that "all men are created equal," they have applied it to religion and have declared that all religions are the same. "We are all going to the same place," they say. "We're just taking different roads to get there." Sin has been banished from our vocabulary; the cross of Christ has been reduced to costume jewelry (the gaudier the better); the blood of Christ has been counted as worthless. Religions that once elicited horror, Satanists and witches, are accorded equality with Judaism and Christianity, and are, in fact, featured in the Religion Sections of the newspaper. And who would have thought that Anton LaVey's *Satanic Bible* would become a collector's item, sometimes selling for as much as $1,000 per copy.

It has been said that a human being has a God-shaped hole in his heart, a place that can only be filled with a relationship with his Creator. It is a spiritual law written on a tablet of flesh. Those who try to fill that void with everything imaginable—drugs, sex, pornography, alcohol, perversion, pagan religions—are only lying to themselves.

There is neither time nor space to fully discuss stem cell research, the divorce plague, child abuse, and the "feminism mystique" of Gloria Steinem. All, however, have contributed to secular America's slide into depravity and debauchery. And the starkest reality of all is that the secularized church has often concurred. Isaiah 5:20 says:

> Woe to those who call evil good and good evil,
> who put darkness for light and light for darkness,
> who put bitter for sweet and sweet for bitter.

We have clearly reached the point that the apostle Paul expressed in his first letter to Timothy:

> The Spirit clearly says that in later times some will abandon the faith and follow deceiving spirits and things taught by demons. Such teachings come through hypocritical liars, whose consciences have been seared as with a hot iron (1 Timothy 4:1–2).

No? When did you last weep for an abuse victim; mourn the senseless death of an innocent and defenseless child; reach out to a battered wife; donate to a clinic that offers an alternative to abortion?

The genie of evil has been let out of the bottle. America has sown the wind and is reaping the whirlwind. Babies die daily, aborted, sacrificed on the altar of self-interest. Abortion has become a valid means of birth control for many women. Have a one-night stand; get pregnant; no problem! Take a morning-after pill, or run down to the abortion clinic on the corner. After all, it's only "tissue," not a real baby. It's a fetus, not a child fearfully and wonderfully made. Is there any wonder Dr. Billy Graham said that if America failed to repent of her evil, God would have to apologize to Sodom and Gomorrah?

A Tolerance for Evil

On September 11, 2001, truly a modern "Day of Infamy" America met evil head on when nineteen Islamic fanatics commandeered four American airliners, piloted two into the World Trade Towers and a third into the Pentagon. The fourth airliner, likely headed for a target in Washington, D.C., was retaken by passengers and crashed into a field in Pennsylvania. It was our first taste of the hatred of jihad as preached by radical Islamic clerics.

Immediately following the attack, the politically correct were hard at work to avoid calling a terrorist a terrorist. Some objected to the use of the words *Islamic* or *Muslim* in describing these mass murders. Others spurned the use of the word *terrorist*. While the American public was traumatized and paralyzed by the horrific events, members of the American press were locked in debate over how not to offend a particular segment of society. Never mind that Osama bin Laden had issued an edict calling on every *Muslim* to kill Americans.

Before the dust had settled over New York City and the fires were extinguished at the Pentagon, these spin doctors were out-lining their campaign to thwart any attempt to hunt down those responsible for the carnage. What followed in the weeks after 9/11 was a succession of antiwar demonstrations reminiscent of the Vietnam era, a series of peace vigils, and other protests. America was declared guilty of aggression, having somehow deserved the attacks due to some perceived ill against Islam and/or its adherents. Those not blaming the US found another scapegoat in Israel. Why was it so hard to place the blame precisely where it belonged, on a group of radical Islamofascists spouting a hate-filled ideology and killing innocent people?

Lesbian writer Susan Sontag wrote in defense of those who called the hijackers "cowards":

> And if the word "cowardly" is to be used, it might be more aptly applied to those who kill from beyond the range of retaliation, high in the sky, than to those willing to die themselves in order to kill others. In the matter of courage (a morally neutral virtue): what-ever may be said of the perpetrators of Tuesday's slaughter, they were not cowards.[210]

Not cowards? Nineteen men merely sauntered aboard four air-liners loaded with passengers, men, women, and children, took control of those giants of the air, murdered not only the passengers but thousands of other innocent bystanders without ever looking them or their families in the eyes; and that is not a cowardly act?

Yet another writer took Americans to task for the upsurge in patriotism and the number of American flags that were raised in the days immediately following the terrorist attack. The flag was purported to be a visual symbol of bigotry, criminality, hatred, and even homophobia in America.

The novelist Barbara Kingsolver jumped into the mêlée with this liberal, enlightening pronouncement:

> Patriotism threatens free speech with death. It is infuriated by thoughtful hesitation, construc-tive criticism of our leaders and pleas for peace. It despises people of foreign birth who've spent years learning our culture and contributing their talents to our economy. It has specifically blamed homosexuals, feminists and the American Civil Liberties Union. In other words, the American flag stands for intimida-tion, censorship, violence, bigotry, sexism, homopho-bia, and shoving the Constitution through a paper shredder? Who are we calling terrorists here?[211]

President Bush was repeatedly denounced for having stated unequivocally that America would hunt down the perpetrators and punish the planners of the attack on America. The president was careful to explain that any strike would be specifically directed at the organizations that funded and harbored terrorists worldwide.

In an address to the joint session of Congress on September 20, 2001, President Bush precisely identified the target:

> Our enemy is a radical network of terrorists, and every government that supports them. Our war on terror begins with al Qaeda, but it does not end there. It will not end until every terrorist group of global reach has been found, stopped, and defeated.[212]

The president warned the American people not to expect the War on Terror to be concluded swiftly:

> Americans should not expect one battle, but a lengthy campaign, unlike any other we have ever seen. It may include dramatic strikes, visible on TV, and covert operations, secret even in success. We will starve terrorists of funding, turn them one against another, drive them from place to place, until there is no refuge or no rest. And we will pursue nations that provide aid or safe haven to terrorism. Every nation, in every region, now has a decision to make. Either you are with us, or you are with the terrorists. From this day forward, any nation that continues to harbor or support terrorism will be regarded by the United States as a hostile regime.[213]

And so the war against bin Laden and the Taliban in Afghanistan was launched, followed by the war in Iraq. Saddam Hussein had for decades provided a safe house for international terrorists. He gave sanctuary to Abu Abbas, the mastermind of the *Achille Lauro* hijacking in 1985, and Abu Nidal, a terrorist mercenary said to be responsible for the deaths of as many as nine hundred people. He also provided safe harbor for the lone escapee from the 1993 World Trade Center bombing, Abdul Rahman Yasin. Hussein doled out large sums of money to the families of suicide bombers that died in attacks against Jews in Israel. It seemed only natural to turn the attention in the War on Terror to Saddam Hussein.

It is interesting to note that the focus on Saddam Hussein began not with President George W. Bush, but with former president Bill Clinton in 1998. In 1998, Hussein ousted the UN weapons inspectors in clear violation of the cease-fire agreement following the First Gulf War. The Clinton Administration requested that Congress draft what was called the Iraqi Liberation Act. The act proposed that a regime change be sought. The bill, as signed by Clinton, stated that "it should be the policy of the United States to seek to remove the Saddam Hussein regime from power in Iraq, and replace it with a democratic government."[214] Furthermore, the Senate approved the use of force in order to achieve that objective. It was overwhelmingly supported by a majority in both the House and the Senate.

With such a show of support for regime change in Iraq, it was only natural that President Bush might expect the same kind of support from Congress when Saddam Hussein began to openly defy UN calls for weapons inspections. The president appealed to the UN to call a halt to Hussein's game playing. In his speech, he reiterated that all of the sanctions and all of the incentives to tempt Hussein to comply had been in vain. Regrettably, a toothless UN was impotent against the "butcher of Baghdad."

Across the country, murmurs of dissent became a roar of antiwar protests. Not surprisingly, Jimmy Carter entered the fray on the side of the dissenters. He averred that Baghdad posed no threat to America. Carter's declaration was soon accompanied by a similar statement from the ubiquitous Al Gore. The cacophony grew as some members of Congress joined in the debate. It seemed that many could not quite understand how a brutal dictator who had at various times invaded both Iran and Kuwait, committed mass murder with WMDs against his own countrymen, and opened his borders to avowed terrorists could possibly pose a threat to anyone.

As the countdown to an Iraq invasion proceeded, the number of antiwar protestors grew, not just in the US but worldwide. Were they protesting the attack on America by al Qaeda? Were they protesting Hussein's brutal attacks against his own people? No, the targets of the demonstrations were the United States and Israel. America was labeled a "terrorist state" and President Bush was unfairly compared to Adolf Hitler. The Washington protest crowd included the likes of Representative John Conyers and Charles Rangel, and New York City councilman Charles Barron. In his comments, Barron placed the United States in the same "axis of evil" category as Iran, Iraq, and North Korea.

Unfortunately, not every liberal in America agreed with talk show host Alan Colmes, formerly a co-host on *Hannity & Colmes* broadcasts. In his book *Red, White, & Liberal*, the very liberal Mr. Colmes wisely said:

> The time to debate going to war was before the fact. Once, American men and women were in harm's way that debate was over and lost by those of us who opposed the intervention.[215]

Conversely, a professor of anthropology at Columbia University, Nicholas De Genova, gave this rousing speech at what was cavalierly call a "teach-in":

> Peace is not patriotic. Peace is subversive, because peace anticipates a very different world than the one in which we live—a world where the US would have no place. . . . The only true heroes are those who find ways that help defeat the US military. I personally would like to see a million Mogadishus. [216]

Oddly enough, these comments were made in reference to, "the ambush of US forces by an al-Qaeda warlord in Somalia in 1993. The Americans were there on a humanitarian mission to feed starving Somali Muslims. The al-Qaeda warlord was stealing the food and selling it on the black market. His forces killed 18 American soldiers and dragged their bodies through the streets in an act designed to humiliate their country."[217]

The hateful rhetoric aimed at American troops engaged in life-and-death battles did not lessen when American troops marched into Baghdad on April 9, 2003; indeed, the hue and cry to bring the soldiers home only escalated. Even as Hussein's heinous prisons were emptied and his monstrous torture chambers taken apart, even as tons of humanitarian aid flowed into Baghdad to feed the hungry and provide much-needed medication to the ill, the Liberal Left was condemning the US incursion into Iraq. Like De Genova, the most open and voluble of the detractors were among America's university elite.

CHAPTER NINETEEN

The Broad Reach of Islamofascism

Islamofascism as the phenomenon manifests itself in our world emanates directly from Islam. The lust for world conquest and the revival of the caliphate, the terrorist violence out of a desire for jihad as commanded in the Koran, the hatred for Jews and Israel, the rejection of democracy and social equality (Taliban ideology prohibits women from working or educating themselves), the Islamic customary demand that women wear the death-shroud burqa, xenophobia (the shunning of foreigners and strangers)— all of these are deeply imbedded in the Muslim world. These things and others are outgrowths of Islam, not fascism. But on account of their barbarity and inhumanity generally, the term Islamofascism is often used so as not to offend the mainstream.

YONATAN SILVERMAN [218]

THERE HAS LONG BEEN a fascination in the Islamic world with all things Hitler. In fact, the Arab states of Syria and Iraq, both Ba'th Party regimes, were patterned after Hitler's fascist concepts. Just as Hitler's vision was a world under the domination of his Nazi regime, so the vision of today's radical Islamic clerics is that of a world under the domination of Islamic, or Sharia, Law. This was never more apparent than when the Ayatollah Ruhollah Khomeini launched his Islamic Revolution even as the shah of Iran was fleeing the country.

The Liberal Left in America took up the banner of the oppressed and downtrodden in Iran and ran with it. What followed was a litany of charges leveled against America for her support of the shah's regime, for supporting an Israel locked in a life-and-death struggle with the Palestinians for bombing Hiroshima and Nagasaki at the end of World War II, for Vietnam, and on and on. Palestinian terrorists became "freedom fighters" and the innocent victims of their atrocious acts became the instigators simply for daring to live in Israel. Suicide bombers who brought devastation to buses, restaurants, busy shopping malls, and even schools were given the righteous designation of "martyr."

Radical Islam has given birth to a weapon that truly cheapens human life: the suicide bomber. But this will be as nothing compared to the weapons of mass destruction under preparation in radical Islamist states—weapons whose targets may begin with Israel but ultimately will be aimed at the world's greatest democracy.

The secular Liberal Left refuses to accept the very serious threat posed by the Islamic radicals. They refuse to accept the fact that every American (place of origin not withstanding), every Jew wherever found, and every Muslim who disagrees with the particular philosophy of the Islamic fanatics is a target. University professors will not be spared simply because they have supported the radical any more than the leftists were when siding with Khomeini in deposing the shah; erudite philosophers will not be spared because of their education; the religious Left will not be spared simply because of their world view on religion. While their support is now welcomed and heralded worldwide by terrorist organizations, once the terrorists reach their goals, they will turn their guns on these as "infidels" just as they did following the Islamic Revolution of 1979. No, all will be required to conform to the doctrines and dictates of the mad mullahs that have hijacked an entire religion—or else.

In fact, on February 26, 1993, Yigal Carmon, counterterrorism adviser to the prime minister of Israel, warned the Pentagon that in his estimation, radical Islam was an imminent threat to America. At the end of his briefing, he was told by smirking critics that they did not consider religion to be a threat to national security.

Following his address at the Pentagon, Carmon flew to New York City, where, while having lunch at 12:18 p.m., a huge explosion took place nearby: Islamic terrorists had attempted to blow up the World Trade Center; six were killed and 1,000 injured.

Islamic terrorists finished the job on September 11, 2001, and still no one wanted to admit *why* we were attacked—just by whom. Osama bin Laden was only the vanguard of a religious hatred that will eventually engulf the entire world if not stopped.

Days before the 9/11 attacks, the UN sponsored a World Conference against Racism, Racial Discrimination, Xenophobia, and Related Intolerance. Hidden behind that grand title was a hate-filled attack against Western democracy in general and the United States and Israel in particular. Charges such as racism, slavery, and colonialism were leveled against these two democracies. It is not surprising that the Muslim regimes still using these practices escaped such criticism. No mention was made of the genocide in Rwanda or Iraq; no condemnation was levied against Iran's use of children as minesweepers during the Iran–Iraq War; nor was there mention of the suppressive regimes in Saudi Arabia or of Syria's subjugation of the Lebanese people.

In attendance at the conference were such stalwart liberals

as Jesse Jackson and Julian Bond and ten members of the US Congressional Black Caucus. In this world forum, the group took its own country to task and called for the US to pay trillions of dollars in compensation for the slavery that had been abolished in the US in 1865. No such demands were made against other states, including those African nations that willingly participated in the trafficking of human beings. Although Cuba is said to have imported more slaves than the United States, favorite son Fidel Castro escaped condemnation unscathed. This only served to underline the double standard still practiced by the UN.

The rhetoric inside the conference became more bitter, and the proceedings deteriorated into a blatant anti-Semitic attack against Israel, President Bush, and Secretary of State Colin Powell. The Israeli delegation exited the proceedings in protest. Some conference-goers took to the streets to parade vile posters with swastikas and pictures of Jews with fangs dripping blood. Richard Heideman, president of B'nai B'rith International, in an open letter to all Jewish community leaders, said of the Durban Conference:

> We and other delegates have been bombarded by Nazi-like propaganda, by caricatures, by hate material, by physical and verbal assaults and by intimidation. And all within sight of U.N. officials, all in clear and open violation of the charters, conventions and declarations which define the very purpose of the world body.[219]

The British representative of the World Jewish Congress, Lord Greville Janner, said it "was the worst example of anti-Semitism I've ever seen."[220]

The conference was attended by a number of nongovernmental organizations (NGOs), funded by the Ford Foundation and drawn from the ranks of the American Civil Liberties Union, The NAACP, the National Lawyers Guild (labeled by J. Edgar Hoover a subversive organization and possibly a cover for the Communist Party), and the pro-Castro Center for Constitutional Rights.

Leftist groups that had once focused on social justice turned their focus almost entirely on Palestine and Iraq. These two terrorist-harboring and supporting states became the darlings of liberals worldwide. Countries and organizations that differed ideologically became frightful enemies. Their venom focused on one group in particular, the World Trade Organization, whose projects were deemed a major cause of environmental concerns worldwide.

The hatred of this organization and its participants congealed into one of the largest protests, some 50,000 strong, ever seen in Seattle, Washington. Anarchy ruled as streets were blocked, Molotov cocktails destroyed local businesses, and chaos reigned. Successive meetings of the World Trade Organization in Czechoslovakia, Canada, and Italy were also disrupted by demonstrators. From these protests was born the World Social Forum, a group whose professed aim is to "mobilize solidarity for the Palestinian people and their struggle for self-determination as they face brutal occupation by the Israeli state." Simply put, this world coalition of leftist liberals has one aim: the emasculation of the United States and the destruction of Israel.

Palestine, the Catalyst

Various wars that have occurred in the Middle East were over what has been perceived to be skirmishes on the periphery of the current war on terror, and therefore completely separate from the jihad declared on the United States. It is easier, then, to view the terrorists as despairing victims and not the murderers and hate-mongers they are.

When the original UN partition plan was drawn for Palestine, the Jews and Palestinians were to occupy twenty percent of the Palestine Mandate initiated by the League of Nations in the 1920s. Great Britain was entrusted with the execution of the mandate. The League and Britain determined in September 1922 that a homeland for the Jews would not include any of the land east of the Jordan River, three-fourths of the territory outlined in the mandate. That area would ultimately become the Hashemite Kingdom of Jordan, an area with a Palestinian majority. Jews were banned from settling anywhere in that area.

In 1937, a royal commission of inquiry was given the directive to try to resolve the differences between Palestinians and Jews. A plan was put forth to divide the territory into two separate states. This was rejected by the Arabs because it called for the creation of a Jewish state in which some Palestinians would live. The Jews resisted the plan because it only allotted them approximately 1,900 of the available 10,310 square miles in the territory. They, however, agreed to negotiate, while the Arabs refused.

Again, in 1939, the British tried to persuade the Arabs to agree to a state in Palestine, and a limitation on the number of Jews that would be allowed to immigrate. This was also declined by the Arabs. How can one explain, then, the vilification of the Jews that has resulted simply because they occupy one percent of Arab lands in the Middle East and only ten percent of the entire Palestine Mandate?

Make no mistake, the Middle East conflict is neither about land, nor about the establishment of a state for the Palestinian people. Both have been offered and rejected various times—in 1939 before the establishment of the nation of Israel, again in Oslo, which introduced the Oslo Accords, at Camp David, and in Washington, D.C. Rather, the conflict is about the destruction of the State of Israel and the annihilation of the Jewish people. The Palestinian Authority doesn't want Jerusalem divided, but instead wants all of Jerusalem. They do not simply desire to occupy the West Bank, but all of Israel from the Jordan River to the Mediterranean Sea. It is not a matter of "land for peace"; it is a matter of using any means possible to rid the Middle East of the Jewish population altogether. They do not wish the subjugation of the Jewish people; they wish their destruction. This was Egyptian leader Gamal Abdel Nasser's agenda. It was Yasser Arafat's agenda, and it has also been the agenda of Bashar al-Assad of Syria and the current leaders in Iran.

Perhaps Yasser Arafat condensed the Arab–Israeli conflict into the most succinct statement of all when he said:

> We shall oppose the establishment of this state to the last member of the Palestinian people, for if ever such a state is established it will spell the end of the whole Palestinian cause [the obliteration of Israel].[221]

Unfinished Business

Political pundits are quick to mistakenly point out that the war in Iraq was President Bush's war, when, in fact, it was an unfinished chapter in the presidency of Bill Clinton. When the World Trade Center was bombed in 1993, Clinton was in office. It was on his watch that Americans were targeted by Islamic radicals. It was the

Clinton Administration that failed to hold their regimes responsible for the attack. It was in 1998 that Saddam Hussein defied the UN and expelled the weapons inspectors. Clinton went so far as to call for regime change, and launched air and missile strikes against Iraq, but considered nothing further. Former CIA director James Woolsey had this to say about the effectiveness of the missile strikes:

> In '93, Saddam [Hussein] tried to kill former president [George H. W.] Bush in Kuwait with a bomb. President Clinton launched two-dozen cruise missiles against an Iraqi intelligence headquarters in the middle of the night, so it would be empty. [He] has his secretary of state explain that we did it in the middle of the night so there wouldn't be anyone there. I don't know what we had against Iraqi cleaning women and night watchmen, but I would not have called that an effective response.[222]

When George Bush picked up the gauntlet thrown down by Saddam Hussein and began his campaign to pursue terrorist-supporting and terrorist-harboring states, he was convincingly supported. Even his previous opponent in the run for the White House, Al Gore, strongly favored the action. However, once the troops were committed to engage Hussein's forces, the detractors began to inexorably rise to the surface. Democratic leaders were urged to abandon Bush and resist the call for the invasion of Iraq.

A petition signed by thousands, including Al Sharpton, Jesse Jackson, Gloria Steinem, and the usual host of Hollywood celebrities caused the political Left to rethink their commitment. Suddenly Al Gore, once a proponent of the war in Iraq, began to criticize

President Bush when he saw that doing the right thing might be politically dangerous to his agenda. He was soon joined by former president Jimmy Carter, who seemed to have conveniently forgotten that President Bush had sought the help of the UN Security Council. He also seemed to have forgotten that Democratic President Bill Clinton had approved strikes against Afghanistan and Iraq, among others, without prior UN sanction.

Carter and Gore proved to be just the tip of the iceberg of quick Democratic opposition to the war. House Minority Leader Nancy Pelosi made her dissatisfaction known just as quickly in a press conference soon after American forces entered Baghdad. Said Pelosi, who voted against going to war with Iraq, "I have absolutely no regret about my vote on this war. . . . The cost in human lives. The cost to our budget, probably $100 billion. We could have probably brought down that statue [referring to the toppled statue of Saddam Hussein] for a lot less."[223]

Before the war began, the Liberal Left set a course to defame, denigrate, and disparage President Bush with no thought of the thousands of troops stationed in and around Iraq. They had no regard for the newly elected Iraqi officials who have continued their struggle to build a stable government on the rubble of Saddam Hussein's evil dictatorship. The president's credibility, voracity, and ideologies have been questioned. He was accused of having conducted a pointless and independent war, devoid of allies such as Russia and France.

It was pointed out time and again that Saddam Hussein possessed no weapons of mass destruction, as the president had led the American people to believe—this despite the fact that Hussein had used chemical weapons in the war with Iran, and again to murder scores of his own people in the Kurdish north. No credence was given to the proposal that Hussein had ample time before the beginning of the conflict to move those weapons across the border into Syria and entrust them to al-Assad. And the fact that some twenty-five million Iraqis had been freed from the control of the vicious Hussein was casually overlooked.

The presidential campaign of 2004 was an all-out assault against the Iraq War, the Bush doctrine on terror, and the American people who strongly supported the president. It proved the truth of the adage that if you're told a lie often enough, it becomes believable. Howard Dean, a rabid war critic, tossed his hat into the candidate ring, soon accompanied by Al Gore, Dick Gephardt, and John Kerry. The candidates vied for the honor of who could produce the most hateful campaign rhetoric against the war in Iraq. It was even suggested by some that the war in Iraq was conceived before the attack on America on September 11, 2001.

At the end of a bitter and divisive campaign during which Senator Kerry proffered that the War on Terror was simply a police action and could easily be handled by occasional military intervention, and accused the White House of assaulting the basic freedoms of the American people, George Bush was reelected to another term as president. The Liberal Left, however, remains firmly committed to the agenda of appeasement and apathy.

Attack of the Liberals

Attacks against America's spiritual and moral foundation have been ceaseless during the past decades. Yet, according to the *Barna Report*, forty-seven percent of American adults attend church on a typical weekend, seventy-one percent believe in God described as the all-powerful, all-knowing, perfect creator of the universe who rules the world today, and fifty-four percent of all Americans identify themselves as Christians. Americans, in general, are still church attendees. Witness the success of the Left Behind series by Tim LaHaye and Jerry Jenkins, *The Purpose Driven Life* by Rick Warren, and Mel Gibson's movie *The Passion of the Christ*. The Bible is still an all-time national bestseller.

Why, then, has a largely Christian nation allowed the marketplace and the political arena to be stripped of everything godly? Why has abortion flourished? Why has God been taken out of schools, while the distribution of condoms is allowed? Everything anti-Christian is promoted, and Christians are ridiculed. The desire to fit in has reduced the average Christian to a spineless jellyfish, afraid to speak up for fear of derision.

The Church, once a stronghold of everything good and right, has too often become just another club where people gather to socialize. It, too, has sometimes fallen prey to the corruption of the secular, and has become a watered-down version of its former self, palatable to all, and effective for none. Christians have become indistinguishable from the nonbeliever down the street. Researcher George Barna had this to say about Christianity today:

If Jesus Christ came to this planet as a model of how we ought to live, then our goal should be to act like Jesus. Sadly, few people consistently demonstrate the love, obedience, and priorities of Jesus. The primary reason that people do not act like Jesus is because they do not think like Jesus. Behavior stems from what we think—our attitudes, beliefs, values, and opinions. Although most people own a Bible and know some of its content, our research found that most Americans have little idea how to integrate core biblical principles to form a unified and meaningful response to the challenges and opportunities of life. We're often more concerned with survival amidst chaos than with experiencing truth and significance.[224]

Even so, the Church remains America's last hope in a hopeless world. And who, in this truth-challenged, politically correct world will dare to stand up and deliver the unadulterated truth according to God's Word? As I ask this question, I'm reminded of the passage in Romans 1:25 (KJV) that speaks of those "who change the truth of God into a lie."

Russian dissident Alexander Solzhenitsyn pinpointed the transformation of Russia into a godless nation:

> If I were asked today to formulate as concisely as possible that main cause of the ruinous revolution hat swallowed up some 50 million of our people, I could not put it more accurately than to repeat: "Men had forgotten God; that is why all this happened."[225]

A new translation of the Bible launched in 2004, and endorsed by the British Archbishop of Canterbury, has done just that—changed the truth of God into a lie. Ruth Gledhill, a religious correspondent for the *London Times*, wrote, "Instead of condemning fornicators, adulterers, and 'abusers of themselves with mankind,' . . . the new version of his first letter to Corinth has St. Paul advising Christians not to go without sex for too long in case they get frustrated."[226]

In the King James Version, the passage in 1 Corinthians 7:8–9 reads in part, "Nevertheless [to avoid fornication] let every man have his own wife, and let every woman have her own husband." In the Good as New version, that passage reads, "My advice is for everyone to have a regular partner."[227]

In modern-day America, churches in general have moved more and more to the left; too often becoming a lobby for liberals, not a lighthouse for the lost. The Church has sometimes become more a launching pad for numerous political candidates rather than a sacred sanctuary of redemption. Organizations such as the National Council of Churches cater to the secularist agenda rather than truly representing millions of Evangelical Christians in America today.

Perhaps most disturbing of all is that the National Council of Churches receives funding from a variety of leftist organizations, i.e.:

> $100,000 from the Ford Foundation in 2000; $149,400 from the Annie E. Casey Foundation in 2000–2001; $150,000 from the Beldon Fund in 2001; $500,000 from the Lilly Endowment in 2002; $50,000 from the Rasmussen Foundation in 2003 and $75,000 from the Rockefeller Brothers Fund . . . [such funding] has done little to counter the contention of critics that the NCC, far from doing God's work, serves as little more than a vehicle to advance the left-wing interests of its leaders.[228]

Another trademark of the NCC is its condemnation of Israel as an aggressor and violator of human rights. Little, if any, acknowledgement is given to Israel's constant bombardment by missiles and suicide bombers via the countries that surround this strong US ally.

In fact, members of the organization have voted at various times to divest holdings associated with Israel in an attempt to cripple the economy of that tiny nation.

The Evangelical Right

The Evangelical Right in America has become, at various times, a scapegoat, the butt of jokes, a laughingstock, and a frequent target of the liberal media. Evangelicals are portrayed as nincompoops who are trying to impose their outdated theology on an enlightened population. In response, the Church has become paralyzed, hypnotized, and ostracized by the very people who most need to connect with it in order to hear the story of the saving grace of God.

It sometimes seems that the Church has given up, and is content to sit idly by watching a world doomed to hell, while placidly waiting for the remnant to be raptured. The Church has abandoned the Great Commission in favor of the Great Omission, taking on many of the characteristics of the church in Laodicea as described by the apostle John:

> So, because you are lukewarm—neither hot nor cold—I am about to spit you out of my mouth. You say, "I am rich; I have acquired wealth and do not need a thing." But you do not realize that you are wretched, pitiful, poor, blind, and naked (Revelation 3:16–17).

John W. Chalfant, author of *Abandonment Theology*, describes it this way:

Clergy and their followers have been teaching, preaching, and saturating the media and their church members with the doctrine of surrender and political non-involvement. They are not teaching us to surrender to Christ through obedience to the commandment of God. Rather, they tell us that America is finished, that the collapse of our heritage and our freedoms has been predetermined within a definable near-future time frame and is therefore beyond our control.[229]

The highly respected theologian, Dr. Francis Schaeffer, penned a sobering book just before his death. In *The Great Evangelical Disaster*, Schaeffer issued a somber and concise overview of the twentieth-century church. He wrote:

> Here is the great evangelical disaster—the failure of the evangelical world to stand up for truth as truth. . . . the evangelical church has accommodated to the world spirit of the age. . . . to accommodate to the world spirit . . . is nothing less than the most gross form of worldliness, we must say . . . with exceptions, the evangelical church is worldly and not faithful to the living Christ.[230]

What a tragic indictment, yet how true.

Rather than walking God's way, many demand their own way, throwing tantrums like wayward children when challenged by what the Bible really says. True to Isaiah 53:6 (KJV), "We have turned every one to his own way."

The desire for acceptance has replaced the hunger to draw close to Christ. Doubt has replaced determination; fear has overcome faith; conformity to the Word has been replaced with conformity to the world; and the voice of one "crying in the wilderness" has been replaced by a cacophony of celebrity seekers. Separation from the world has evolved into separation of church and state, and the consequences of removing God from the political process have had dire results for the true Church.

The good news is that there is a remnant. Not all Christians have bought in to the secular, Liberal Left agenda. It is because of these men and women, unnamed giants of the faith, prayer warriors all, that there is still hope. It is because they firmly hold to the truth in 2 Chronicles 7:14 (KJV):

> If my people, which are called by my name, shall humble themselves, and pray, and seek my face, and turn from their wicked ways; then will I hear from heaven, and will forgive their sin, and will heal their land.

America doesn't have to reap the whirlwind; we do not have to get what we deserve. God has graciously made a way of escape. The answer is in humility: "Humble yourselves, therefore, under God's mighty hand, that he may lift you up in due time" (I Peter 5:6.) We, like the apostle Peter after his denial of Christ, must become broken before the Lord in order to find forgiveness and restoration. Integrity must triumph over deception; the desire to do what is right must overcome the desire to conform to the mores of this world.

The Church must undergo the scrutiny of the Light. No longer can the Church tolerate the incursion of darkness; evil must be acknowledged and defined as such. The Church still has a choice. The words of Joshua ring in my spirit:

> But if serving the LORD seems undesirable to you, then choose for yourselves this day whom you will serve. . . . But as for me and my household, we will serve the LORD (Joshua 24:15).

The choice is yours and the day of reckoning could be closer than we might imagine.

As Christians, we believe in the blessed hope of the return of Jesus Christ. When He does, the combined military might of all the world powers will not be able to hinder His prophetic plan for the nation of Israel. The so-called New World Order will pass into oblivion when God's new order is finally revealed. When things look bleak, when the prospects for peace look dim, look up—for our Redemption is near.

Our Lord was asked by His disciples in Matthew 24:3 (KJV), "What shall be the sign of thy coming, and of the end of the world?" He began to tell them the signs beginning with the destruction of the Temple. In verse 2, Jesus prophesied that the Temple would be taken apart stone by stone forty years before it happened in AD 70. Jesus then revealed all the signs of His Second Coming and in verses 32–36 laid out a key sign: the sign of the fig tree, which has always been a symbol of the nation of Israel. That fig tree bloomed on May 14, 1948, according to Isaiah 66:8 (KJV): "Shall the earth be made to bring forth in one day? or shall a nation be born at once?" Jesus warned that no one would know the day or the hour of His return (Matthew 25:13). But He taught that the generation that saw the blooming of the fig tree would not pass away before He came.

Similarly, millions of Iranians are listening to the teachings of Ayatollah Yazdi, preparing for the second coming of the Islamic messiah, the Mahdi. There is an eerie correlation between the belief in the second coming of the Mahdi and the unfulfilled prophecies of Ezekiel, which describe a massive invasion of Israel by a great confederation of nations. It will be led by Gog and Magog, identified by Bible scholars as modern-day Russia.

Another of the countries identified in the attack is Persia, which is modern-day Iran—no surprise there. Many Evangelical

Christians see this as an alliance formed between Russia and Iran for the purpose of attacking the Jews in Israel. The war of Gog and Magog was predicted to strike Israel after the Jews came back. The prediction also speaks of a time when Israel is "brought back from the sword." In other words, the war will occur when Israel is at peace (Ezekiel 38:8, 11–12).

There is a fundamental difference between the Islamic prophecies of the second coming of the Mahdi and the Christian prophecies of the Second Coming of Jesus Christ. In Christian theology, the Apocalypse *follows* "the blessed Hope" or "Rapture" for which Christians await.

This is the opposite sequence from the apocalyptic event awaited by the Muslims who believe in the Twelfth Imam or Mahdi. The Rapture is a unique moment in history as Christ returns to Earth, when the "dead in Christ" shall rise to join living Believers and all are taken up to heaven to be with Jesus.

In other words, if a war is coming where Russia and Iran are allied against Israel, as Christians believe is foretold in the book of Ezekiel, the time sequences are different. For Muslims this war of the Apocalypse must take place before the second coming of the Mahdi.

As the nuclear crisis with Iran deepens, and Russia again rears its insatiable head on the international stage, millions of Christians worldwide are consulting their Bibles and praying to sort out how current world events fit into "last days" prophecies. Ezekiel 38:21–22 predicts massive human carnage as a result of the war. That Israel will win this great war is little consolation given the massive number of deaths Ezekiel predicts as a result of the conflict. When the president of Iran speaks from the podium of the United Nations

General Assembly and references the second coming of the Mahdi, should we be surprised that Christians are searching the prophecies of Ezekiel?

The apostle John received a vision on the Isle of Patmos in AD 95 that became the book of Revelation. In that vision he saw four riders on horseback, galloping across the earth, bringing deceit, destruction, death, and devastation. Those four riders are commonly known as the Four Horsemen of the Apocalypse. If you listen closely, you can almost hear the hoofbeats across the airwaves, Internet, and the pages of today's newspapers and magazines: wars, rumors of wars, earthquakes, drought, floods, and mayhem.

Revelation 5 begins with the unveiling of a scroll written on both sides and sealed with seven seals. Seals, in that day, were impressions made with wax, clay, or some other soft material that assured no unauthorized person had accessed the contents. The seals in John's vision had to be broken, one by one, to divulge the scroll's contents. Only Jesus was qualified to do this. As He broke each seal, another portion of God's revelation about the final days of the earth was disclosed, each time divulging a horror worse than the revelation before.

Daniel, the prophet who lived in ancient Babylon (modern-day Iraq) during Israel's captivity there, wrote of the mystery of the end times in Daniel 12:1–4, 8–10. It begins with these words from the angel Gabriel:

> At that time Michael, the great prince who protects your people, will arise. There will be a time of distress such as has not happened from the beginning of nations until then. But at that time your people—everyone whose name is found written in

the book—will be delivered. Multitudes who sleep in the dust of the earth will awake: some to everlasting life, others to shame and everlasting contempt. Those who are wise will shine like the brightness of the heavens, and those who lead many to righteousness, like the stars forever and ever. But you, Daniel, close up and seal the words of the scroll until the time of the end. . . . So I asked, "My lord, what will the outcome of all this be?" He replied, "Go your way, Daniel, because the words are closed up and sealed until the time of the end. Many will be purified, made spotless and refined, but the wicked will continue to be wicked. None of the wicked will understand, but those who are wise will understand."

In Matthew 24:3, when His disciples asked Him, "What will be the sign of your coming and of the end of the age?" Jesus replied (vv. 6–7): "You will hear of wars and rumors of wars, but see to it that you are not alarmed. Such things must happen, but the end is still to come. Nation will rise against nation, and kingdom against kingdom."

In the Museum of Modern Art in New York City, Umberto Boccioni's *The City Rises* shows the Four Horsemen of the Apocalypse in a modern urban setting. The museum is not far from Ground Zero, the spot where the World Trade Center towers were struck and collapsed. Ground Zero is also the term used to indicate the point at which a nuclear explosion occurs.

The massive oil painting is six feet by nine feet and singles out the horror of the third horse and its rider. Boccioni painted the black horse flailing wildly above the other horsemen. This is symbolic of what transpired in Hiroshima and Nagasaki, bringing an end to World War II. Even more frightening is the reality of a nuclear bomb or bombs in the hands of terrorists. The turmoil boiling in the cauldron that is the Middle East could make it infinitely easier for radical Islamic terrorist organizations to acquire nuclear devices.

Did the prophet Zechariah envision a nuclear holocaust? He was prompted by the Holy Spirit to write, "And this shall be the plague with which the Lord will strike all the people who fought against Jerusalem: Their flesh shall dissolve while they stand on their feet; Their eyes shall dissolve in their sockets; And their tongues shall dissolve in their mouths" (Zechariah 14:12 NKJV).

It may startle you to know that God doesn't predict the future; He foretells events to His prophets, who in turn prophesy to the people those things that God has foretold. God revealed His future plans to the prophets of old—Isaiah, Jeremiah, Daniel, Ezekiel, Zechariah, and others. Then, in His perfect timing, He allowed the prophesied events to become reality. He used ancient kings and kingdoms to chastise His errant children—the nation of Israel—and He used those same kings and kingdoms to return them to their homeland.

Seventy years after Nebuchadnezzar took the Jewish people captive, Cyrus allowed them to return to Israel. (This is what Daniel had prayed for in Daniel 9:17–19.) Not only were they allowed to return, but also Cyrus provided everything they needed to rebuild the Temple and the walls of the city. With their return to Jerusalem, he also relinquished into their care the items the Babylonians had taken from the Temple. It is ironic that the descendants of the very nation that was instrumental in returning the Jews to Jerusalem during the reign of King Cyrus of Persia, the Iranians, now want them "wiped off the map."

While the exact players in end-time events are not clearly defined in Scripture, the present situation depicts all of the nations of the earth aligned either with or against Jerusalem. Although a belief in the rise of the Mahdi through an apocalyptic world struggle is terrifying in and of itself, we are not without hope. Listen, for a moment, to the words of Jesus: "See to it that you are not alarmed. Such things must happen, but the end is still to come . . . . The one who stands firm to the end will be saved" (Matthew 24:6, 13).

God did not give us the Scriptures to instill fear and a desire to run and hide. He has called us to pray. In other words, the severity of those last days—the days we live in—depend greatly on the prayers and actions of Christians today. The Bible is not about trying to bring the end of the world as the Islamofascists hope to do; it is about bringing salvation and God's love and mercy to a world going increasingly mad. It is not difficult to see who is behind these activities when Jesus plainly told us: "The thief [the devil] comes only to steal and kill and destroy" (John 10:10).

It is up to Christians to face the present situation in the Middle East with moral clarity, to pray for the peace of Jerusalem, to oppose evil in this world, and to pray for justice and righteousness to prevail. It is time for citizens of the United States to remember her heritage in God, recalibrate her moral compass of right and wrong to God's way of thinking, and pray for her salvation both for this world and the world to come. Prayer is not the best answer; it is the *only* answer. It is not the last resort; it is the only resort.

There is a war going on between light and darkness. I am certain that the terrorist attacks of our day are not the prophetic will of God for this time but are the will of hell. Daniel, who had been carried captive from Jerusalem to Babylon, turned to the Lord and repented for the sins of his nation, asked for forgiveness on their of the last chapter in the history of mankind? What events must yet take place to trigger the ticking of God's prophetic clock? Bible scholars say there is nothing to delay the return of the Messiah for those who serve him. It could take place at any moment, and no mortal can say for sure when that will be.

The Bible tells us no one will know the day or the hour of Jesus Christ's return, but we are exhorted to recognize the season. The rebirth of Israel, then, is a sign that His return will occur within the lifetime of some of us now living. Nothing stands in the way of its happening tonight or tomorrow. With every day that passes, the dream becomes more a reality.

APPENDIX A

Excerpts from an Interview with Benjamin Netanyahu

BENJAMIN NETANYAHU was prime minister in Israel from 1996–1999 and has been a good friend since before he was appointed as the deputy chief of mission in the Israeli Embassy in Washington in 1982. More recently, in 2002, he served as Israel's foreign minister, and was appointed finance minister in 2003, where he served until he resigned in protest of the withdrawals from the Gaza in 2005.

Mike Evans: Talk to me about Iran's involvement with the recent outbreak of fighting in southern Lebanon.

Mr. Netanyahu: I think there is no question that Hezbollah would not last a day without Iranian support—and, of course, Syrian support. They have been funding them, directing them, arming them, inspiring them, and there is no question that of the two, Iran is the more serious threat. It is guided now by a mad Shi'ite militancy that wants to throw the world back 1,000 years. I was going to say to Medieval times, but it is almost pre-Medieval times, and to do this with an apocalyptic slaughter of millions. They have this creed which you think would already have passed from the world. After all, 300 years ago was the end of the religious wars, but they want to reconstruct it.
The danger is, as you can see, we've been given

a wake-up call here. Using their proxies in Lebanon and coincidentally in Gaza, the Hamas, they are rocketing Israeli cities with these weapons they have now. Imagine what would happen later if Iran were to have missiles that would reach into every European capital. Within a decade into the Eastern coast of the US, and would be armed not with explosives, but with nuclear weapons. I think that is a very grim possibility for the world. I think this has to be stopped. I think it has to be stopped today by a division of labor. Israel will deal with Hezbollah cutting its military force and dismantling its missile arsenal; and the US should deal with Syria and especially with Iran by applying massive international pressure on them. Down the line, I think the most important statement is the one President Bush and Vice President Cheney have made, that Iran must not be allowed to acquire nuclear weapons. And when you see Israel's cities being hurled by Iran's proxies, to understand that we are just the forward position. They are really after you, not after us. We are just the front position of the West.

Mike Evans: We have proxies that are attacking your country and no one is using the word *Iran* any longer. Is it possible that if America sleeps that America could be experiencing proxies coming across our borders?

Mr. Netanyahu: Yes, but the more likely thing you would experience is a world we don't even want to contemplate. Up until now, nuclear weapons have been in the hands of responsible regimes. You have one regime, one bizarre regime that apparently has them now in North Korea. There aren't a billion North Koreans that people seek to inspire into a religious war. That's what Iran could do. It could inspire the 200 million

Shi'ites. That's what they intend to do—inspire them into a religious war, first against other Muslims, then against the West.

The reason they despise us so much, the reason they want to eradicate us is that they don't hate you because of us, they hate us because of you. They say we are the "Small Satan" and that America is the "Great Satan." Europe is the "Middle-Sized Satan," although they don't know it. It is important to understand that they could impose a direct threat to Europe and to the United States—and to Israel, obviously. They don't hide it. They don't even hide the fact that they intend to take on the West.

The only thing they are hiding is their nuclear program, which is being exposed by the international community. Many think that what they've done in Lebanon was merely a decoy strategy to deflect attention to growing pressure to their nuclear program. So we have to have our eyes fixed on the two objectives: One, dispatch Iran's proxy in Lebanon and give Lebanon a hope for the future, and give Israel security; but equally, deal with Iran's nuclear and missile program while there is still time, while that regime has not armed itself with weapons of mass death.

Mike Evans: On 9/11 you spoke to the nation and you described 9/11 as a "wake-up call from hell." What would America look like, and what could happen to our nation if Iran goes nuclear?

Mr. Netanyahu: Iran has said in unequivocal terms that first of all its target is Israel and they do it with a particular brand of malevolence because they deny that the Holocaust took place—the murder of 6 million Jews—while they're openly declaring their intention to create another Holocaust to destroy the six million Jews of Israel. Number one, Israel could be in great jeopardy. Number two, so will everybody else. That is, in short order, the Western-oriented regimes of the Middle East would fall by the wayside. That is why you see the Arab countries are siding against Iran, against Hezbollah, because they understand what I am saying. So, the Middle East could be taken over, and that means the oil fields—the oil spigot of the world—would be in Iranian hands. If you are worried about oil prices today, and what that does to the Western economy, just think about tomorrow. And, number three, of course, is the ability of Iran to use its nuclear arsenal and its missile arsenal to threaten Europe and the US directly.

Make no mistake about it; their mad, apocalyptic vision would be perfectly possible for them to do. This is not the Soviet Union; this is not China. These are not rational forces. Whatever you could say about the Soviet Union, it acted fairly carefully on the world scene. Every time their ideology of world domination conflicted with their survival, they always backed off . . . in Cuba, in Berlin. They always backed off; they were very rational in that regard. But you can't count on the ayatollahs of the world armed with nuclear weapons to back off. They often prefer their zeal over their survival. Have you ever heard of a Communist suicide bomber? No. But militant Islam produces battalions of them, and they smash into buildings in Manhattan, and they smash into the Pentagon, into US warships, into buses, schools, you name it. So, this is a different ideology; it is a different threat. It must not be allowed to be armed. It is the new barbarians who are seeking the weapons of mass death, and we have all been forewarned. This is another wake-up call. That's all it is.

Mike Evans: What was going through the minds of the nineteen who attacked America on 9/11, and what is in the minds of the Islamic fascists in Iran? Is it any different?

Mr. Netanyahu: It is a particular creed, and the creed that guides Iran is a particular brand of Shi'ism. Shi'ism dates back to the early years of Islam, and the battle for the inheritance of Mohammad's legacy. It was a splinter group that lost out from the main trajectory of Islam that went to the Sunnis. It had a kind of mystical leader, the Mahdi, who was a great religious leader that disappeared about a thousand years ago. This Mahdi will come back in a great apocalyptic war that will claim the lives of millions. It almost mandates this kind of conflagration, and you really don't want the only country in the world with ninety percent Shi'ites, Iran among them, the most extreme part of this religious sect, to acquire the horrific weapons of atomic bombs and missiles to carry out their twisted ideology. It is very dangerous; people don't realize.

Mike Evans: Do they think they can usher him in with an apocalypse?

Mr. Netanyahu: That's what they think.

Mike Evans: A Christian thinks of the coming of Jesus Christ as the blessed hope. So, you are saying there is an Islamic faction that would prefer a mushroom cloud in Israel and America, a world without Zionism and America, and that somehow they think we are all going to submit to Islam?

Mr. Netanyahu: Prefer, no! That's what they want; it's not a preference. It's like they are ordered to do it. This is the danger of this creed; it's not a choice, it is almost like an order from Allah. That's why these people are willing to commit suicide. The question is: Do we have suicidal regimes? Do we have regimes that will actually go the distance for this mad apocalyptic vision, believing they will somehow inherit paradise while they sow hell for everybody else, and for their people as well? The answer is that this is probably the first time that such a mad militancy on a global scale would seek to acquire weapons of mass death. There was, sixty years ago, another mad militancy, Hitlerism, that was racing to produce the bomb, but happily was defeated before this happened. Imagine a world in which Hitler had atomic bombs. That's pretty much the world you could have if the ayatollahs have atomic bombs.

Mike Evans: Having served as the prime minister of Israel and also the ambassador of Israel to the UN, this president of Iran spoke to the UN about the second coming of the Twelfth Mahdi, and he wrote an eighteen-page letter to the president of the US challenging him to convert to Islam. He ended it with, "I hear the glass shattering and the towers falling of your liberal democracy." As a world leader, what in the world would cause a president of a country to write the president of the US such a bizarre letter?

Mr. Netanyahu: It is precisely this mad ideology that people underrate. They think that this is a normal country with a normal susceptibility to the calculation of cost and benefit, basically a country that operates on the world scene with a modicum of responsibility. That's not the case. Iran is an outlaw state; it fans terrorism and militancy worldwide; it is now organizing the rocketing of civilians in Israel because Hezbollah without Iran collapses in two seconds. And it is preparing to be able to launch atomic warheads into an enormous radius. It's not just targeting Israel. If they only wanted Israel, they would not build those long-range rockets that now can pretty much cover every European capital, and soon will cover the US

Mike Evans: Is it a coincidence that your soldiers were taken hostage, that Katyushas were fired at your nation during the same period of time that President Bush was going to G8 to try to put pressure on Iran.

Mr. Netanyahu: It has been said, not without reason, that Iran used this ploy of kidnapping and murdering of our soldiers by two of its proxies, Hamas in the south, and Hezbollah in the north of Israel, to deflect international attention from its nuclear program. I think this may work in the short term, but I think it will backfire in the midterm. I think right now people in America, not only the president of the US, and the American administration, but I think people in America and in other countries can start asking themselves, "Wait a minute; is this what is in store for us?"

If they are willing to do this to Israel, which they openly say is merely a surrogate for the US—that's the way they view it—then you know what they have in mind for America—and that's what underlines everything we are talking about. This is undoubtedly in their view a skirmish in a larger war, and the larger war is not against Israel. It begins with Israel, but just as was the case with the Nazis, you begin with the Jews, and then you proceed to everyone else.

Mike Evans: How important is Christian support for the State of Israel at this time?

Mr. Netanyahu: I think it's fundamentally important. But the fact is that we are very lucky that in the US there is a great body of citizenry that understands that we have a common heritage. It is a heritage of freedom, of respecting individual rights, of respecting individual conscience, of allowing choice, protecting freedom and democracy—and that comes from many quarters in the US, and most especially from many in the evangelical community and others across the political spectrum. The US in this regard is different. It's different from Europe because it has a core belief.

America, like Israel, was built as the Promised Land, almost the new Promised Land. It is a carrier of so many universal values of freedom and justice that the Jewish people gave the world. I think that this is one of the great blessings of our time that the world in the beginning of the twenty-first century is being led by the US The first half of the twentieth century, the world was not led by the US and the consequences were horrible indeed—World War II and the Holocaust. I think we are fortunate that the US today is leading the world because it has its moral sights very, very clear.

Mike Evans: When you were prime minister, we had a president in office that did not respond to you with moral clarity. At this present moment, we have a president in office that is responding to the State of Israel with moral clarity; how important is that?

Mr. Netanyahu: I think it's all-important. I think in America, everyone wanted to see through a change in administration peace for Israel and security for Israel. And that is not changing, but what is required is to identify the source of the threat. Leadership is charged with two great tasks, to identify the threat to a society or a country, or a civilization, and to see the opportunity to protect it and make it survive and thrive. And

I think, right now, America has such leadership. I think the world right now has such leadership.

Mike Evans: How do you see the current Iranian nuclear situation?

Mr. Netanyahu: Now, you have one regime, North Korea, that seeks to inspire a nuclear war. That's what Iran could do; inspire 300 million Shi'a to a religious war—first against other Arabs, then against the West. They don't hate you because of us; they hate us because of you. They say we are the Small Satan; you are the Great Satan, America. It is important to understand that. They don't hide the fact that they intend to take on the West. The only thing they are hiding is their nuclear program. They face growing pressure from their nuclear program. They are using a decoy strategy to deflect attention.

Many think that what they have done in Lebanon is merely a decoy strategy to deflect the growing pressure from their nuclear program. We have to have our eyes on the two objectives: One, to take care of Iran, especially Iran's part in Lebanon—and two, deal with Iran's nuclear missile program. Iran must not arm itself with weapons of mass destruction.

APPENDIX B

Excerpts from an Interview with Former IDF General Moshe Ya'alon

LT. GENERAL MOSHE YA'ALON served as the Chief of Staff for the Israel Defense Forces from 2002 until 2005. He is currently a Distinguished Fellow at the Shalem Center Institute for International and Middle East Studies.

Mike Evans: General, can you tell us on how Iran intends to defeat the West?

Gen. Ya'alon: Western like-minded people should understand the Iranian ideology to impose new Caliphate over the entire world. They call it Nation of Islam. They perceive the West is a threat to their ideology, to their culture, and they believe that they'll be able to defeat the West from the cultural point of view and to impose this new government by use of terrorism. Today the Iranian regime is determined to acquire military nuclear capability first of all to use it as an umbrella for their terror activities. They prefer to use proxies to deal with the West and with Israel—to undermine our moderate regime, and then to dominate the Middle East. Of course to dominate the oil by undermining those regimes who are linked to the West and later on to try to export what they call the Iranian Revolution—the Iranian ideology to Europe and to other Western countries using proxies with terrorism—exporting the ideology by force.

Mike Evans: What is the foundation theology that drives this?

Gen. Ya'alon: It is interesting what we are facing today—we are facing different Islamic ideologies. In the Iranian case it is a Shi'ite ideology, but today the al Qaeda ideology, which is very different—but shares the same agenda and the same strategy. This is the case of the Muslim Brotherhood coming from this different ideology calling to impose the Nation of Islam all over the world. The Iranian ideology actually is to dominate the Islamic world and to dominate the world by imposing Islam. The ideology is [ultimately] to reach peace and tranquility all over the world.

All the people all over the world should be Muslims. This is the idea. They use this idea of what they call the Mahdi—like their messiah—in order to encourage [people] to be proactive—to [perform] terror activities. By acquiring nuclear military capabilities [they hope] to convince by force those infidels who do not believe in Islam to become Muslims in order to reach peace and tranquility all over the world.

Mike Evans: Do they believe that an apocalypse would usher him in?

Gen. Ya'alon: I'm not sure the idea is apocalypse—they are trying to convince people to convert themselves; like [when] President Ahmadinejad in his eighteen-page letter to President Bush actually recommended he be converted to Islam—not by force, but he tried to convince him. He really believes in it. For Westerners it might seem ridiculous, but he says what he means and he means what he says. In the letter—in calling to wipe Israel off the map and so forth—he means what he says. He really believes in it, so they prefer to convince the Westerners.

This is the idea of Hamas. Hamas is part of the Muslim Brotherhood. We have it in a speech in Damascus. Last February, after they won the elections, he was talking about the Nation of Islam, and he recommended the Westerners to be converted or not to support Israel, otherwise they will be full of remorse. They speak the same language although they do not share the same ideology—but the most tenuous force today regarding this kind of ideology is no doubt Iran.

Mike Evans: Talk to us about Iran's nuclear program.

Gen. Ya'alon: No doubt today there is not any dispute in the Western intelligence community that Iran is determined to acquire military nuclear capability. This is not just a civilian project. We have information in the last decade that there is a clandestine Iranian military nuclear project. They will try to overcome the problems in the enrichment process, but they're on their way to overcoming it—they're on their way to acquiring it. And according to the experts, it's a question of a couple of months—I'm not sure how many months—to reach what they need to have—[that is] the indigenous know-how to be able to enrich the materials and to be able to produce a bomb. Then they will have a couple of years to build—to actually produce—the bomb, but no doubt they are determined to acquire the military nuclear capability. What we [have] faced in the last couple of years—especially since 2004 when the IAEA exposed their clandestine project—[is Iran] trying to gain time in order to go ahead with the process. Unfortunately, they feel like they are succeeding to manipulate—to deceive—the West, and to go on with the project.

Mike Evans: How big is their project and are the Russians involved?

Gen. Ya'alon: You know, I was the head of the intelligence of the Israeli Defense Force in the years '95–'98, and actually I personally met Russian officials and introduced them to the information that we had about Russian experts involved in the missiles project—and of course a nuclear project at that time. Russian administration at the time denied it, but we had evidence of Russian involvement at the time. So no doubt when we are talking about the missile project it was even before the Shahab-6, which is already operational today. We had all evidence about Russian involvement in this project.

Mike Evans: How many sites are we talking about?

Gen. Ya'alon: This is not one site like it was in Iraq. We are talking about dozens of facilities dealing with this project.

Mike Evans: And what is the difference between their sites now and the Iraq site?

Gen. Ya'alon: In the Iraqi case, it was one reactor, Osirak, that was destroyed by the Israeli air strike in 1981. Today, the Iranian regime has learned a lesson from the Iraqi case and they have many facilities—[they] know it's a challenge for intelligence, but we can cope with it.

Mike Evans: Are they built underground?

Gen. Ya'alon: Yes. They're built underground; they're built in well-protected facilities.

Mike Evans: And do they face the Gulf? Are they lined up on the Gulf?

Gen. Ya'alon: The Iranian intention strategically is to dominate the Gulf—to become a hegemony regarding all sources, which is the Gulf States of the Middle East. So this is a combination of religious ideology and political strategy. This is a combination in which they are trying—this regime—to dominate the religion and of course, to harm or [control] Western interest regarding oil in the Gulf.

Mike Evans: What kind of threats has the president of Iran made against the State of Israel?

Gen. Ya'alon: President Ahmadinejad declared that Israel should be wiped off the map. He referred to it at a conference with the title "The World without Zionism." They had another conference about "The World without America." So they see Israel as a spearhead of Western culture—Western civilization—and believe that on the way to defeat the West, Israel should be defeated, and this is the reason that he supports all the terror organizations that operate against the State of Israel—like the Hezbollah in Lebanon, the Palestinian Islamic jihad, the Hamas, Fata activists— on an individual basis. He believes that this is a step on the way to defeating the West. In this stage, Israel should be wiped off the map—and he really believes in it—and he believes that he's able to implement it.

Unfortunately he's encouraged from our decisions like the fighting in Lebanon and in the Gaza Strip. We did it especially because of Israeli internal considerations. It was perceived—and is still per- ceived—by the Iranian regime as weakness—and he is encouraged by Israel like he is encouraged by the US difficulties of the coalition—the difficulties in Iraq. Of course he's accountable for it as well because he does his best not to allow any political stability in Iraq behind the scene, and he provides the know-how—the terror know-how—he provides it to the insurgencies like the IEDs, improvised explosive devices, Iranian-made. And of course he does his best to undermine those moderate regimes who are linked to the West like in Jordan, in Egypt, in Persian Gulf states, and unfortunately he feels like he's winning because he doesn't face any determination from the West and he goes on with his policy using the proxies and acquiring the military nuclear capability for his benefit.

Mike Evans: You're saying that many of our troops that are blown up are actually blown up by military devices that are coming from Iran?

Gen. Ya'alon: No doubt about it. The coalition troops—the Americans, the Brits, the Italians—who are blown up today in Iraq are blown up by Iranian-made improvised explosive devices. We faced the same devices in Lebanon used by the Hezbollah—Iranian-made devices—the same. We intercepted these kind of devices on the *Karine-A*—the ship that came from Iran—and we intercepted [it in the Red Sea] trying to smuggle these kind of devices to the Palestinian terrorists—so no doubt this is Iranian-made.

Mike Evans: When Iran uses the term the "Great Satan," referring to America, what do they mean?

Gen. Ya'alon: Israel is perceived by this regime as a small Satan. The Great Satan is America—and actually the Iranian regime is challenging the United States as the leader of the Western culture. Israel is a marginal issue on the way to defeating the United States. Today, the Iranian regime is concentrating on dealing with the Americans' interest in the region—like in Iraq, in the Persian Gulf state, and in Israel. [They see America] as a spearhead of Western culture and religion. But the strategic goal is to defeat the United States—to defeat the Western culture—to defeat the Western values—and to impose the new Caliphate and the Nation of Islam.

In the end, I believe that if they are successful in the Middle East, they will approach Europe, and of course the United States—and actually the Iranian regime has the terror infrastructure even today—a sleeping terror infrastructure everywhere. Like they did it in Argentina in '92 and '94 against the Jewish communities, like they did it in Europe against their opponents in Germany, and elsewhere—in Asher. Everywhere they have the sleeping terror infrastructure to be used on the day to come.

Mike Evans: If Iran gave the nod for those with the infrastructure to harm us that are living within our country, what are they capable of doing?

Gen. Ya'alon: You can look to what happened in Germany towards assassinations, and you can look back to what happened in Argentina, which was blowing up huge buildings—the Israeli Embassy and the Jewish Community Center—so they have the capability to send a truck loaded with explosives to blow any building in the United States or anywhere in the world.

Mike Evans: Israel has dealt with—in the last six years—over 20,000 attempted suicide attacks. Obviously it has worked for them to achieve their objectives with Israel.

Crime has paid for them in many ways, from their perspective.

Is there any possibility that they could try that in the United States?

Gen. Ya'alon: Why not? Using homicide bombers—I don't call them suicide bombers but homicide bombers—it becomes very effective from their perspective—from their perception—it becomes very effective. They believe that Israel retreated from Lebanon because of these kinds of terror attacks. Talking about the radical Islamists, they believe—all of them—al Qaeda, Muslim Brotherhood and the Iranian regime—they believe that they defeated Russia as a superpower— why [would they not believe they are] able to defeat the second superpower, or the first one—the United States—by using their determination or their will?

Not all of the West has the power, but actually I'm not sure that the West has an understanding— the awareness, the will and the determination—and [Islamofascists] have the will and the determination— and believe that they will win by their advantage of will and determination, and that we just have to listen to them—to Osama bin Laden, to Ahmadinejad, to Khaled Mashal [leader of Hamas]—and of course to the main generator today for any terror activities all over the world—the Iranian regime.

Mike Evans: When you said that they believed they defeated the Russian Soviet Union, were you referring to the Afghan war?

Gen. Ya'alon: Yes, of course. The radical Islamists today, they feel like they are winning. They feel like they are winning, although they do not have the power—but they believe they have the will and the determination.

Why do they feel that they are winning? First of all, they believe [that if] they defeated the Soviet Union in Afghanistan, then [they] will be able to defeat the United States. Secondly, they believe the Hezbollah defeated Israel in Lebanon. It was a victory for terror according to their perception. They believe that they changed the Spanish policy because of the devastating attack in Madrid in 2004. They believe that Israelis withdrew from Gaza because of the Hamas terror attacks, and of course they are encouraged from the Hamas political victory in the [Palestinian] elections.

They're encouraged by the Muslim Brotherhood gaining power in Egypt. They're encouraged today from what's happening in Mogadishu in Somalia, and of course they're encouraged from the coalition troops' difficulties in Iraq, and from the political difficulties here in Washington for the president—for the administration. So they feel like they are winning and they are very self-confident today that they are on the way to defeating the West.

Mike Evans: How important is the support of Americans who have moral clarity in this battle?

Gen. Ya'alon: In order to win this kind of war, we need the awareness of Westerners. Then we need moral clarity, and then a clear strategy. We sleep. We in the West are sleeping, and we need a wake-up call to understand this threat is imminent. It's not a theoretical threat, and as long as [Islamofascists] feel like they are winning—as long as they do not witness Western determination to deal with this politically, economically and militarily, they will go on with it. They will use first of all the proxies against Western targets anywhere—not just Israel, but Western moderate regimes in the Middle

East—and they will go on with it from the Middle East to Europe to the United States.

Mike Evans: If nothing is done, if the world continues to sleep—if the West continues to sleep—and we wake up a decade from now and nothing has been done—can you describe what America could be like in comparison to your nation when you were Chief of Staff—as it relates to terrorism and the threat—what it could be like in the streets of America?

Gen. Ya'alon: It will be more difficult to any administration or government in the West to deal with nuclear Iran because of the nuclear umbrella. Cane said recently that the only worse option—rather than exercising the military option regarding the military nuclear project in Iran—is to have a nuclear Iran. I agree with him because to have a nuclear Iran with this kind of non-conventional regime—with these non-conventional capabilities—this is not even rational. We're not talking about a Soviet Union–type of leadership. They were rational. This regime is not rational. They have a strong religious belief—and they are driving this strong religious belief to defeat the West.

So first of all, they will use terror like we faced in Lebanon from the Palestinian authority. They will oppose other countries by undermining them, blackmailing them, by terror activities—a combination of terror activities under a nuclear umbrella—and they will approach Europe and the United States with the use of proxies—not to use missiles, [they will] use proxies—and they have many proxies: Hezbollah, Palestinian terror organizations, and of course [those] run by the Iranian intelligence who were responsible for the devastating attacks in Argentina—special Iranian intelligence used covertly to launch terror attacks against Western targets. So it might come to the United States as well.

Mike Evans: What part did Iran play in 9/11?

Gen. Ya'alon: al Qaeda elements used Iran as a safe haven. [We] can't say that the Iranian regime was involved directly or in any other way with 9/11, but in no doubt al Qaeda elements used Iran for a certain period of time as a safe haven.

Mike Evans: I'd like to be able to describe to the American people a visual thing. What visually would they be seeing and hearing if homicide bombers began this strategy in the United States. What would it be like? What would be the particulars?

Gen. Ya'alon: There is a sleeping infrastructure—terror infrastructure—today all over the world like we have not seen—not simply in Canada—and this is the case everywhere because we are talking about ideology, which is spread by many radical Islamists. In many cases it's the Iranian regime talking with Shi'a elements, and in other cases the al Qaeda organization— which is an umbrella—an ideology to encourage radical Islamists. I'm not talking about all Muslims. I'm talking about radical Islamists who become terrorists and are ready to sacrifice their life by becoming homicide bombers—killing infidels as they call us—Christians, Jews, Buddhists—whatever other than Muslims are infidels—to kill them, and in this way to convince them to be converted to Islam. All over the world there are radical Islamists who are ready to be become homicide bombers. It might be Osama bin Laden or others. They are ready, so if the Iranian regime decided to implement it here in the United States, they will have the capabilities to do it.

Mike Evans: Explain what it would be like practically if it happened in New York or D.C.

Gen. Ya'alon: I think practically today in Israel we assume that any minute a homicide bomber might try to approach any public facility, so we have a guard in the entrance of any public facility—which is any mall, any restaurant, any café, any public transportation—to defend the civilians from homicide bombers. So it might happen even here.

Mike Evans: But the American people have never really experienced that type of terror. I know that when they do this, sometimes they work in pairs of twos. They strategically plan it. Describe for us what it would be like if it actually happened here in Washington, D.C., or New York. What would it be like?

Gen. Ya'alon: Of course people will not feel secure because of the idea of being blown up in a public facility—in the Metro, or in the restaurant, or in the concert hall, or in the theater, or anywhere—to lose your personal feeling of security on a daily basis and to be aware of any suspicious movement—not to trust anyone who goes with a suitcase or with any other bag—which might be an explosive bag—it changes the whole way of life when you face it.

Mike Evans: You mentioned that this president had the audacity to write a letter to try to convert the president of the United States. If you would attempt to convert the president of the United States—obviously he would certainly want to attempt to convert the American people.

Gen. Ya'alon: Oh, of course.

Mike Evans: Could you talk about that for a minute? Start with the letter.

Gen. Ya'alon: Actually, President Ahmadinejad recommended that the president of the United States be converted to Islam—of course this recommendation is for all the American people to be [converted] to avoid the conflict—to avoid the war that he declares on the West. Actually, he declares war against Western culture, and yes, he recommends—like any other radical Islamist today—like Osama bin Laden and Khaled Mashal, who also talks about not supporting Israel and adopting Islam—otherwise you will be full of remorse—you will regret it in the end. Yes, this is the proposal to be converted.

Mike Evans: The American people have a tendency to think this is just one person who believes this.

Gen. Ya'alon: Actually, in Iran we should distinguish between the Iranian regime and the Iranian people—but when we are talking about the regime we should talk about the ayatollahs, the conservatives—the conservatives who do not allow any reforms and are trying to manage Iran using the Islamic Law—who do not allow democracy or democratic values. So we should distinguish between the regime and the people. I believe that most of the Iranian people do not like the ayatollahs—but the problem is not with one man. The problem is with the system—with this ideology of the ayatollahs.

Mike Evans: How many are we approximately talking about, and how long has this ideology been fed to them?

Gen. Ya'alon: We are talking about the Iran revolution that emerged

in 1979 quite successfully in Iran, although they are
not able as a regime to convince all the Iranians
to believe in this ideology, they have succeeded
in running the country successfully, and actually
they succeeded in strengthening their grip in governing—building the intelligence, intimidation, discrimination, pressure against the people—and they
are quite successful in their way. So we have to talk
about the Iranian regime, not just the Iranian people
like we have to talk about the radical Islamists—not
all the Muslims—and the Iranian regime is radical
Islamist regime.

Mike Evans: Most people think of nuclear bombs as missiles, fired
through missiles—but could there be a period of time
where a nuclear bomb could be put in a cargo container or even brought across a border?

Gen. Ya'alon: Actually, the bomb, according to my understanding,
might be used by the Iranian regime as an umbrella,
then by proxies—not by the regime itself, which
means by aircraft or by missile—by proxies—the dirty
bomb to be used by terror organizations as proxies.
This is the best way to deny accountability and this
is the way this regime is thinking about how to gain
the benefits of these kinds of activities—like terror
activities—and not to be considered accountable.
That's what they are doing now in Iraq, in Lebanon,
in the Palestinian authority, and all over the Middle
East against moderate regimes—denying accountability, but no doubt generating, financing, equipping,
supporting and encouraging these kinds of proxies.
So the idea of using proxies is the most probably scenario, even when it comes to nuclear capability

Mike Evans: Would you describe what a dirty bomb is and what kind
of damage that could do in a high-population area?

Gen. Ya'alon: You can bring a dirty bomb to any city using maritime cargo or air cargo or ground cargo. It doesn't matter. It might be brought by ship, by airplane, or by truck—to be used in a very highly populated urban area like a city anywhere. It might be Tel Aviv, it might be Berlin, it might be New York—and of course to cause devastating collateral damage—to kill as many civilians as they can—but to contain it to a certain area like a big city.

Mike Evans: Our worst horror was 9/11—and we know the number of deaths. Just approximately what would be a rough number [of casualties] if a dirty bomb went off in a highly populated city?

Gen. Ya'alon: It might be dozens of thousands; it might be hundreds of thousands of casualties. It depends on the quantity of the materials in a dirty bomb.

Mike Evans: If Iran is not stopped and they go nuclear, then are you saying that they cannot be stopped—or if they were stopped—what consequences would that take?

Gen. Ya'alon: I believe that in one way or another they should be stopped. They shouldn't have nuclear capability. I prefer that a military option would be the last resort. We haven't experienced yet the political and economic option. It should be used early on—and I prefer that by not using the political and economic option—which means political isolation and economic sanctions—we will have to use the military option. I'm talking about the West—like my people—and no doubt Iran will respond to any option. They even might respond to economic sanctions—not talking about military option. They might respond using proxies, terror organizations—special Iranian apparatus—to execute terror attacks against certain targets.

APPENDIX C

A 21-Day Study of Iran (Persia), Iraq (Babylon), and Israel in Biblical Prophecy

Week One

Day 1: Daniel's Prayer and the Seventy Weeks — Daniel 9

Day 2: Daniel's Vision of the Man — Daniel 10

Day 3: The Kings of the North and South — Daniel 11

Day 4: The End of Days — Daniel 12

Day 5: Israel Reborn — Ezekiel 36:1–11, 22–36

Day 6: Nations Shall Rise Against Israel — Ezekiel 38

Day 7: Those Nations Are Judged — Ezekiel 39

Week Two

Day 8: Jesus on the End Times in Matthew — Matthew 24

Day 9: Jesus on the End Times in Mark — Mark 13

Day 10: Jesus on the End Times in Luke — Luke 21

Day 11: John Before the Throne of God — Revelation 4–5

Day 12: The Seven Seals — Revelation 6–8:5

Day 13: The Seven Trumpets — Revelation 8:6–11:19

Day 14: The Beasts and the Great Harvest — Revelation 12:1–14:20

Week Three

Day 15: The Seven Plagues and the Seven Bowls — Revelation 15–16

Day 16: Babylon Rises — Revelation 17

Day 17: Babylon Falls — Revelation 18–19:5

Day 18: The Marriage Supper of the Lamb — Revelation 19:6–10
The Coming of He Who Is Faithful and True — Rev. 19:11–21

Day 19: The Defeat of Satan — Revelation 20

Day 20: The New Heaven and Earth — Revelation 21

Day 21: "Surely, I Am Coming" — Revelation 22

ENDNOTES

1. David Crary, Associated Press, January 7, 2015, http://www.cbc.ca/news/world/charlie-hebdo-shooting-st%C3%A9phane-charbonnier-bernard-maris-among-those-killed-1.2892946; accessed January 2015.

2. "French forces kill Charlie Hebdo attack suspects, hostages die in second siege," *Reuters*, January 9, 2015, http://timesofindia.indiatimes.com/world/europe/French-forces-kill-Charlie-Hebdo-attack-suspects-hostages-die-in-second-siege/articleshow/45828052.cms; accessed January 2015.

3. http://en.wikipedia.org/wiki/Allahu_Akbar_(anthem); accessed January 2015.

4. "Charlie Hebdo, Firebombed French Newspaper, Starts Blog, Fights Hackers," http://www.huffingtonpost.com/2011/11/04/charlie-hebdo-blog-firebombed-french-paper_n_1075702.html; accessed January 2015.

5. Guy Faulconbridge, "Britain's MI5 chief warns al Qaeda in Syria planning mass attacks on West," Yahoo News, January 8, 2015, http://news.yahoo.com/britains-mi5-chief-warns-al-qaeda-syria-planning-220625665.html; accessed January 2015.

6. Ibid.

7. Ibid.

8. Riyadh Mohammed, "ISIS Closing in on Israel from the North and South," *The Fiscal Times*, http://www.thefiscaltimes.com/2014/12/23/ISIS-Closing-Israel-North-and-South; accessed December 2014.

9. Prime Minister Benjamin Netanyahu, http://www.imra.org.il/story.php3?id=65006; accessed September 2014.

10. Moshe Phillips and Benyamin Korn, "Hillary's Hand in Hamas' Terror Tunnels," August 26, 2014, http://www.frontpagemag.com/2014/moshe-phillips-and-benyamin-korn/hillarys-hand-in-hamas-terror-tunnels/; accessed October 2014.

11. Rory Jones, Hamas Tunnel Network Sparks Recriminations in Israel, *The Wall Street Journal*, August 23, 2014, http://blogs.wsj.com/middleeast/2014/08/12/hamas-tunnel-network-sparks-recriminations-in-israel/; accessed October 2014.

12. "ISIS Spokesman Who Promised To 'Raise The Flag Of Allah Over The White House' Killed In Syria," http://www.inquisitr.com/1425478/isis-spokesman-who-promised-to-raise-the-flag-of-allah-over-the-white-house-killed-in-syria/#LxhkzurqLkdybyTk.99, accessed October 2014.

13. Jenna McLaughlin and Dana Liebelson, "Top Al Qaeda Bomb Maker Reportedly Killed in Air Strikes" September 23, 2004, http://www.motherjones.com/politics/2014/09/what-is-khorasan-why-did-us-bomb; accessed October 2014.

14. Vicki Needham, "FBI Director Warns of Khorasan Attack," http://www.msn.com/en-us/news/us/fbi-director-warns-of-khorasan-attack/ar-BB7HrLP; accessed October 2014.

15. "ISIS Leader al-Baghdadi Calls on Muslims to Rush to 'Your State'"; http://www.nbcnews.com/storyline/iraq-turmoil/isis-leader-al-baghdadi-calls-muslims-rush-your-state-n145521; accessed September 30, 2014.

16. "Jimmy Carter Pushes US to Recognize Hamas, slams Israel in op-ed," August 5, 2014, http://www.foxnews.com/politics/2014/08/05/jimmy-carter-pushes-us-to-recognize-hamas-slams-israel-in-op-ed/; accessed October 2014.

17. Dwight L. Schwab, Jr., "Jimmy Carter doesn't know when to shut up," October 12, 2014, http://www.examiner.com/article/jimmy-carter-doesn-t-know-when-to-shut-up; accessed October 2014.

18. Asadollah Alam, *The Shah and I: The Confidential Diary of Iran's Royal Court 1969–1977* (New York: St. Martin's Press, 1993), 500.

19. Craig Whitlock, "Rift widens between Obama, US military over strategy to fight Islamic State," *Washington Post*, September 18, 2014, http://www.washingtonpost.com/world/national-security/rift-widens-between-obama-us-military-over-strategy-to-fight-islamic-state/2014/09/18/ebdb422e-3f5c-11e4-b03f-de718edeb92f_story.html; accessed October 2014.

20. F. Michael Maloof, "Purge Surge: Obama Fires Another Commander," http://www.wnd.com/2013/11/purge-surge-obama-fires-another-commander/; accessed October 2014.

21. Major General Patrick Brady, "Obama's Dangerous Emasculating of Our Military," *World Net Daily*, October 29, 2012, http://www.wnd.com/2012/10/obamas-dangerous-emasculating-of-our-military/#HscU2i0ZjByx0sKX.99; accessed October 2014.

22. "Nuclear Summit: Barack Obama tells Russia's Dmitry Medvedev More Flexibility After Election," March 26, 2012, http://www.huffingtonpost.com/2012/03/26/nuclear-summit-barack-obama-medvedev_n_1379422.html; accessed October 2014.

23. http://en.wikipedia.org/wiki/Wahhabi_movement; accessed October 2014.

24. http://en.wikipedia.org/wiki/Pogo; accessed October 2014.

25. Anna Molin, "Sweden Recognizes Palestinian State," *The Wall Street Journal*, October 30, 2014; accessed November 2014.

26. Walid Shoebat, personal interview with Mike Evans, August 26, 2006. (Former Palestinian terrorist recounting the teaching he received about Islamist Eschatology as a child and "terrorist in training.")

27. Dr. David Jeremiah, *Agents of the Apocalypse* (Carol Stream, IL: Tyndale House Publishers, 2014), 142.

28. "Cyrus the Great: Cyrus II, Kourosh in Persian, Kouros in Greek," *Iran Chamber Society*, http://www.iranchamber.com/history/cyrus/cyrus.php; accessed December 19, 2006.

29. *The Encyclopedia Britannica*, Vol. 6 (1958), 940; quoted in Wayne Jackson, "Cyrus the Great in Biblical Prophecy," *ChristianCourier.com*, September 28, 2000, http://www.christiancourier.com/articles/read/cyrus_the_great_in_biblical_prophecy; accessed December 2006.

30. "History of Iran," *Wikipedia, the free encyclopedia*, last updated December 7, 2006, http://en.wikipedia.org/wiki/History_of_Iran (accessed December 8, 2006); and Ehsan Yarshater, "When 'Persia' Became 'Iran,'" last updated December 8, 2006, http://www.cais-soas.com/CAIS/Iran/persia_or_iran.htm; accessed December 2006.

31. Alan Dershowitz, personal interview with Mike Evans, August 18, 2006.

32. Golda Meir, http://izquotes.com/quote/284823; accessed October 2014.

33. Daniel Greenfield, "Why Putin Invaded Ukraine," http://www.frontpagemag.com/2014/dgreenfield/why-putin-invaded-ukraine/; accessed October 2014.

34. http://www.foundingfatherquotes.com/quote/677#.VDQ3UI10w3E; accessed October 2014.

35. http://historicwords.com/american-history/john-adams-our-constitution-was-made-only-for-a-moral-and-religious-people/; accessed October 2014.

36. Natan Sharansky, *The Case for Democracy: The Power of Freedom to Overcome Tyranny & Terror* (New York: PublicAffairs, 2004), 40–41.

37. George W. Bush, http://www.brainyquote.com/quotes/quotes/g/georgewbu145057.html; accessed December 2006.

38. "Bush Calls for Greater Religious Tolerance in US," *Voice of America*, October 29, 2009, http://www.voanews.com/content/a-13-a-2002-02-07-1-bush-67418692/383769.html; accessed November 2014.

39. Ronald Wilson Reagan, http://www.quotationspage.com/quote/33737.html; accessed December 2006.

40. Alexander I. Solzhenitsyn, "A World Split Apart," June 8, 1978, Harvard University Graduation, http://www.orthodoxytoday.org/articles/SolzhenitsynHarvard.php; accessed October 2014.

41. Fay Voshell, "The Choice Before Us," *American Thinker*, http://www.americanthinker.com/articles/2014/11/the_choice_before_us.html, November 2, 2014; accessed November 2014.

42. Ronald Reagan, "The Evil Empire: Remarks at the Annual Convention of the National Association of Evangelicals," *American Rhetoric*, March 8, 1983, http://www.americanrhetoric.com/speeches/ronaldreaganevilempire.htm; accessed November 2014..

43. http://www.allthelyrics.com/lyrics/charles_wesley/a_charge_to_keep_i_have-lyrics-1129014.html; accessed October 2014.

44. http://www.searchquotes.com/search/Moral_Clarity/; accessed October 2014.

45. Joseph Goebbels, "The Jews are Guilty," http://research.calvin.edu/german-propaganda-archive/goebl.htm; accessed October 2014.

46. Aleksandr I. Solzhenitsyn, "A World Split Apart," June 8, 1978, http://www.orthodoxytoday.org/articles/SolzhenitsynHarvard.php; accessed September 2014.

47. Lee Edwards, "The Conservative Consensus: Frank Meyer, Barry Goldwater, and the Politics of Fusionism," The Heritage Foundation, January 22, 2007, http://www.heritage.org/research/reports/2007/01/the-conservative-consensus-frank-meyer-barry-goldwater-and-the-politics-of-fusionism; accessed November 2014.

48. Ronald Reagan, "Inaugural Address, January 20, 1981," Ronald Regan Presidential Archives, University of Texas online, http://www.reagan.utexas.edu/archives/speeches/1981/12081a.htm; accessed October 2014.

49. George W. Bush, "Remarks at the Swearing-In Ceremony for Tom Ridge as Director of the Office of Homeland Security," October 8, 2001, *The American Presidency Project*, http://www.presidency.ucsb.edu/ws/print. php?pid=62592; accessed December 2006.

50. Kathleen Parker, "Vote for the Ones Who Know What's at Stake," *Houston Chronicle*, October 9, 2014, http://www.chron.com/opinion/outlook/article/Parker-Vote-for-those-who-truly-know-what-s-at-5809942.php; accessed October 2014.

51. George W. Bush, "President George W. Bush addresses the Nation, World Congress Center, Atlanta, Georgia," WhiteHouse.gov, November 8, 2001, http://georgewbush-whitehouse.archives.gov/infocus/ramadan/islam.html; accessed October 2014.

52. "White House rejects proposal to partition Iraq," NBC News.com, October 19, 2006, http://www.nbcnews.com/id/15334267/ns/world_news-mideast_n_africa/t/white-house-rejects-proposal-partition-iraq/#.VGO2x41AQ3E; accessed November 2014.

53. T. Becket Adams, "Panetta directly contradicts Obama's account of US withdrawal from Iraq," *Washington Examiner*, October 2, 2014, http://washingtonexaminer.com/panetta-directly-contradicts-obamas-account-of-us-withdrawal-from-iraq/article/2554290; accessed October 2014.

54. David Remnick, "Going the Distance," *The New Yorker*, January 27, 2014, http://www.newyorker.com/magazine/2014/01/27/going-the-distance-2?currentPage=all; accessed October 2014.

55. Peter Baker and Eric Schmitt, "Fault Is Shared in Misjudging of ISIS Threat," *New York Times*, September 30, 2014; accessed October 2014.

56. Barry Farber, "Iraqi Soldiers: Spectacular Cowards," *World Net Daily*, http://www.wnd.com/2014/06/iraqi-soldiers-spectacular-cowards/#RF0yBkYx16Z4BPTI.99; accessed October 2014.

57. "700 'beheaded, crucified and shot' after revolt against militants," http://www.msn.com/en-us/news/world/700-beheaded-crucified-and-shot-after-revolt-against-militants/ar-BBaghq6?ocid=U142DHP; accessed October 2014.

58. Walter E. Williams, "Will the West Defend Itself," *Townhall.com*, http://townhall.com/columnists/walterewilliams/2014/10/01/will-the-west-defend-itself-n1898118/page/full; accessed October 2014.

59. Mike Levine, "Homeland Warns of ISIS Retaliation in US by Sympathizers," ABC News, August 22, 2014, http://abcnews.go.com/US/homeland-warns-isis-retaliation-us-sympathizers/story?id=25087995; accessed October 2014.

60. Jenna McLaughlin and Dana Liebelson, "What Is Khorasan and Why Did the US Just Bomb It?" September 23, 2014, http://www.motherjones.com/politics/2014/09/what-is-khorasan-why-did-us-bomb; accessed October 2014.

61. Ibid.

62. Charles Krauthammer, "Islamic State dependent on US ambivalence on airstrikes, Turkey," *Houston Chronicle*, October 9, 2014, Outlook, B9.

63. From a 2007 interview with Dr. Mike Evans

64. Naftali Bendavid, "Removal of Chemical Weapons from Syria Completed," *The Wall Street Journal*, June 23, 2014, http://online.wsj.com/articles/removal-of-chemical-weapons-from-syria-is-completed-1403529356; accessed October 2014.

65. Paul Alster, "Gruesome photos may show ISIS using chemical weapons on Kurds, report says," October 13, 2014, http://www.foxnews.com/world/2014/10/13/gruesome-photos-may-show-isis-using-chemical-weapons-on-kurds-says-report/; accessed October 2014.

66. Arthur Ahlert, "Saddam's WMDs: The Left's Iraq Lies Exposed," June 23, 2014, http://www.frontpagemag.com/2014/arnold-ahlert/saddams-wmds-the-lefts-iraq-lies-exposed/; accesses October 2014.

67. Joe Herring & Dr. Mark Christian, "The Return of the Arab Spring," *American Thinker*, September 1, 2014, http://www.americanthinker.com/2014/08/the_return_of_the_arab_spring.html; accessed October 2014.

68. Yifa Kaakov, "Netanyahu: War on terror won't be over unless Iran is contained along with IS," *Times of Israel*, October 3, 2014; http://www.timesofisrael.com/netanyahu-iran-must-be-contained-along-with-is/#ixzz3G8K6LPg5; accessed October 2014.

69. David Kupelian, "Games Obama Plays," *World Net Daily*, November 10, 2013, http://www.wnd.com/2013/11/games-obama-plays/; accessed October 2014.

70. Ibid.

71. "Obama Addresses Students at St. Xavier," http://www.ndtv.com/article/india/obama-addresses-students-at-st-xavier-full-transcript-64877?cp; accessed September 2014.

72. "Under Obama 'War on Terror' Phrase Fading," White House on MSNBC.com; http://www.msnbc.msn.com/id/28959574/ns/politics-white_house/, accessed October 2014.

73. http://en.wikipedia.org/wiki/Hajj; accessed October 2014.

74. The Azusa Street Revival was an historic Pentecostal revival meeting that took place in Los Angeles, California, and was led by William J. Seymour, an African-American preacher. It began with a meeting on April 14, 1906, and continued until roughly 1915. http://en.wikipedia.org/wiki/Azusa_Street_Revival, accessed April 2014.

75. Michael Cook, *The Koran: A Very Short Introduction* (Oxford: Oxford University Press, 2000), 43.

76. *Encyclopedia of Islam and the Muslim World* (Farmington Hills, MI: Thomson Gale, 2004).

77. Emmanuel Sivan, *Radical Islam: Medieval Theology and Modern Politics* (New Haven: Yale University Press, 1990), 101.

78. Comptroller General of the United States. "Iranian Oil Cutoff: Reduced Petroleum Supplies and Inadequate US Government Response." Report to Congress, General Accounting Office, 1979.

79. Don A. Schance, Tehran, *Los Angeles Times*, April 24, 1980, p. 1: The Iranian government, in the words of Ayatollah Ruhollah Khomeini, has condemned both "Westoxification and Eastoxification."

80. CIA intelligence memorandum, January 19, 1979, entitled "Iran: Khomeini's Prospects and Views."

81. Cited by Dariush Zahedi in *The Iranian Revolution Then and Now* (Boulder, CO: Westview Press, 2000), 136.

82. http://www.brainyquote.com/quotes/authors/e/elliott_abrams.html; accessed October 2014.

83. Karim Sadjadpour, "June 2010: Even Iran's regime hates Iran's regime," *Foreign Policy, Revolution in the Arab World*, Rumblings; 15.

84. Simon Robinson, "Five reasons to suspect Iran's election results," *Time*, June 15, 2009; http://www.time.com/time/specials/packages/article/0,28804,1904645_1904644_1904643,00.html; accessed April 2011.

85. "Report: Thousands protest in Iran," *United Press International*, February 14, 2011; http://www.upi.com/Top_News/World-News/2011/02/14/Report-Thousands-protest-in-Iran/UPI-92661297665320/; accessed February 2011.

86. Judith Levy, "Iran and Syria: BFFs?" *Washington Times*, March 1, 2011; http://communities.washingtontimes.com/neighborhood/israel-online/2011/mar/1/iran-syria-ahmadinejad-assad-khameini-israel/#; accessed March 2011.

87. "Cairo ready to re-establish Iran diplomatic ties," *The Jerusalem Post*, April 4, 2011; http://www.jpost.com/MiddleEast/Article.aspx?id=215154; accessed April 2011.

88. Michael Slackman, "Arab unrest propels Iran as Saudi influence declines," *The New York Times*, February 23, 2011; http://www.nytimes.com/2011/02/24/world/middleeast/24saudis.html.; accessed February 2011.

89. Michael Slackman, "Arab unrest propels Iran as Saudi influence declines," *The New York Times*, February 23, 2011, http://seattletimes.com/html/nationworld/2014314450_saudi24.html; accessed October 2014.

90. "Full Text of Prime Minister Netanyahu's speech before the United Nations General Assembly 2013," October 1, 2013, *Times of Israel*, http://www.timesofisrael.com/full-text-netanyahus-2013-speech-to-the-un-general-assembly/; accessed October 2013.

91. Rep. Lee Terry, "Can We Afford to Trust Obama on Iran?" *Real Clear Politics*, November 24, 2013, http://www.realclearpolitics.com/articles/2013/11/24/can_we_afford_to_trust_obama_on_iran_120769.html#ixzz3GFkBP0JX; accessed October 2014.

92. Tom Watkins, "Netanyahu: Iranian president is 'wolf in sheep's clothing,'" *CNN*, October 2, 2013, http://www.cnn.com/2013/10/01/world/meast/israel-netanyahu-iran/; accessed November 2014.

93. Josep Federman, "Netanyahu: Iran Nuclear Deal a 'historic mistake,'" *Huffington Post*, November 25, 2013, http://www.huffingtonpost.com/2013/11/24/netanyahu-iran-deal-israel-nuclear_n_4332906.html; accessed November 2014.

94. "Arabs not allied with Iran not quiet over nuclear deal," *USA Today*, November 24, 2013, http://www.usatoday.com/story/news/world/2013/11/24/iran-nuclear-deal-arab-reactions/3691289/; accessed November 2014.

95. David E. Sanger, "Role for Russia Gives Iran Talks a Possible Boost," *The New York Times*, November 3, 2014, http://www.nytimes.com/2014/11/04/world/middleeast/role-for-russia-gives-iran-nuclear-talks-a-possible-boost.html?_r=0; accessed November 2014.

96. Ibid.

97. Paul Richter, "Iran nuclear talks again stuck on Arak reactor's future, official says," *Los Angeles Times*, October 16, 2014, http://www.latimes.com/world/la-fg-iran-nuclear-talks-arak-reactor-20141016-story.html; accessed October 2014.

98. Alan Dershowitz, personal interview with Mike Evans, August 18, 2006.

99. Yossef Bodansky, *The Secret History of the Iraq War* (New York: Regan Books, a division of HarperCollins, 2004), 9.

100. Jane Arraf, "Iraq insurgents' bombmaking gets more lethal," *NBC News*, December 8, 2006, http://www.msnbc.msn.com/id/16110075/; accessed December 12, 2006).

101. James Woolsey, personal interview with Mike Evans, August 16, 2006.

102. http://www.brainyquote.com/quotes/keywords/iran_2.html; accessed October 2014.

103. Personal conversation between Mike Evans and Israeli Prime Minister Isaac Hertzog, August 2006.

104. "UN: Sanctions loom, Iran keeps enriching," *CNN.com*, August 31, 2006, http://www.cnn.com/2006/WORLD/meast/08/31/iran.deadline/index.html; accessed November 2006.

105. George Jahn, "Iran Expanding Enrichment," *The Washington Post*, October 23, 2006, http://www.washingtonpost.com/wp-dyn/content/article/2006/10/23/AR2006102300326_pf.html; accessed November 2014.

106. Iran has begun uranium enrichment in second centrifuge cascade, agency says," http://usatoday30.usatoday.com/news/world/2006-10-27-iran-enrichment_x.htm. October 27, 2006, http://news.yahoo.com/s/ap/20061027/ap_on_re_mi_ea/iran_nuclear; accessed November 2014.

107. "Bush condemns Iran nuclear move," *BBC News*, October 27, 2006, http://news.bbc.co.uk/2/hi/middle_east/6092540.stm; accessed November 2006.

108. "Iran bomb 'within next 10 years,'" *BBC News*, June 2, 2006, http://news.bbc.co.uk/2/hi/middle_east/5039956.stm; accessed November 2006.

109. "1983 Beirut barracks bombing," *Wikipedia, the free encyclopedia*, last updated November 2, 2006, http://en.wikipedia.org/wiki/Beirut_barracks_bombing; accessed November 2006.

110. Alan Dershowitz, personal interview with Mike Evans, August 18, 2006.

111. Benjamin Weinthal, "Iran's non-Muslims face prison, execution, despite 'reform' claims, says new UN report," October 27, 2014, http://www.foxnews.com/world/2014/10/27/iran-non-muslims-face-prison-execution-despite-reform-claims-says-new-un-report/; accessed October 2014.

112. Ibid.

113. Ibid.

114. Clifford D. May, "France Derails Iranian 'Sucker's Deal,'" November 14, 2013, http://www.defenddemocracy.org/media-hit/france-derails-iranian-suckers-deal/; accessed November 2014.

115. "UT Overview: Background," University of Tehran website, 2004, http://www.ut.ac.ir/en/main-links/overview.htm; accessed December 2006.

116. John Dumbrell, *The Carter Presidency: A Re-evaluation* (Manchester, England: Manchester University Press, 1993), 181.

117. Asadollah Alam, *The Shah and I: The Confidential Diary of Iran's Royal Court 1969-1977* (New York: St. Martin's Press, 1993), 500.

118. Cyrus Vance, *Hard Choices: Critical Years in America's Foreign Policy* (New York: Simon & Schuster, 1983), 318.

119. Farah Pahlavi, *An Enduring Love* (New York: Hyperion, 1987), 269-270.

120. James A. Bill, *The Eagle and the Lion* (New Haven: University Press, 1988), 233.

121. Amir Taheri, *The Spirit of Allah: Khomeini and the Islamic Revolution* (Bethesda, MD: Adler and Adler, 1985), 194, 197, 199-200.

122. Raymond Tanter, personal interview with Dr. Mike Evans, 2007.

123. William Sullivan, White Paper, 06556, 62.

124. Ofira Seliktar, *Failing the Crystal Ball Test,* (Westport, CT: Praeger Publishers, 2000), 133.

125. Robert E. Huyser, *Mission to Tehran* (New York: Harper & Row, 1986), 17.

126. Michael D. Evans, *Showdown with Nuclear Iran* (Nashville: Nelson Current, 2006), 3-4.

127. Huyser, *Mission to Tehran,* (New York: Harper & Row, 1986), 293

128. Ibid, 296

129. George Sharoui, "America's Security: The Genesis of the Problem," April 26, 2005, *IntellectualConservative.com*, http://www.intellectualconservative.com/article4303.html; accessed December 2006.

130. Baqer Moin, *Khomeini: Life of the Ayatollah* (New York: Thomas Dunne Books, 2000), 204.

189. Paul L. Williams, *Osama's Revenge* (Amherst, NY: Prometheus Books, 2004), 41.

190. Dr. Hugh Cort, *The American Hiroshima: Iran's Plan for a Nuclear Attack on the United States* (Bloomington, IN: IUniverse, 2011), 7.

191. Hoda Osman, "Alleged Terrorists Used Social Network Sites," *CBSNews.com*; May 19, 2010, http://www.cbsnews.com/news/alleged-terrorists-used-social-network-sites/; accessed September 2014.

192. "Al-Qaeda plans to wage holy war on Facebook," *The Telegraph*, December 21, 2008, http://www.telegraph.co.uk/news/worldnews/3885367/Al-Qaeda-plans-to-wage-holy-war-on-Facebook.html; accessed March 2011.

193. Hoda Osman, *"Alleged Terrorists Used Social Network Sites."*

194. Gina Vergel, *"Security Expert: Social Networking Sites Are Hotbeds of Terrorism,"* Fordham University, http://www.fordham.edu/Campus_Resources/enewsroom/topstories_1916.asp; accessed October 2014.

195. Ronald Kessler, "Facebook, YouTube, and Terrorists: A Deadly Mix," *Newxmax.com*, February 19, 2011; http://www.newsmax.com/RonaldKessler/Facebook-YouTube-FBI-Terrorists/2011/02/18/id/386589; accessed March 2010.

196. Ibid.

197. http://en.wikipedia.org/wiki/2010_Portland_car_bomb_plot; accessed October 2014.

198. Rebecca Savastio, "Three Young American Girls Returned Home After Trying to Join ISIS," October 22, 2014, http://guardianlv.com/2014/10/three-young-american-women-returned-home-after-trying-to-join-isis-in-syria/#WE0AvMCvPWOMpvgd.99; accessed October 2014.

199. http://guardianlv.com/2014/10/three-young-american-women-returned-home-after-trying-to-join-isis-in-syria/#WE0AvMCvPWOMpvgd.99

200. Adam Goldman and Matt Apuzzo, "How bin Laden emailed without being detected," *Associated Press*, May 12, 2011; http://hosted2.ap.org/APDefault/*/Article_2011-05-12-US-Bin-Laden/id-3c1efb3e86da4863bb2c29fd7254eeb8; accessed May 2014.

201. Romesh Ratnesar and Stuard Ramson, "Can We Stop the Next Attack?" *Time.com*, March 11, 2002 http://www.time.com/time/magazine/article/0,9171,1001961,00.html; accessed December 2006.

202. Andy Serwer, "The Oracle of Everything," *Fortune*, November 11, 2002, http://archive.fortune.com/magazines/fortune/fortune_archive/2002/11/11/331843/index.htm; accessed November 9, 2004.

203. Mort Zuckerman, personal interview with Mike Evans, August 22, 2006.

204. Marshall Kirk and Hunter Madsen, *After the Ball: How America will Conquer its Fear and Hatred of Gays in the '90s* (New York: Penguin, 1989), 188.

205. Ibid, 221

206. Michael D. Evans, *The American Prophecies* (Nashville: Warner Faith, 2004), 21.

207. "First Amendment," *Constitution of the United States of America.*

208. John T. Elson, "Toward a Hidden God," *Time Magazine*, April 8, 1966, http://www.time.com/time/magazine/article/0,9171,835309,00.html; accessed November 2006.

209. "Dr. Dobson Urges: Head to Alabama," *WorldNetDaily.com*, August 26, 2003, http://www.worldnetdaily.com/news/article.asp?ARTICLE_ID=34267; accessed November 2006.

210. "Top Ten Reviews," *Internet Filter Review,* http://internet-filter-review.toptenreviews.com/internet-pornography-statistics.html; accessed November 2006.

211. Susan Sontag, "The Talk of the Town," *The New Yorker*, September 24, 2001, http://www.msgr.ca/msgr-3/talk_of_the_town_susan_sontag.htm; accessed December 2006.

212. Barbara Kingsolver, *Milwaukee Journal Sentinel*, September 27, 2001, http://www.rightwingnews.com/quotes/left.php; accessed November 2006.

213. George W. Bush, "Address to a Joint Session of Congress and the American People," *Voices of Democracy*, September 20, 2001, http://voices-of-democracy.org/bush-an-address-to-a-joint-session-of-congress-speech-text/; accessed November 2014.

214. Ibid.

215. "Iraqi Liberation Act of 1998," *Iraq Watch*, http://www.iraqwatch.org/government/US/Legislation/ILA.htm; accessed December 2006.

216. Alan Colmes, *Red, White & Liberal* (New York: Regan, 2003), 53.

217. David Horowitz, "Moment of Truth (For the Anti-American Left)," http://www.frontpagemag.com/Articles/ReadArticle.asp?ID=6962; accessed November 2006.

BOOKS BY: MIKE EVANS

Israel: America's Key to Survival

Save Jerusalem

The Return

Jerusalem D.C.

Purity and Peace of Mind

Who Cries for the Hurting?

Living Fear Free

I Shall Not Want

Let My People Go

Jerusalem Betrayed

Seven Years of Shaking: A Vision

The Nuclear Bomb of Islam

Jerusalem Prophecies

Pray For Peace of Jerusalem

America's War: The Beginning
of the End

The Jerusalem Scroll

The Prayer of David

The Unanswered Prayers of Jesus

God Wrestling

The American Prophecies

Beyond Iraq: The Next Move

The Final Move beyond Iraq

Showdown with Nuclear Iran

Jimmy Carter: The Liberal Left
and World Chaos

Atomic Iran

Cursed

Betrayed

The Light

Corrie's Reflections & Meditations

GAMECHANGER SERIES:

GameChanger

Samson Option

The Four Horsemen

THE PROTOCOLS SERIES:

The Protocols

The Candidate

The Revolution

The Final Generation

Seven Days

The Locket

Living in the F.O.G.

Persia: The Final Jihad

Jerusalem

The History of Christian Zionism

Countdown

Ten Boom: Betsie, Promise of God

Commanded Blessing

Born Again: 1948

Born Again: 1967

Presidents in Prophecy

Stand with Israel

Prayer, Power and Purpose

Turning Your Pain Into Gain

Christopher Columbus, Secret Jew

Finding Favor with God

The Jewish State: The Volunteers

See You in New York

COMING SOON:

The Columbus Code

Finding Favor with Man

MICHAEL DAVID EVANS, the #1 *New York Times* bestselling author, is an award-winning journalist/Middle East analyst. Dr. Evans has appeared on hundreds of network television and radio shows including *Good Morning America, Crossfire* and *Nightline*, and *The Rush Limbaugh Show*, and on Fox Network, *CNN World News*, NBC, ABC, and CBS. His articles have been published in the *Wall Street Journal, USA Today, Washington Times, Jerusalem Post* and newspapers worldwide. More than twenty-five million copies of his books are in print, and he is the award-winning producer of nine documentaries based on his books.

Dr. Evans is considered one of the world's leading experts on Israel and the Middle East, and is one of the most sought-after speakers on that subject. He is the chairman of the board of the ten Boom Holocaust Museum in Haarlem, Holland, and is the founder of Israel's first Christian museum—Friends of Zion—in Jerusalem.

Dr. Evans has authored a number of books including: *History of Christian Zionism, Showdown with Nuclear Iran, Atomic Iran, The Next Move Beyond Iraq, The Final Move Beyond Iraq*, and *Countdown*. His body of work also includes the novels *Seven Days, GameChanger, The Samson Option, The Four Horsemen, The Locket, Born Again: 1967*, and coming soon, *The Columbus Code*.

Michael David Evans is available to speak or for interviews.
Contact: EVENTS@drmichaeldevans.com.

218. Yonatan Silverman, "Understanding Islamofascism," *American Thinker*, January 22, 2012, http://www. americanthinker.com/2012/01/understanding_islamofascism.html; accessed October 2014.

219. Richard Heideman, "An Open Letter to all Jewish Community Leaders by Richard D. Heideman, International President B'nai B'rith," September 3, 2001, http://www.join.org.au/Releases/Durban_Open_Letter.htm; accessed November 2006.

220. Herb Keinon, "Festival of Hate," *Jerusalem Post*, Daily Edition, Features, (September 7, 2001).

221. David Horowitz, *Unholy Alliance: Radical Islam and the American Left* (Washington, D.C.: Regnery Publishing, Inc, 2004), 135–136.

222. James Woolsey, personal interview with Mike Evans, August 16, 2006.

223. "Saddam Hussein is Losing Grip on Northern Cities in Iraq," *CNN.com,* Transcripts, April 10, 2003, http:// transcripts.cnn.com/TRANSCRIPTS/0304/10/ip.00.html; accessed November 2006.

224. George Barna, "A Biblical Worldview Has a Radical Effect on a Person's Life," *The Barna Update*, December 1, 2003, https://www.barna.org/barna-update/article/5-barna-update/131-a-biblical-worldview-has-a-radical-effect-on-a-persons-life#.VGUJAo10w3E; accessed November 2006.

225. http://www.searchquotes.com/quotation/If_I_were_asked_today_to_formulate_as_concisely_as_possible_that_main_cause_of_the_ruinous_revolutio/363299/; accessed October 2014.

226. "A New Bible Translation Promotes Fornication," http://hissheep.org/kjv/new_bible_translation_promotes_fornication.html; accessed November 2014.

227. Ibid.

228. Jacob Laksin, "The Church of the Latter-Day Leftists," *FrontPageMagazine.com*, January 13, 2005, http://www. frontpagemag.com/Articles/ReadArticle.asp?ID=16625; accessed November 2006.

229. John W.Chalfant, *Abandonment Theology: The Clergy and the Decline of American Christianity* (Winter Park, FL: Hartline Marketing, 1997), 8.

230. Dr. Francis A. Schaeffer, *The Great Evangelical Disaster* (Westchester, IL: Crossway Books, 1984), 37.

231. Dr. David Jeremiah, vii.

232. Lisa Jenkins Moore, "We WILL War," *Living Magazine,* November 2014, 38.